Design Is Invisible

Lucius Burckhardt

Design Is Invisible

Planning, Education, and Society

Silvan Blumenthal and Martin Schmitz (eds.)

Birkhäuser
Basel

Editors

Silvan Blumenthal
CH-Zurich

Martin Schmitz
D-Berlin
martin-schmitz.de
lucius-burckhardt.org

Translation from German into English: Jill Denton, D-Berlin
Copyediting: Andreas Müller, D-Berlin
Layout, cover design and typography: Ekke Wolf
Typesetting: Sven Schrape, D-Berlin
Printing and Binding: BELTZ Bad Langensalza GmbH, D-Bad Langensalza

Originally published in German as
Lucius Burckhardt
Design ist unsichtbar. Entwurf, Gesellschaft und Pädagogik.
ISBN 978-3-927795-61-7

Library of Congress Cataloging-in-Publication data
A CIP catalog record for this book has been applied for at the Library of Congress.

Bibliographic information published by the German National Library
The German National Library lists this publication in the Deutsche Nationalbibliografie; detailed bibliographic data is available on the Internet at http://dnb.dnb.de.

This publication is also available as an e-book (ISBN PDF 978-3-0356-1071-0).

P.O. Box 44, 4009 Basel, Switzerland
Part of Walter de Gruyter GmbH, Berlin/Boston

Printed on acid-free paper produced from chlorine-free pulp. TCF ∞

Printed in Germany

ISBN 978-3-0356-1201-1

9 8 7 6 5 4 3 2 1 www.birkhauser.com

Content

[Square brackets indicate a translator's note]

Foreword

Lucius Burckhardt was a man who persistently questioned the world about him. The science of strollology[1] is an especially cogent expression of this resolute disposition. It demonstrates the unconventional breadth and idiosyncrasy of Burckhardt's philosophical inquiry, which transcended the bounds of individual faculties and indeed, of the university itself.

The science of strollology, which he founded, also simultaneously attests the great pleasure Burckhardt took in juxtaposing clearly distinct or even disparate fields, such as everyday life and scholarly research. It derives from his recognition that to overcome such divisions is imperative. Theory and practice, expert and layman are seemingly immutable categories—yet declaring a stroll to be a science sweeps them aside. Taking a stroll—or "promenadology," as Burckhardt also called it—has an explosive effect. All that previously appeared matter-of-fact is suddenly no longer clear-cut. Hierarchies collapse, giving rise to a wonderful open space in which a comprehensive endeavor to deal with the environment in more meaningful ways can be pursued.

How to design this open space is no classic architectonic exercise—and nor is the present book a guide to surmounting such a specific challenge. However, the conception of the science of strollology as an independent discipline typifies the field into which we

1 Strollology developed out of Lucius Burckhardt's teaching practice at the University of Kassel in the 1980s. This new perspective on the environment and perception thereof is explored in detail in: Markus Ritter and Martin Schmitz (eds.), *Why Is Landscape Beautiful? The Science of Strollology*, Birkhäuser, Basel 2015.

hope the present text compilation—and likewise the concise study *Lehrcanapé*[2]—will offer insight.

The anti-authoritarian student protests of 1968 shook up traditional structures—also at the ETH in Zurich, and particularly in the architecture faculty, where shock waves continued to reverberate for several years. Disastrous urban planning in the postwar period had already badly dented public confidence in architects' expertise. In consequence, the structure of the profession itself came under scrutiny. Calls went up for a reform of the architect's role. The *Lehrcanapé* experiment[3] launched by Burckhardt prompted further debate of the issue. Altering the pattern of the architect's education and training was to forge him anew. The reform was radical. Academic roles were rewritten, pedagogic traditions were thrown overboard, new methods were tested, relevant problems were identified, and discussion of the university itself was never-ending.

Those involved at the time were agreed: the form of the architecture degree course is not written in stone. This awareness propelled them to fight for the freedom to redesign professional education and training; and the rigor of their demands was honed not least by an appreciation of how powerfully education shapes people's minds and hence also their worlds.

Design was already invisible back then—and, in the case of Burckhardt's own world, it was very closely and specifically bound up with the current form of tertiary education. It was impossible

2 Silvan Blumenthal, *Das Lehrcanapé: Lucius Burckhardt und das Architektenbild an der ETH Zürich 1970–1973*, Basel 2010

3 The *Lehrcanapé* (professorial sofa) was instituted at the ETH Zurich from 1970 to 1973 as an alternative approach to teaching. Unlike the chair of design's usual introductory course in traditional design techniques, the sociologist and architect who jointly occupied the *Lehrcanapé* sought to confront students with the real issues unfolding at the time beyond the university precincts. Cf. also Footnote 2.

to talk about teaching design without examining the design of teaching. The *Lehrcanapé* and—incomparably broader in scope—the science of strollology are equally emblematic of this paradigm shift. The university is that world in which the university professor Lucius Burckhardt pursued design. It is here that he formulated "Design is invisible" as a theory and here too that he put it directly into practice.

The present new text compilation seeks to render palpable the most important aspects of this broad-ranging field. Divided by theme into three sections, the texts lead from the theory "Design is invisible" to its sociologically informed background then to the pedagogic practice that ensued. These are stand-alone, critical articles on design in the broadest sense of the term and in part date from as far back as the 1960s. Burckhardt provocatively takes "good form" in his sights and highlights the relevance of the invisible: a well-designed streetcar is worthless if it doesn't run. A web of integrated systems is at work behind the object hitherto examined in isolation. The resolute call to review and rethink such systems is accompanied by words of warning, namely to resist the temptation of the all-encompassing, exclusive, conclusive design. For it is only in school, only in textbooks that sums can be solved so neatly, Burckhardt explains, thereby alerting us to solutions to a reality that cannot be wholly grasped while hinting at a further system of influence. Our patterns of thought and speech put us in a specific relationship to the world with specific consequences. That which society defines as a remainder or as dirt is cleared away. In Lucius Burckhardt's view, this norm marks the first step on the fatal path to environmental pollution. Other narratives are therefore needed—alternative designs in the midst of our social patterns of thought and speech. A suitable place for this attempt at renewal is the university, Burckhardt believes, in particular the university of his own invention, where students are awarded the diploma on the very first day, the better then to begin their studies on the second day.

Lucius and Annemarie Burckhardt in their office at the faculty of architecture and urban and landscape planning at the University of Kassel in 1993. Photo: Reinhard Franz

DESIGN

Design Is Invisible (1980)

Design objects? Of course we can see them: the whole gamut of designs and devices, from a building to a can opener. The designer gives them a logical, ready-to-use form, premised on certain external parameters: in the case of the can opener, on the structure of a can. The designer of cans, for his part, considers how a can opener functions. That is his external parameter.

So we can perceive the world as a realm of objects and divide these, for example, into houses, streets, traffic lights, kiosks, coffee makers, washing-up bowls, tableware, or table linen. Such classification is not without consequences: it leads namely to that concept of design which isolates a certain device—a coffee maker, let's say—acknowledges its external parameters, and sets itself the goal of making a better or more attractive one; that is, of producing the type of thing likely to have been described in the 1950s as "good form."[1]

But we can divide the world up in other ways too—and, if I have understood *A Pattern Language*[2] correctly, that is what Christopher Alexander strives to do. He does not isolate a house, a street, or a newsstand in order to perfect its design and construction; instead, he distinguishes an integral composite, such as the street corner,

1 [Max Bill's book *Die Gute Form* (1957) decisively shaped the criteria propounded at the time for functional yet aesthetically pleasing "timeless" design. The German Ministry of Economics and Technology awarded the "Federal Prize for Good Form" for the first time in 1969. Since 2006, it has been presented annually under the name "Design Award of the Federal Republic of Germany."]

2 [Christopher Alexander: *A Pattern Language. Towns, Buildings, Construction,* Oxford University Press, New York 1977]

from other urban composites; for the newsstand thrives on the fact that my bus has not yet arrived, and so I buy a newspaper; and the bus happens to stop here, because this is an intersection where passengers can change to other lines. "Street corner" simply tags a phenomenon that encompasses, above and beyond the visible dimension, elements of an organizational system comprised of bus routes, timetables, magazine sales, traffic light sequences, and so on.

This way of dividing up our environment also triggers a design impulse—yet one that takes account of the system's invisible components. What we need, perhaps, so that I won't miss my bus while scrabbling for change, or because the newsagent is serving another customer, is a simplified method of paying for a newspaper. Some people instantly dream up a new invention—an automatic magazine dispenser with an electric hum—while we imagine somehow intervening in the system: selling magazines for a round sum, or introducing a subscription card that we can simply flash at the newsagent—in any case, some kind of ruling to tackle magazine distribution and that institution "the morning paper."

What are institutions? Let us forget Christopher Alexander's street corner in favor of a clearly identifiable institution, the hospital. What is a hospital? Well, a building with long corridors, polished floors, glossy white furniture, and little trolleys loaded with tableware for mealtimes.

This view of the hospital takes us back to the traditional design brief: the architect and the designer are called upon to plan hospitals with shorter corridors, more convivial atmospheres, and more practical trolleys. As everyone knows however, hospitals are now bigger, their corridors longer, the catering service more anonymous, and patient care less caring. That is because neither the architect nor the designer were allowed to intervene in the institution per se, but only to improve existing designs and devices within the given external parameters.

So, let's describe the hospital as an institution. Despite all its visible features, it is first and foremost a system of interpersonal relationships. Interpersonal systems are also designed and planned, in part by history and tradition yet also in response to the people alive today. When the Ministry of Health decrees that hospital catering is not the responsibility of medical staff but a management issue—or vice versa—this ruling is part and parcel of the institution's design.

The hospital owes its existence above all to the three traditional roles of doctor, nurse, and patient. The nurse's role evokes a myriad of associations, from the Virgin Mary through to Ingrid Bergman, and appears to be clear-cut. In reality, it is far from clear-cut, as it incorporates a great number of more or less vital activities. The doctor, historically only a minor figure on the hospital stage, shot to the top in the nineteenth century on a wave of scientific claims swallowed whole with religious fervor, and perpetuated to this day by TV and trashy novels, with the result that a formidable whiff of heart transplants now permeates even the most backwoods county hospital. And what about the patient? He has no role to play at all, you say? He simply falls ill, through no fault of his own? — *Come, now, please make up your mind whether you want to be sick or healthy!* — Evidently there is an element of choice in the matter. We can—and must—decide one way or the other, otherwise we will irritate our boss—our boss at work, or the hospital boss. A patient lies down—in Chodowiecki's day he used to sit—or ambles gratefully around the park, convalescing. He resigns himself in any case to the three-role spiel, although it has long been due for an overhaul; but more of that later.

Do other similar institutions exist? Yes, indeed: the night. Yet night is a natural phenomenon, you say? The sun is shining on the Antipodes and so it is dark in our neck of the woods? Anne Cauquelin was the first to posit that the night is artificial. And there is no disputing that human behavior shapes the night, one way or another, in line with various man-made institutions. In Switzerland I can work undisturbed after 9 p.m. then go to bed. To give someone a call at that hour is considered impolite. In Germany my telephone is quiet all evening then springs to life at 11 p.m.—for the cheap-rate period begins at 10 p.m., whereupon all international lines are immediately overloaded, and it takes around an hour to get a connection.

Thus the night, which evidently originally had something to do with the dark, is a man-made construct, comprised of opening hours, closing times, price scales, timetables, habits, and streetlamps. The night, like the hospital, is in urgent need of redesign. Why does public transport cease to run at precisely the moment people drain their last glass in a wine bar, leaving them no option but to take the wheel? Might not a rethink of opening hours make the streets safer for women obliged to return home on foot, late at night? Are we going to live to see the day also in these climes, where car ownership is the sole guarantee of a measure of safety?

Let's take another institution, the private household. For the traditional designer, the household is a treasure trove of devices clamoring to be planned. There are endless things here to invent or improve: coffee makers, food mixers, and dishwashers, to name only a few appliances. The planner deploys novel means to ensure everything stays the same. Moves to reform the household were made around 1900: early mechanization fostered collectivization as well as untold experiments with canteens, public laundries, and built-in, centralized vacuum cleaners. Thanks to the invention of small motors these amenities were reinstated later in the private household. Kitchen appliances save housewives' time, you say? Don't make me laugh!

The war on dirt is a sub-system within that institution, the private household. What is dirt? Why do we fight it? And where does it go after we emerge from the battle, supposedly victorious? We all know the answer. We just don't like to admit it. The dirt we fight along with the detergents we use to do so is simply environmental pollution by another name. But dirt is unhygienic, you say, and one cannot avoid a spot of cleaning? Strange! Because people used to clean, even before they knew about hygiene. And besides, the filters used in vacuum cleaners are not fine enough to contain bacteria effectively. Which means that vacuum cleaners merely keep bacteria in circulation. What a shame for the vacuum cleaner, the designers' favorite brainchild!

Then how do people clean in hospitals, where hygiene is truly vital? As far as I can see, hygiene in hospitals rests on three pillars. The first pillar is purely symbolic—for sparkling white surfaces and the shine on polished (which is to say wax-smeared) floors are considered the epitome of cleanliness. The second is antiseptics—toxins, in other words: an endless flow of new disinfectants designed to kill bacteria. Any success in these stakes is unfortunately short-lived however, for resistant strains never cease to develop, and are engendered selectively in fact, by these very toxins. And the third pillar is vacuum cleaning. In contrast to the domestic vacuum cleaner that releases dust back into the same room it was captured, hospitals' centralized air conditioning and vacuum-cleaning systems spread dangerous spores all over the place. Is there a remedy for such unpropitious circumstances? Of course—but it falls neither in the designer's brief nor within his external parameters! The key to the problem is to redesign the health care system, above all by promoting decentralization.

Let's name one last institution: the production site. A lot could be said on this topic but let us stick to one point only: workplaces—by which we mean jobs—are also man-made design objects. We're not talking here about making chairs at work more comfortable, or about cheering the place up a bit with fresh wallpaper and a few potted plants. The object of design in this context is that particular part of the production process assigned to each individual laborer, as well as the degree of energy, knowledge, and skill—respectively of ignorance, boredom, or mindlessness—that must be invested at a particular point in the production process. This applies not only to production sites in the narrower sense of the word, i.e. to factory jobs, but also to administrative and clerical work. Workplaces—jobs—are designed ostensibly for productivity; yet productivity of a sort akin to counter-productivity. Automation, as it is called, destroys jobs that have hitherto been a source of satisfaction while other jobs in the manual sector, which could and should most urgently be rationalized, remain unchanged. Here we can touch only briefly on the problem, without offering concrete evidence of our claim. Yet the main point is this: jobs are also designed; not only in the traditional sense of design but in terms of the way the production process is broken down into various types of task, which actively demand or render redundant the laborers' skills range, and foster or hinder cooperation.

The previous comments were intended to show that design has an invisible component, namely an organizational-institutional dimension over which the designer always exercises a certain influence yet which, given the way we classify our environment in terms of objects, tends to remain hidden. Inasmuch as the world is divided into object categories and the invisible dimension only marginally acknowledged as an external parameter, the world too is designed. Furthermore, institutions' resistance to change—especially given the wealth of technological objects now under development—is also a form of design: radiology equipment is designed for the use of *nurses in radiology*.

In the following we wish to consider whether these insights are of any use to us, or simply sad proof of the fact that the world is badly designed.

Whenever we think about design, we must address two phases: the phase of actual design or planning through to production; and the consumption phase, up to and including an object's disposal on the trash heap, or in a museum. Let us take a look first at the established hypothesis on each:

- On design: the objective is a functional object, whereby one might discuss endlessly whether functionality per se is identical with beauty, or whether the designer must add beauty as an extra.
- And on consumption: technology and technical devices are neutral; their misuse stems from people's villainy. The *Werkbund Almanac* from 1914 featured warships as design objects while the journal *Werk* from April 1976 described the cooling towers of nuclear power stations as an appealing venture for architects.

And now, two contrary viewpoints, as a possible premise for a new way of describing the two processes, design and consumption:

- On design: objects owe their form to the interactions inherent to the design process.
- And on consumption: such objects in turn exert influence on social interaction; objects are not neutral; *Tools for Conviviality*[3] exist (asserts Illich!), as well as their opposite, objects that impede social interaction.

And let us test a third hypothesis while we are at it, a hypothesis on counter-productivity:

- Every new invention that is put to use effects change, and such change in turn necessitates new inventions. If all the problems that successively arise are dealt with conventionally, namely one by one, as isolated phenomena, the outcome is counter-productivity.

3 [Ivan Illich: *Tools for Conviviality*, Harper & Row, New York 1973]

Here is a brief example: a central heating system serving several apartments allegedly gave rise to the need to monitor each individual tenant's energy consumption. Gauges based on the evaporation of liquid were installed and, as a result, each tenant now turns off his radiators when he goes out. However, each tenant also wants his apartment to be warm, the minute he turns the radiators back on. Consequently, water in the heating system is kept at such a high temperature that every tenant, even the most thrifty, ultimately pays more for heating now than when heating costs were split between tenants, without individual monitoring.

Let's begin therefore with the design process. Here, as we observed in our opening remarks, the designer classifies the world in terms of object categories rather than problem categories. This rests on linguistic determination, for to name a problem is simultaneously to identify the appliance that can remedy it. When I complain that my electric onion chopper may indeed save me a moment's work but then takes ten minutes to clean, what springs to mind is not so much a return to the simple kitchen knife but a design for an appliance able to clean my onion chopper. The objective, once named, becomes an instant remedy, and supersedes any general endeavor on my part to cook more efficiently when time is limited.

A further effect of this direct link between naming and remedy is the suppression of secondary considerations: with the exception of the appliance to be designed, no technical or organizational changes should be necessary. Whatever can be integrated in existing systems, however overloaded these may be, is considered successful: a waste disposal unit built into the sink drainage, an oven that self-cleans through pyrolysis, etc. This type of troubleshooting is rooted in the designer's position within policymaking bodies: his job is to deliver ideas—but he bears zero liability.

In the late 1950s, the Ulm School of Design was the first professional institution to recognize that industrial design is counter-productive—yet the solutions it proposed were technocratic. They were based on a radical analysis of the desired outcome but failed to consider that outcome in its broader context. Students in Ulm were hence likely to submit papers that began something like this: *The exercise consists in raising ten to twenty gram portions of semi-solid substances from a dish circa thirty centimeters in diameter then transferring them horizontally to an open mouth, where a movement of the upper lip relieves the supporting structure of its load…* The result is not Charlie Chaplin's eating machine but a fork with a Modernist profile.

In the meantime, of course, it has been recognized that objects that have great symbolic value yet require only minimal inventiveness—flatware, for example—do not fall into the design field. Conversely, those things yet to be invented, or at least their technical aspects, are too complex for designers. So design must broaden its scope and embrace socio-design: a way of thinking about resolving problems that results from coordinated changes made both to roles and to objects. One example may be to design a kitchen so inviting, it inspires guests to help the host chop onions…

Before leaving the field of design to consider aspects of consumption, I want to slip in a comment or two on shopping and its "*hidden persuaders*."[4] Of course the marketing and advertising professionals who use depth psychology to sell either soap powder, or instant cake mix that makes a mother feel she is breastfeeding the

4 [Vance Packard's book *The Hidden Persuaders* (David McKay Co, New York 1957) was a pioneering and prescient work revealing how advertisers use psychological methods to tap into unconscious desires in order to "persuade" the consumer to buy promoted products.]

whole family, have not yet thrown in the towel. But the hype in the design field has pretty much died down: I now buy a new refrigerator when the old one breaks down, not simply because I want one with rounded contours. Rearguard action continues on the car market, where revivals are a flourishing trade, and the avant-garde has already discovered the flea market for other retail sectors. The flea market will be the place where dwindling numbers of throwaway consumers meet the swelling ranks of post-industrial society.

This is not to say that progress—in its positive as well as its counter-productive guise—has come to a standstill. But the sector in which progress is still being made is straightforward. Progress holds sway in production for the white (official) market but gray market trading, moonlighting, self-sufficiency, barter systems, and informal mutual aid are on the increase too. White trading is still scoring points also in these areas: DIY hobby products have slipped onto the shelves among the detergent battalions. Yet these might be fleeting epiphenomena on the road to greater self-sufficiency. Whether we should welcome all this wholeheartedly remains uncertain: it panders to lower middle-class aspirations, and harbors a threat of social isolation; but perhaps a retrograde step or two is the price society must pay for a springboard to new realms of experience.

With regard to usage and consumption, we wanted to point out that objects are not neutral. Is there such a thing as *evil* objects? Goods are harmful when they foster our dependence on systems that ultimately pillage our resources, or desert us. Without doubt we are all attached to such systems, and this makes us liable to blackmail. However, we can still influence the extent of our dependency. We should avoid those objects that compel us to buy more accessories. We should distrust media that provide a one-way flow of information, even though we can no longer do without them. We should exercise restraint in buying and using any goods that isolate us. The car is a major case in point, especially as it tends also to foster inconsiderate behavior in its user.

The car has destroyed not only our cities but also our society. One can commission as much research as one likes, as to why juvenile delinquency is on the rise, why more women are attacked, why districts are becoming derelict, or slums, or no-go areas by night. As long as the defense against motorized crime is a motorized police force, as long as the pedestrian is advised to use his car, the solution can be named without any need for further research: motorization based on private car ownership has abandoned the non-motorized populace to greater insecurity, and to an increasingly uncompetitive mass transit system.

This leads to our last remark: on counter-productivity. We already mentioned the example of monitoring heating costs. That is only a minor aspect of the outrageous counter-productivity of the central heating system, every failure of which has been countered by a new remedy that proved subsequently to be a failure, to the point where we now use our electronically controlled, overheated, and, in terms of air hygiene, unhealthy central heating system in devastatingly wasteful fashion as a boiler; and the central heating system is being superseded now by an even greater evil, air conditioning. Counter-productivity, as we have said, arises when inventions are used in such a way as to cause a break in the overall system, a break that is patched up in turn by an isolated invention. The sum of these successor-inventions equals the counter-productivity of the overall system.

To return to the car: since the average inner-city speed for cars has been lowered to match that of cyclists, or pedestrians even, automobile manufacturers are pursuing research into the automobile's successor. And what are they developing? A car fitted with an additional gadget that allows the car to be steered to its destination by an electronic short-wave remote control system, whenever it enters the city limits. Or, to return to the vacuum cleaner: since the public has grown aware that vacuum cleaners are all the more damaging the more efficient they are, i.e. the more powerfully they can whizz bacteria through the filter, the industry is looking at a successor gadget—and guess what that may be? You're right: a vacuum cleaner with a built-in bacteria filter!

Invisible design. Today, this implies conventional design that is oblivious to its social impact. Yet it might also imply tomorrow's design—design that consciously takes into account the *invisible* overall system comprised of objects and interpersonal relationships.

Invisible Design (1983)

When an association has existed for a lifetime—the Deutsche Werkbund (German Work Federation) celebrated its seventy-fifth anniversary in 1982, the Swiss counterpart its seventieth just recently—it is high time to ask whether its goals have been attained or remain unattainable: either would be reason enough to consider disbanding the association.

On the still valid catchphrase "everyday life"

Well, the goals of the Werkbund are not so easily dealt with or, to say the least, can be articulated only with a high degree of abstraction—and not even then in a language that remains unchanged for a lifetime. Faced as we are today with CCTV-surveilled production chains, Werkbund founder Friedrich Naumann's notion of "the spiritualization of production"[1] barely raises a smile while Naumann, for his part, would find it hard to grasp modern notions such as "design for everyday life."

And nevertheless, the catchphrase "everyday life" is perhaps the common thread connecting several decades, even if it is always interpreted anew, in the light of each specific era. Before the First World War it implied the revival of the quality production of handcrafted articles of daily use, the goal being to end the alienation of hand and

1 ["Durchgeistigung der Arbeit," here, as translated by the architecture critic Rayner Banham in *Theory and Design in the First Machine Age*, New York and London 1960, p. 72.]

head by means of artisanal production methods that involved them both. Yet the rise of First World War munitions factories quickly rendered the philosophy obsolete and the best that could be hoped for in the interwar period was an improvement in cheap industrial products. After the Second World War, given Germany's Wirtschaftswunder (economic miracle) and the booming Swiss economy, the functionalist ethics born of war and crisis became obsolete in turn. The goal of the Werkbund now was "good form," and this good form proved to be a perpetuation of the utilitarian and economic forms of the interwar period yet without the latter's conditions of crisis, hence to be functionalism without a function, as it were.

The flawed ideological basis of "good form"

The flawed aesthetic and biological premise for the term "good form" made it prone to derision and scorn from all quarters. In particular in the years of student revolt around 1968, the Werkbund had to put up with being asked whether incessant improvements to essentially unaltered products really benefitted the everyday life of the masses, it being evident that industry had long since factored in formal obsolescence, i.e. accelerated the aging of its products by recurrently varying their design but to no practical purpose. This question gave rise to considerable tension within the Werkbund, which even recourse to the founding principles and declarations of the forefathers Naumann, Behrens, Muthesius, Schumacher, and so on, did little to dispel. For their articulation of goals, in calling for neat, premium, purposive design as the highest guiding principle, bore out the arguments of the older generation; and in equal measure, in calling for the fundamental social competence of design and its pervasive relevance to the everyday lives of the working population, also those of the youngsters.

This situation led the Deutsche Werkbund to launch a series of conferences at its headquarters in Darmstadt six years ago, in order to review the theoretical foundations of the goals of the Werkbund and tailor them to this day and age. "Design Is Invisible" was the catchy hypothesis behind this undertaking. This was not to claim that useful objects cannot be seen, however, but highlighted rather that they are all embedded in invisible systems, which are likewise man-made and hence "designed." Not only the form of products but also the rules determining their usability must accordingly be the object of research: the streetcar that takes us to work or brings us home is of interest to us not because of its streamlined design, elegant gray synthetic upholstery, or—by no means!—the electronic hum of its ticket machine; for what we want above all is a very frequent service, a network that does not get jammed in private traffic, and a user-friendly ticketing system that is cheap or, preferably, completely free of charge. The streetcar schedule, network, and ticket prices are just as "designed" as the driver's cabin, the seating, and the doors of the streetcar itself. And this is why we must address the phenomenon streetcar network not merely in its visible dimension but in its entirety.

Invisible, networked systems

If one continues thinking along these lines, the world reveals itself to be not a set of building blocks composed of individual elements, but rather a network of systems that can be divided—with caution—into subsystems. According to Alexander,[2] the intersection is one

2 [Christopher Alexander: *A Pattern Language. Towns, Buildings, Construction*, Oxford University Press, New York 1977]

1907

1920

1930

"A Brief History of the Werkbund"
Drawing: Lucius Burckhardt

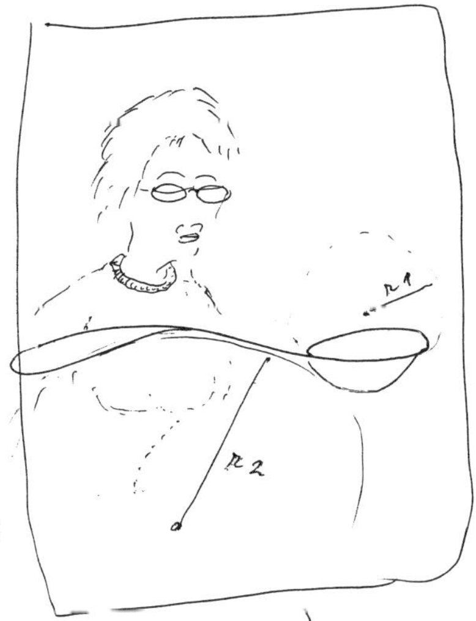

1960

1980

such subsystem. If we wished to improve it then it would not suffice to widen the street at the expense of the sidewalk, as planners generally do. Nor would it be helpful to install automated ticket vending machines, since those hulks would then have to await our coins while we searched through our pockets in vain. More pertinently, consideration should be given to integrated systems: Could I buy a subscription at the kiosk for a daily newspaper that contains my preprinted streetcar ticket? This subscription would be paid for with a round sum each Monday morning.

If we look about us we come upon a whole string of everyday phenomena, the invisible aspects of which are likewise manufactured by someone, somewhere. Just think of nighttime. It is a natural phenomenon, certainly: the sun sinks on the horizon and darkness falls. At the visible level, we counter the dark with streetlights. But institutional nocturnal frameworks are of far greater importance: businesses close while restaurants, cinemas, and theaters have opening hours. Transport schedules most decisively shape the night: anyone reliant on the bus or streetcar must be aware when the last one runs. Not even metropolises provide a round-the-clock service. In her book *La ville la nuit* [The City By Night], French philosopher Anne Cauquelin described how Paris falls asleep; and she proved that the night respectively the way we have to spend it is the outcome of a string of "design decisions."

Nighttime—ill health—dirt—death

Let's move on now to things that it is difficult to perceive as "design:" ill health, for example. At best we might think that hospitals could stand some improvement: fewer long corridors, fewer white walls, and a private room for each patient. Traditional design takes this approach. However, to perceive ill health itself as something subject to design is difficult. And yet, if we look at old engravings, we can see that ill health used to be different. We used to be propped up, mostly, whereas today we tend to lie down. We used to be comforted by friends, neighbors, and priests, whereas today we are alone and call the doctor. Ill health is therefore "designable." What has remained is that relic, the nurse. Her role, not only her uniform, is shaped by historical decisions; and it is now in need of a redesign.

Let's move on now to another topic: dirt. As Mary Douglas has pointed out (in *Purity and Danger*), purity is an ancient dictate of mankind, one that has taken different forms in different cultures in the course of history, but has always been put on an equal footing with cleanliness. That means: neither impurity nor dirt consists in specific materials but is a socially determined phenomenon. Cleanliness is justified today by hygiene. Yet people used to clean, even before bacteria were discovered. A sign of cleanliness today is to wash one's hands before eating; people used to wash them after eating. We consider gypsies dirty because they do not wash; gypsies believe our way of handling water is extremely unhygienic and, moreover, that cleanliness in any household that keeps cats is inconceivable. A Brahman peasant bathes in the same water as an "untouchable" but would never thresh corn with an untouchable given that straws transmit dirt. — Our image of dirt leads to a regime of cleanliness that ultimately causes environmental pollution—for we cannot rid the world either of dirt or our detergents. It is high time, not for more powerful vacuum cleaners that use more energy than ever to whirl up bacteria and blast them through inadequate filters but for a rethink of dirt itself.

Do these examples suffice? — Other sets of issues could be presented. Housework: a quite coincidental package of personal achievements and purchased commercial services that has taken shape organically throughout history. — Household gadgets have by no means lightened the housewife's load. In fact they have actually returned to the private domestic sphere a number of activities that were transposed to communal public spaces as early as the 1920s. — The street and the motorcar: a broad field opens up here. It encompasses the destruction of the city in both physical and social respects, as well as a nascent sense of urban insecurity that it was long believed the modern state had successfully overcome. — Death: its repression in society's consciousness diminishes its dignity and worth. Which society but ours would ever permit a hospital bathroom or corridor alcove to become the ignoble setting for this awesome occurrence?

From the individual object to thinking in terms of systems

Then what conclusions might the Werkbund draw from such deliberations? — Influenced by the Bauhaus, the nascent design of the 1920s dared take preliminary steps towards reforming the traditional tools and gadgets of everyday life. After the [Second World] war, academies and schools of applied arts pursued the same line of thought and established the profession of designer. This profession was always focused on the object: the goal of design was namely "good form," defined by the function of the individual object in a context that was held to be immutable. Improvements were hence soon limited to formal modifications that sought to approximate the International Style. The fact that "good form" had long been criticized and derided behind the scenes yet continued to be presented to the general public as a criterion of award-winning, acclaimed design gave rise to a situation bordering on dishonesty. The Italian designer Ettore Sottsass and his associates dealt the deathblow to "good form." They created critical objects and furniture, the exaggerated functionality of which made them ridiculous and impractical.

Others, such as Raggi and his circle, demonstrated through ironic references to 1950s design how even allegedly good design sank in just a few years into kitsch banality. Against the backdrop of these—at the visible level—critical positions, the Deutsche Werkbund endeavored through conferences and internal debate to pursue the concept of "integral design," that is, the incorporation also of invisible systems in the design process. It is not by changing the product itself but only by influencing cooperative subsystems that the everyday life of an individual can be improved.

Criteria For A New Design (1977)

Those were the days, back when the Werkbund commission descended with all-important faces on the MuBa design fair (*Mustermesse Basel*) to grant its annual "Good Form" design award (*Die Gute Form*), before going on to dine in style at Gerstner & Kutter. Producers with their eyes on this prestigious prize had to register for the competition in advance. The product range under consideration was accordingly quite limited: candidates had to be initiates, aware of the Werkbund's existence. Even the commission realized this, one fine day, and thereupon decided to swarm through the MuBa's extensive halls personally, in search of good form. Well, the Church too believes in heathens who lead a Christian life without knowing a thing about Christianity. Therefore, if ever the commission happened upon examples of *anima naturaliter christiana*, it warmly encouraged them to pay the judgment fee, so that their products too might be assessed. It thus came to pass that the award went to Lux & Schoechlin's lilac tie, which, although soon to be supplanted by the black roll-neck sweater (which never won the award), was at the time still an emblem of the middle-aged, dynamic, progressive architect. Another time, the award went to a clean-cut, right-angled fitted kitchen with a white PVC finish. The same fitted kitchen went on display at MuBa the following year too, but this time with an imitation zebrano wood finish and the "Good Form" seal of quality to go with it. An outraged letter to the manufacturer prompted an unruffled inquiry in return: whether the point in question here was the good form or good color…

As it strode around the halls of the design fair, passing judgment, the commission seemed very sure of what it was about: right angles, sharp edges, and plain surfaces in light gray or white—no room for error there. The sole exceptions to this rule were jewelry, which had to be "natural" and "real," and children's toys, which had to be made of wood. It had a tough life, that good old good form; and now it is dead. But who killed it?—In the following, I endeavor to name certain stations in its slow demise; and these will serve perhaps to point us towards those "criteria for quality design today" recently called for in *werk-archithese*.

- Semi-conductor technology spelled the end of visible functionalism; in the absence of a sign it is impossible to tell from looking at a gray metal box whether it makes music or processes data.
- The postwar generation's tastes oscillated between several forms of variously apparent purposiveness.
- The obsolescence rate of the look of a thing came to outstrip that of its technology.
- Perception of functionalism proved to be linguistic; forms are not read directly but as signs.
- The demand for precise research into human needs led to paradoxes that challenged the very definition of need. In any case, human needs are not a describable set that can be "satisfied" by a corresponding set of objects.
- The man who consumes in order to satisfy his needs destroys his own environment and that of his fellow human beings.
- The attempt to "solve" the urban traffic problem has such disastrous repercussions as to give rise to the term "livability," namely the first term ever to incorporate a social and a material component.
- Youth protests [in 1968], the greatest intellectual movement since 1945, were by no means anti-form. Rather, they invested form with new values. In 1960, London youth began to dress in a Victorian style. In 1970, students squatted vacant villas in the bankers' district of Frankfurt Main, thereby giving expression to a greater sense of freedom than the modern architects who demolish such villas.

- The *Whole Earth Catalog* demonstrates the feasibility of life beyond the capitalist production of consumer goods and "good form."
- The oil crisis is bearing surprising fruits: a rethink. The Royal Institute of British Architects' new motto—"long life, loose fit, low energy"—is a rap on the knuckles of modernist dogma.
- In his renowned article, Alexander Tzonis counters "welfare" design with populism and compiles a list of participatory concepts now emerging in the design field.
- Herbert J. Gans discovers in Levittown that not objects per se but the organization of objects determines our lives. Accordingly, it is not the house itself but the lease and house rules that foster or hamper livability.
- Ivan Illich discovers that objects have properties likely to edify or destroy society: vehicles for personal use that exceed 20 km/h, apparatuses with over 10 volt, or medicinal systems of exaggerated scientificity are all a hindrance to democracy.

And now you're asking about criteria for new design? I could indeed name a few. So please imagine a new Werkbund commission descending on the MuBa trade fair in Basel, picking up some product on display, and asking:

- Is it made from raw materials sourced without oppressing anyone?
- Was it manufactured in meaningful, non-rationalized labor processes?
- Is it multi-purpose?
- Is it built to last?
- In what state is it discarded, and what becomes of it then?
- Does it make its user dependent on central supply systems or services, or can it be used independently of these?

- Does it privilege the user alone, or stimulate a sense of community?
- Is it freely selectable, or does it compel the user to make additional purchases?

A collection is still underway for the post-jurying party.

On the Design of Everyday Life (1979)

I do not intend to deliver solid theory in this lecture, just some speculation to stimulate you—and it will be easy to attack what I say. If things go well, we'll end up with a new job description, one I would call "the integrated designer." My intention is to identify the organizational context of designed or planned systems, which is to say, the rules that govern usage and actually comprise our environment—in other words, to correlate the invisible part of our lives with its planned, visible, physical dimension.

To make that perhaps a little less abstract, I'll tell you first about something I have observed. I usually spend my vacation on a farm, at which the mailman used to call by each day. He never knocked on the door, just opened the door so loudly that one could tell he was in the house. He then put the mail on the table and waited expectantly for someone to come talk to him a while. Then he went to the next farm. Then the post office decreed that farms should install a mailbox on the road, in order to save the mailmen's time: a beautiful design task. We therefore acquired a mailbox, a yellow one with a black trim and very distinguished-looking metal moldings that were flat enough to let the rain pour in, and we installed it. After that, we noticed that our farmer and all other farmers in the area no longer had any information, as the dissemination of information in rural areas does not take place through letters. Namely, neighbors do not write to one another; they tell their stories to the mailman, who passes them on at the next farm. The post office actually had no idea of how it conveyed news. It believed it transported letters containing news. In reality, however, an invisible system was at work, which actually conveyed news in a most appropriate way.

We who are interested in visual culture have partly forgotten to reference the organizational, social dimension, as well as other dimensions that we will deal with later. If we take modern architecture to begin with, I must point out immediately that this dimension was not initially overlooked. Modern architecture of the 1920s certainly had a social dimension inasmuch as it strove to reorganize society. It strove perhaps to do so in a way we would no longer pursue today—the Frankfurt kitchen—by regulating daily life in a very rigid yet nonetheless well-considered way. That this stimulus (or this mission) turned into a style that subsequently allowed context to fall into oblivion is another matter. The paradoxes of this non-ornamental style then gave rise to all sorts of other approaches. The endeavor to make architecture more expressive by integrating in it elements of everyday life was pursued in theoretical terms—*Learning from Las Vegas*, Advertising is Beautiful, etc.—yet these did not address more than the purely visual realm.

I would like to examine a different strand of development, namely the growing appreciation in the 1960s of the fact that this form of architecture and design cannot save the world. Then, sometime around the mid-1960s, we began to hear terms such as "livability" or—negatively—the notorious "inhospitableness of our cities" (Mitscherlich): hence terms that appeared to integrate the visual context, namely the house or the city, as well as the invisible dimension: How does one use this? Are there rules that hamper its use, or make its use impossible? Does not the housing question imply that one ask also who owns the house, whether the janitor is a nice man, what the house rules are, who has the authority to lock the house, etc., etc.? The 1960s also witnessed the emergence of a word with very far-reaching connotations: "environment"—environment as something with a systematic character, with carefully balanced properties, and self-regulatory capacities that we have evidently disrupted. I do not wish to discuss here the extent to which this reading may be tenable; rather, I want to cite it as a further example of the endeavor to integrate the visible and invisible dimensions, i.e. the physical environment and rules.

The 1960s introduced a remarkable new approach into the architectural field, yet one that could be read in two ways. I mean Kevin Lynch's approach in *The Image of the City*,[1] in which he asks: "How do people actually see their city" and "What do they see of the city?" Lynch observed that people do not see urban planners and architects' input in the city. When someone asks the way to the railroad station, he is not told in reply, "You must go to the beautiful house designed by Le Corbusier, then take a right, then comes a building designed by Mies van der Rohe, then you go straight ahead, and you'll be at the station!" He is told rather, "You must go as far as this road sign then, if no one is looking, you just cut through the flower bed, go past the tobacconist's, and right behind that is the best way to the station!" So people see the city from their everyday perspectives: Where is the short cut? Where can I buy cigarettes? Where is there a slot machine? And so forth …

Lynch's theory was understood in a dual sense, or misunderstood—one cannot be too sure whether Lynch himself misunderstood himself, if that is possible. For he, or at least his successors, called for the construction of expressive buildings by which people could orientate themselves, whereby actual observations suggest people are orientated not to forms per se but to forms plus usages, which is to say, to everyday signs rather than aesthetic signs.

Herbert J. Gans's book *The Levittowners*[2] was published likewise in the 1960s. The author asked himself, why people live in or buy

1 [Kevin Lynch, *The Image of the City*, MIT Press, Cambridge MA 1960]

2 [Herbert J. Gans, *The Levittowners: Ways of Life and Politics in a New Suburban Community*, Routledge & Kegan Paul, New York 1960]

houses in Levittown, in those monotonous settlements made up of detached houses that are built moreover, in a strange, old-fashioned colonial style, with terrible lawns out front that one is not allowed to use, and so forth. So these detached family homes have everything the architect or the initiated layman abhors—yet they sell like hot cakes. Mr. Levitt & Sons are doing good business, and the buyers are satisfied. Herbert J. Gans also bought such a house, spent two years there, studied the phenomenon, and ascertained that people's environment is not the visible environment; rather, the Levitts had succeeded in creating an invisible, social environment that was perfectly suited to a certain class of income and social standing. Such people find there what they need, namely families of the same age who have children who also want to go to schools that lead to university, and who also belong to certain churches of certain denominations, churches that offer a social as well as an ecclesiastical perspective; families in similar professional positions. Levitt pitches people's environment correctly, because his plans are based on a classification system in which the house itself, its lawn, its garden, its driveway, and all the things we find so horrible rank very low whereas invisible factors rate very highly.

Finally, let me name a very different discovery made by Ivan Illich, namely that properties of a social nature are inherent to objects. Illich expresses this thus, in his striking manner:

Everything that moves faster than 20 kilometers per hour is undemocratic. I do not agree with that. I think the railroad—it is democratic—should have a special permit. Yet we must take advantage of the discovery itself. There are objects that create liberties and there are objects that create dependencies; there are objects that foster social relations and there are objects that foster isolation.

What we are looking for here, is—to use my term of choice—an integrated or integrative theory of design or planning; one that incorporates regulatory systems as well as the visible dimension of our environment. Until now, architects and designers have said: Spaces regulate life—regulate where entrances are, what shape rooms are, and how objects look. Then there is a profession that says: laws regulate life. And then along come the sociologists and say: no, behavioral patterns and systems of relationship regulate life. And since these professions go about their business so perfectly in parallel, the architects build their buildings; they build schools, and rave on the opening day about how this school will be a community center, a hub of the neighborhood; and they never suspect (or perhaps already suspect), that it will never become a community center, not because any architectural failing precludes this possibility but because the janitor locks up at 8 p.m.—which is good for business of course, for the construction of a community center can be commissioned next. Traffic is approached in a similar manner, namely as an isolated phenomenon. It is calculated how many people will move to an area. A basic presumption is that growth will be continuous. It is then calculated how many people have a car nowadays, and how long it will take until the last baby also has a car. Then road width is adjusted accordingly. Here, the English term "self-fulfilling prophecies" should be taken quite literally: the roads will fullfill, i.e. will fill until they are full, because once roads have been built, they are used, naturally, for this kind of extrapolation of course forces people to use a car to get around. That other possibilities exist, that one might move beyond full capacity calculations, for example by introducing staggered work schedules and the like, can never be grasped—simply because the expert in this field is not available.

Now, the built, physical world certainly has defining properties. There is a saying in German: "We cannot go through the wall." Therefore a door must exist. But hidden doors and non-doors exist too, namely laws and prohibitions. And walls are not as important as dos and don'ts are. The streetcar stop I have to use each day is organized in such a way that I miss the streetcar whenever I use the cross-walk with traffic signals that leads to the streetcar stop, because the streetcar can drive off the exact same moment the cars do. And I cannot board the streetcar at that moment, because the cars do not stop for me when they have a green light. So, if I don't want to miss my streetcar, I have to jump over the flowerbed that lies outside the traffic signal zone. What is decisive here is not the physical access point per se but rather, the regulation. A streetcar stop is thus an integrated system comprising design, laws, and regulations—and is obviously still in search of its designer.

I would like now to speak about an important aspect of non-physical organization, about time. Time and temporal rhythms, timetables and transport schedules: these are the things that govern our lives. I was recently sent a book from France, Anne Cauquelin's *La ville la nuit*.[3] Can one write a book about the night? The night is a natural phenomenon of course, yet since electric light was invented we can light up the night, at least as far as we need to. But the night is an institution, says Anne Cauquelin. It is determined, not by the fact that nature creates darkness and light, but by rules. When are lights turned on? When are they turned off? In consequence, public transport ceases to operate at a particular time, for example, and bars close—hence, infrastructure is not used to full capacity, and our freedom to do as we like is restricted: the freedom, for example, to spend an evening having a drink with friends then return home by public transport with alcohol in our blood. We cannot do so, because public transport does not run after midnight. In Hamburg's City Nord district or in the City of London there are restaurants that close in the evenings. Other restaurants in more outlying districts open only in the evenings, because people in the evening go to other

3 [Anne Cauquelin, *La ville la nuit*, Presse Universitaires de France, Paris 1977]

places than they do at midday. The institution night necessitates a dual infrastructure.

Let us linger a moment on this issue of time and temporal rhythms. The history of labor struggles, of safety at work, and of the acceptability of labor also includes the struggle for a shorter working week. But one gets the impression that those responsible on both fronts in this struggle, or on its three fronts—the state, the employers, and the trade unions—do not think the temporal rhythm concept through to its end. Their hitherto legitimate struggle therefore enters a new phase, for we are obliged now to consider how to use leisure time. I'm not talking here—and I should stress this three times over—about the problem of leisure per se. That does not exist in any case. Everyone is convinced that everyone else has problems with leisure, but no one believes he himself does. If only everyone would admit this once and for all, it would put a stop not only to all this talk of the problems with leisure but also to the leisure facilities that are built in order that other people spend their leisure time properly.

So, that is not my issue here. Rather, I am concerned with the issue of how these temporal rhythms determine our lives, namely the daily rhythm, the weekly rhythm, hence also the weekend, the annual rhythm, vacation time, and the rhythm of life—at what age do we embark on our working lives and at what age do we retire? We really ought to know more about the consequences these rhythms have, as well as about how life can be organized under the conditions imposed by temporal rhythms. I consider this really is an issue when it comes to designing our lives. It is, moreover, also a visible problem: the daily rhythm leads to congestion on our roads, the annual rhythms to congestion in our tourist resorts, etc. In France at the moment, the planners' watchword is "de-synchronization," by which they mean that the masses' working day, and likewise their weekend and vacation schedules, should not follow a uniform temporal rhythm. It is hoped that de-synchronization will render redundant the famous announcements that tell us on certain Friday evenings and Saturday mornings in July that roads from Paris to the South have become impassable. Of course, this is functionalism once again: traffic becomes jammed and so organization is called for; yet this is far from being a redesign of the problem.

I would like also to make a passing reference to the other places where such invisible, organizational problems crop up. I already mentioned Ivan Illich and his discovery that objects have a certain authority, and are discriminatory. They can create dependency on power supply systems, for example. Some objects are created such that one has to buy a further object if one wishes to use them; then, when one has done so, one realizes one needs to buy yet another object in order for them to function. In addition, objects have production histories. They may be the product of inhumane labor operations, obtained through the exploitation of nature or people; but they may also be made from recyclable raw materials.

It is not difficult nowadays, to give the car a beating. We generally think the car is to blame for the destruction of society, namely because it is discriminatory. There are areas that can be reached solely by motorists, or that cannot be reached on Saturdays and Sundays because public transport provides no service. Another form of social destruction is the isolation that ensues from the fact that the majority population is sitting in cars. The minority population, which is not protected by steel and speed, no longer risks using the roads, roads that previously were considered safe, because previously there were always enough people standing around or walking by who were able to rush to a person's aid, or to fetch help. When everyone is sitting in his tin can and only one person is unprotected, that person feels unsafe: actually unsafe or potentially unsafe. This is not an argument for pedestrian zones, however. I consider the impact of pedestrian zones on peripheral areas to be a disaster. But that is another matter.

I would like to examine the social characteristics of objects, such as are exemplified here by the car, in reference also to other objects. A year ago we talked about building technology and the issue of the individual's access to building technology. Our power supply is not just a physical phenomenon; it is also wrapped up in regulations. We are not allowed to tinker with it, firstly—officially; everyone does tinker with it, however, and can buy everything that is outlawed in any department store. But given our high voltage it is not entirely safe to do so. Why cannot a part of our power supply run at a lower voltage, one that wouldn't kill us if we happened to touch it? That is impossible, the experts say—yet in the car it is possible. The car headlights are as bright as our lamps, have 12 volts, and anyone can tinker with them. But that, apparently, is impossible in the home.

Nor are we allowed to tinker with our water supply. Licensed tradesmen must do that; and everything must be installed, and under lock and key. The fittings are such that a wrench of the sort we can obtain is unable to open them; only fully trained tradesmen have the right type of wrench to repair our wash basins and replace the seals—whereby that really is something just anyone could do. But, we are told, it is impossible for safety reasons, and we would all have drowned already, and our houses been swept away, if any Tom, Dick, or Harry had access to the water pipes. I too believed all that, at least until we bought a washing machine; for then suddenly, everything was allowed. A rubber hose serves as a drain; we hang it over the washtub when the machine is running, and otherwise we hang it on the wall. The water functions here pretty much as it does when we use it in the garden: it arrives through a hose and leaves through a hose. Evidently, the washing machine lobby has political power enough to break the rules and return to common sense, to the common sense we could all do with actually, when it comes to house building. Then we could namely help ourselves. It would be more fun too.

I would like to mention a further arena—the sickness system—in which an institutional context should be integrated, although this notion initially may seem rather alien. We think of disease as something contagious that flies at us out of the blue. But it has a highly institutionalized aspect. When one is sitting around at work, tired, it may happen that the boss arrives and says: So, please make up your mind whether you want to be sick or healthy! Apparently one can decide such a thing. There are two rituals: either I decide, although I am sick, to be healthy, and carry on as before; or I embark on the ritual of being sick, and tell my boss, "Yes, I would be very grateful if you would call a cab for me, then I will call from the hospital to say how bad it looks." This, although there's nothing wrong with me today that a cup of tea and a couple of hours peace and quiet wouldn't put right. But I have triggered the sickness system already—doctor, nurse, and the whole caboodle. I decided to be sick and must consequently accept sickness as a context and an institution. And the hospital is also such an environment, designed by architects and managed by organizers, and these two things do not go together. Let's not broaden the topic even further: I could show you points where organization does not work, because the context is not properly designed.

So we evidently live in systems that are partly visible but also contain some invisible reference systems, regulatory systems, or temporal rhythms. The transitions between these systems are a type of invisible door, namely the rules that facilitate or assure this transition. At some point our work is done and we can go home. The next question might be, whether we can still go shopping, whether our working day, our company's closing time corresponds to the stores' closing time. Some stores close a little later than our company, if we are lucky, and perhaps we can make it to the post office too, although it is naturally too late to go to any other office. These institutional doors govern how we organize our everyday lives. It is evident therefore, that we are surrounded by an invisible functional system of sorts, which is integrated in the social system comprised of our participation in working life, in our circle of friends, and in hierarchies.

And now, the final question: Who actually designs this environment by combining the organizational aspect and the visible aspect? Who has even a clue as to who designs what, and as to who determines the regulatory aspects of our environment? Allow me therefore to reiterate the provocative challenge: be an integrated designer! For only then will you be a true designer of everyday life, or an architect of everyday life.

Design—Rite and Expression of a Hopeful Society (1984)

That hopeful society we keep hearing about is actually comprised of designers. It is they who are happy and pursue a healthy lifestyle, they who choose to be awoken each morning by a machine that also makes them a cup of tea. It is they who begin the day with a run in the woods before taking their shower and briefly calling their girlfriend, who is likewise enjoying carrot juice, a run in the woods, and a shower before rushing off to work—and she provides training in computer-assisted basket-weaving to blind Afghan children with speech defects, by the way, and has already made quite a success of it.

Adornometer,
Drawing: Lucius Burckhardt

Habermaster:
Insert cash—Retrieve cash,
Drawing: Lucius Burckhardt

Also for our dear D., it is time now to set the air conditioning to daytime temperatures and pick up a pencil. He's happily sketching a hairdresser's table in Sottsass style, just to warm up, as well as a kidney-shaped table with Mendini frills. Ultimately, however, he turns his attention to the serious matter of a fire-resistant electrical socket. But although D. could deliver a really neat idea for the form of the grounding lug, his design today is not going very well. He's mulling over the words of the fire insurance boss to whom he had tried the previous day to sell the socket: "The fire risk is minimal now. More security merely increases the risk."

So no hope of progress there, for the moment. And what about the great coffee-making machine? The manufacturer hasn't been back in touch—doubtless he too is feeling the crisis. And what about the bathroom? The client fears conflict with the union of master plumbers. Is there anything doing anywhere else? Crockery? Silverware?—All done with. Furniture? The market is in ruins. Cars? Televisions?—It would be nice, if ever ... But there is that packaging job for an anti-sweaty-feet spray. The can itself is revolver-shaped so the packaging has to convey something more conciliatory, but without lessening the product's masculine appeal. Difficult indeed. And one ought really feel ashamed for the client.

When this mid-morning mood swing is as low as it can go, D. sweeps the bookshelf with a gaze until the cover of a large book catches his eye. "Design is invisible," D. shouts. "Design is invisible. How on earth did I manage to forget that?" He stands up and walks into the adjacent room: his laboratory, as he calls it, a laboratory for the design of certain rites. Here one can find all his major developments, which he keeps secret from the world: the Adorno-Meter, the Habermaster, and the Stein of Wittgen. He is presently working on a Levi-Strauss.

The Levi-Strauss is under development as a bouquet—a "Strauss," in German—that one can present to the lady of the house when invited to be her guest. Whereas bouquets in general wilt and therefore cannot be given back to the original donor on a return visit, the Levi-Strauss is designed specifically for the purpose of such ritual recycling. Based on the exchange of brides, the origin of all hospitality gifts, it is meant to inspire wife swapping and thus lend a new dimension to hospitality.

But the Levi-Strauss is just a byproduct of a comprehensive design project that is intended not only to bring about D.'s breakthrough but also to put an end to the crisis overall: the alarm-clock-as-needed project. While of the size and appearance of a common or garden alarm clock, this device spreads hope and joy thanks to its very existence. And when it starts up, God forbid that the stores are not yet open; for then no one can stop us from purchasing the ballpoint pen that functions perfectly up to a depth of 30 meters underwater, nor save us from moving voluntarily into a newly built apartment. And now there's the front door bell: the girlfriend is here, ready to whisk D. off to satisfy needs he doesn't yet know he has.

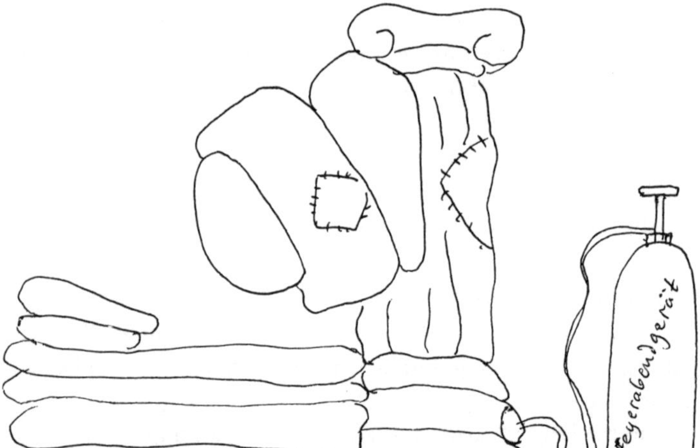

Feyerabend device,
Drawing: Lucius Burckhardt

Design Implies Processes, Not Just Forms! (1970)

Faith in design's ability to produce a humane society is one of the fundamental mistakes of the modern movement's pioneers. Human environments are visible and subject to formal design to a limited extent only; they are comprised to a far greater extent of organizational and institutional factors. To alter these is a political challenge.

When faced with the monotonous rows of pseudo-colonial-style houses in the sprawling suburb of Levittown, the American sociologist Herbert J. Gans pondered whether the clients of Mr. Levitt & Sons were struck by the ugliness of this housing. But in the clients' eyes, as he soon discovered, the environment was comprised of quite other factors than the beauty or ugliness of buildings and gardens: factors such as a society that showed them respect, good schools for their children, access to a church of their own denomination, the pleasure they took in owning a property as well as the freedom this gave them to convert it, and low-risk access to the highway and their place of work. By contrast, the environment they had fled was marked by their fear of being fired, neighborhood discrimination, bad company for their children, and schools that did not lead to a university education. Such are the environmental factors faced by anyone dealing with life's constraints. Should he manage to finance his son's tertiary studies at a school of design then the son is likely to let him know, during semester vacation, that Levittown is badly planned and the parental home a design disaster. The father may then reply that any environment deserving of the term humane is one in which people can live free of fear, exploitation, and surveillance by third parties, is one that any of its members can freely choose, and help to shape, one in which no one is subject to design terror, not even that of "good design."

In so-called ethnological museums, attempts are made to familiarize the visitor with alien peoples by exhibiting their cultural artifacts; thus one finds, for example, a spear, a canoe, or a musical instrument from some tribe or other. Let's imagine that an alien people wishes to acquaint itself with our culture and we send off a tea's-made, poultry scissors, a sewing machine, and a hairdryer—for our "good design" exhibitions display that sort of thing, we must admit.

This "modern" design has been dead at least since the invention of semi-conductor technology. While, until the Second World War, it was still possible to imagine that technology would find its way back to a form of organic design that expresses the purpose of a device as clearly as tongs or a coffee pot do, we note today that similar elements (certain transistorized aggregates) culminate in different devices depending on how they are arranged: a box full of wires and batteries may be a music machine or a calculator: the difference between them lies in their inner organization, metaphorically expressed as "soft-ware."

Under these circumstances, design's role as a means to improve the environment is viable only if consideration is given to the real meaning of the term. Design implies processes, not just forms. The aim of design is first and foremost to determine not the form of a device but rather its potential use, its applicability, its broadest possible viability, and its non-contribution to chicanery and regression. I'm thinking here of a typical exercise in traditional design. Tickets for public transport are available today from the automated vending machines proliferating on our streets: dynamic-looking hulks with award-winning distinctions and a discreet electronic hum. But what about the old lady with two handbags, numb fingers, and eyeglasses that have steamed up in the cold? Have such automated hulks improved her environment? If she could still pay her fare inside the bus, she'd gladly do without this design, wouldn't she? And surely the best design would simply be to do away with bus tickets once and for all.

The discipline I aspire to represent teaches that we should focus not on objects but, as people often say, "on human beings." Wrong! The modules of which our environment is comprised are neither people nor objects but the invisible rules that shape social processes, which is to say roles, relationships, behavioral norms, or however else one chooses to call them.

Our visible environment is shaped only minimally by designers. Even visible elements retain or modify their appearance primarily owing to the impact of productive forces. Let's cast our minds back to our last weekend excursion, which took us through a picture-book landscape in the Swiss Alps. That landscape is an outcome neither of sophisticated design nor the blind impact of nature but, rather, of the work of the farmers who maintain it, mow the grass, plant new fruit trees, and keep the hedgerows trim and tidy. If ever methods of agricultural production change, so too does the landscape. Or let's call to mind a busy city center with its stores and old and new buildings: it too is no more the work of town planners than it is "organically grown." It is a snapshot of the interplay of economic circumstances and speculative forces, of political power relations and shopping habits grown dear to us. The preservation or systematic improvement of such environments can be assured only minimally by design but to a far greater extent by shaping social circumstances.

This is what my discipline teaches: the environment is a product of the interaction that takes place between all the stakeholders involved, which is to say, between planners, civic authorities, property owners, and residents; or between designers, and users, and one's like-minded peers; or finally, in the learning process of any individual who never ceases to learn to interpret his environment anew.

The Grammar of Reality (1967)

My memories of drawing class: the teacher was a zoologist and thwarted artist. He drew with the precision one finds in old botany books and his painting style lay somewhere between the Impressionists and Segantini. In drawing class there were colored crayons only. They were marvelously suited to the master's goals: to let some violet glint there, on the trunk of a tree, a midnight blue there, in the deep shade; to highlight that distant lawn with a touch of orange, and have the nearby fir trees softly glow, midway between ultramarine and purple. If the student's sheet appeared to approximate these goals, the teacher would take a seat and add the finishing touches himself. But usually he merely said: "See that sun-kissed cliff? Crayon No. 23 with a dash of No. 7."

Was that good so? Yes, it was good so. One penned a note to Santa Claus in fervent hope, topping the list with a set of colored crayons, a butterfly net, a flower press, and a magnifying glass (20:1). I devoted to botany the one afternoon each week when I didn't have school, and presented the findings next morning in class. "Let me see," he'd say then. "Where did you find that? Bring it to the drawing class. That deep purple interests me." It was a world in harmony and at peace with itself, in which a young boy could have formative experiences.

But was it truly harmonious? It was the 1930s. In Paris, Merleau-Ponty and Sartre were discussing perception; Koffka was writing his *Principles of Gestalt Psychology*, Brunswik his *Perception and the World of Objects*; and beyond seven mountains, among the seven dwarfs, Portmann was already musing on the form of animals. None of this penetrated our Darwin-inspired Biedermeier temple. It was the 1930s. From the radio crowed the voice of the Führer. One day a catalog landed on the table at home: "degenerate" art was being auctioned off at Fischer's in Lucerne. My schoolboy self leafed through it, helplessly: "This is supposed to be art? Collectors pay hundreds of francs for that? And the sable-rattling Führer is afraid of it? What did these things ever do to him?"

One may well ask: Why indeed was he afraid of them? And by what reason or implacable logic did his ally and opponent in the East persecute them? Their hate was directed not only at artists such as George Grosz, who clearly exposed their ridiculousness. No, they were equally afraid of landscapes, animal portraits, and still lives; yes, of paintings in which we could see nothing at all that we might have put a name to. How might anything so anodyne do harm? Here was something for which there was no place in our artistic natural history museum. When we drew, we believed we were drawing nature as it really is; and whatever we brought to paper was to our minds a part of nature, just as a luminous sheen and colored crayon number-so-and-so were. The master said: "You must learn to see the colors in the colors."

So no one solved for us the riddle the dictators had posed. No one told us that it is not the portrayal of a thing but the way it is portrayed that puts the message across. No one shook our faith in the fact that Mother Nature speaks to us in her own language, that there is a natural grammar as well as an appropriate way to paint, one that our teacher had mastered and now was passing on to us. So we made it all cozy, drew down the blinds to keep out the sun, and beat a path to the world with colored crayons. By the time the war broke out some of us were painting the soldiers and canons that could be seen on the streets back then; and by the time it was no longer possible to draw the things afoot in that war ... Well, by then we were no longer in school.

Today I think that art teaching must at the very least make the problem of communication transparent in design. Nature consists not of the signs, forms, and colors we use to produce its likeness but emits its own stimuli from which we fashion our impressions, musings, and models. These reflect not nature but our fellow human beings. Accordingly, recurrent reinterpretation of the world is the process that shapes society; and it is also the most sensitive political seismograph—if only one leaves it free rein.

Urban Design and Its Significance for Residents (1975)

People would be hard put to come up with a word to match our German word "Gestalt."[1] It says a great deal and veils even more. Its implicit assertion that "the whole is greater than the sum of its parts" is fruitful; yet it fails to convey that to make a whole of various parts is not a natural process but a social act, an act which reflects history, culture, hegemony, and education.

How modern this concept of the city as a conscious design, as a planned object or cityscape is, and how tightly interwoven it is with our—possibly Romantic—way of seeing becomes evident when we try to glean from the historical travelogues of Montaigne, Felix Platter, or even such a late author as Madame de Staël something of the appearance of the cities they visited. We learn the name of the city as well as that of the river on which it stands—both are traced back to their Latin roots, perhaps—then we learn about the churches. Some Roman antiquities are sure to be mentioned and, before we know it, we are on nodding terms with several more or less famous personalities. The cityscape corresponds to the pictograms of an artist such as Matthäus Merian. His etchings appear to render urban form visible; in reality they collate information about the actual location, fortifications, major churches, and curiosities of a place. Baedecker takes a very different angle: human beings vanish, except when in the guise of the typical "Volk" or commoners. Buildings and streets, especially historic ones, acquire

1 [The German word "Gestalt" has several meanings, among which number design, form, guise, cast, and stature.]

importance. It is they, taken as a whole, which constitute the picturesque and photogenic city—which admittedly encompasses only the inner city. Actual residential areas, villa districts, and social housing projects, to say nothing of supermarkets, are still neither an object of "urban design" nor part of the cityscape as such, even today.

The cityscape as seen by the urban dweller, the city resident, is a construct too, which is to say, an image engendered by learning processes that unfold in a social setting. The resident's city differs from that of the tourist presumably inasmuch as the resident processes a greater amount of information to a lesser degree of picturesqueness. The resident has a more precise knowledge of the city than the visitor, but he feels no need to distill what he knows into a souvenir image. It is more likely that familiar features—the street he lives on, his workplace, local stores, his Sunday excursions—are fixed in his mind's eye solely for the purpose of getting about the place, in a skeleton framework whose extreme form is the subway map. A series of research projects on this theme have shown that a resident takes his bearings from features of relevance to him personally, i.e. those that foster or prohibit his activities. Conspicuous landmarks that play no part in his personal sphere are registered consciously only when no other pointers are available.

Beyond this personal experience of the environment, the resident's cityscape is no different than that of the tourist. He describes his city by drawing on those very clichés established by the local tour guide or tourism office. The familiar hometown, which one tends a priori to regard as nothing out of the ordinary, is imbued with flair thanks to foreign forces and the slogans coined to market it: "The City of Gorgeous Gables," for example, or "The Ruhr District's Showcase." A resident adopts such slogans, even if he has no personal experience of the feature in question but has simply heard that others set great store by it.

This leads to an important insight. The resident observing parts of his city is unsure how to interpret them whenever he comes across phenomena that have no relevance to his own life, which is to say, no social relevance. Picturesqueness alone, combined with existential irrelevance, is not conducive to legibility. Such parts of the city or architectural structures are read more easily in terms of secondary characteristics, which are more indicative of the social background. A residential street lined—from the connoisseur's viewpoint—with striking nineteenth-century buildings, let's say, is judged by any passer-by one cares to ask in terms either of the make of car parked in front of the buildings or the matter of how well-kept, neglected, or full of trash their front yards happen to be. And it is such secondary characteristics, in fact, which tell us something about the street's current social significance.

For any city resident unbiased by knowledge of art history, the objects in question are significant not as architectural monuments but as institutions. The city resident's visible environment is therefore only of secondary importance; the invisible circumstances that shape his environment are of much greater relevance. What types of people live here? How high is the rent? Who owns the house? What are the house rules? Are children allowed to make noise? Are the local stores affordable? Will the street be considered a good address when I apply for a job? This sort of information outweighs by far the fact that the street was built around 1880, or that its style reflects English Neo-Gothic of the 1840s, which derived in turn from certain Tudor revivals in eighteenth-century English castles. Given this primacy of the "invisible" dimension, the apparently contradictory insights acquired through primarily sociological research (such as that of Herbert J. Gans),[2] and primarily cognitive research (in

2 [Herbert J. Gans: *The Levittowners: Ways of Life and Politics in a New Suburban Community*, Routledge & Kegan Paul, New York 1960. For more on Gans and Lynch, cf. also "On the Design of Everyday Life."]

Kevin Lynch's sense of the term),[3] seem to me to lead to the same results.

If we acknowledge, in consequence, that the city resident's environment is first and foremost a social environment, and that urban design has a role to play only insofar as it conveys social information, and hence a sense of social belonging, we can now hazard certain conclusions that perhaps throw some light on what has happened to our cities and their residents over the last twenty years. We all know the score: land not earmarked for construction became the most sought-after location; residential buildings shot up like mushrooms on cheap land in places neglected by public transport planning; and the state reneged on its lovely plans, namely by opening up undeveloped land between major traffic arteries to private traffic, and neglecting public transport in the already built-up areas. The repercussions for the city center were catastrophic. The areas devoted to traffic tore apart the inner cities to an extent such that the center, hitherto a compact destination, completely fell apart; and all that remained was parking lots and department stores, along with some older apartment buildings on odd lots, which have long since been in the hands of speculators and are generally leased to immigrant workers. What information does a city in this condition convey to its residents?

From 1957 to 1967, that decade of planning and economic optimism known also as the Golden Sixties, public applause for such development was still forthcoming. Profiteers were numerous, and only a very few felt the damage, namely those young married couples or new arrivals in town in search of an apartment, who ultimately had to move into the most expensive and least favorably situated housing developments. Anyone who already had an apartment still

3 [Kevin Lynch, *The Image of the City*, MIT Press, Cambridge MA 1960]

paid a low rent, and benefited moreover from the wage raises that had to be granted, given the higher rent levels in the growing number of new apartments on offer.

Only in the late 1960s, the era of student protests, wildcat strikes, and environmental shock did this state of affairs begin to change. Large sections of the population were affected by developments, because either their apartments had been demolished, or their street was threatening to turn into a slum, or to drop considerably in value owing to the amount of traffic whizzing by. The city had become the enemy. In London, under the rallying cry "Let us be," ad hoc residents' committees marched in protest against every new initiative launched by the authorities. In Turin in the summer of 1967, workers at FIAT rose against the city authorities, and were bloodily beaten down by police on the Corso Traiano. In 1968, the city of Paris was brought to a standstill for more than the month of May. Student protests in German cities, which were partly the outcome of social disintegration, simply strengthened the resolve of other urban dwellers to turn their backs on the city. Like it or not, city residents realized that an urban lifestyle is a viable proposition even without setting foot in the city. In the triangle between suburban residence, shopping mall, and workplace ghetto, a form of existence came into being, far removed from anything the aesthete still imagines "urban design" to mean.

The question of urban design, the face of the city, consequently took a back seat to the question: Will cities even continue to exist? Optimists in the fields of technology and media development had envisaged that information systems would take the place of cities, quasi as a natural progression. They believed city life would be possible in the future also in isolation, for social contacts would be able to be successfully maintained regardless of one's location. However, we have as yet seen nothing to suggest that the media are developing as tools of democratic debate. It is far truer to say that they continue to represent the one-way street of indoctrination, permitting a response only when it suits their agenda. Moreover, the car-free Sundays introduced during the oil crisis in the winter of 1973–74 illustrated very clearly this new rural "urban dweller's" lack of independence as well as the level of isolation he suffers once the trade in motor cars, to which public transport has been sacrificed, shows its true colors.

Meanwhile, however, given the menaced, slum-ridden city centers wrecked either by the economic boom or its counterpart, the crash, we face the grave problem of preserving the city. Preserving the city in the first instance implies landmark restoration, which is to say, the care and maintenance of cultural heritage. How worthy of preservation a building is deemed to be depends on art historical factors as well as on its picturesque context, or anecdotal city history. Landmark restoration insofar accomplishes only a fraction of what actually needs to be done, namely to preserve the city also as a place fit to live in. Therefore, the issues are, firstly, to save the still quite considerable reserves of comfortable and affordable living space in our inner cities and, secondly, to put this preservation strategy on a firm footing by creating social conditions that make the city viable not only for extravagant bachelors, student couples, and immigrant workers, but also for average members of the population with their normal age and family structures. We showed at the start of this paper that the prerequisites of doing so lie only to a limited extent in the visible dimension, which is to say, in "physical planning."

If, in this regard, we assert that the legibility of the environment has little to do with architecture per se, but a great deal to do with a building's current function—viz., that an imposing building may be redundant in social terms, and a modest one currently of major importance—the question arises as to why anyone ever strives to create good architecture? Or in other words: What is design? Architectural and social significance have coincided at certain moments in history, perhaps purely by fluke. Such good fortune in any event allows us a brief glimpse of paradise; what becomes visible is the ideal of a society rid of conflict and living in harmony with its self-built environment; without history, certainly, but happy (perhaps). In our constantly shifting society, such buildings immediately become monuments; they become historical because history refutes the supposedly happy moment and exposes its contradictory foundations. So buildings of the past, thanks to their design and fragmented condition, make us aware of the shifts in power relations that lie behind us as well as of those that lie ahead.

To recapitulate: urban design as such does not exist; rather, it is a construct, the outcome of how we have learned to interpret whatever we see. For the eye schooled in art history, visible elements merge in a certain design; for the average city resident, social relations constitute the environment. The latter primarily reads this, his own environment, not in terms of architecture but in terms of the secondary characteristics that inform him about the current use and ranking of streets and neighborhoods.

The destruction of cityscapes has progressed to an extent such that large sections of the population who pursue an "urban" lifestyle no longer experience the city—or experience it only as a stomping ground for commercial activities, or for male indulgence in vice and danger. However, family life between the private suburban residence, the workplace, and the shopping mall is no replacement for the city. To preserve and revive the city is primarily therefore not simply a matter of caring for historic buildings but of creating an urban environment that fosters a strong sense of community.

Heritage Preservation Is Social Policy (1976)

The current shift in public opinion regarding heritage preservation as well as the growing number of landmarked monuments are summed up most tellingly in the following two statements: traditional heritage preservation engages with the cultural heritage epitomized by monuments of architectural interest; future heritage preservation will have to engage with all the building stock in existence. Patrimony as epitomized by monuments of architectural interest is collated as a list of such landmarked buildings. The task of the preservationist consists, firstly, in expanding this list—or in striking a building off the list, if necessary—and secondly, in the measures he may take to preserve and restore a building before introducing restrictions on its use.

By contrast, the sort of heritage preservation now looming large on the horizon engages with our man-made environment. It follows therefore that the term must now be interpreted much more broadly, and also relativized. On the one hand the term encompasses existing building stock in its entirety, including all the horrors bequeathed us by the recent past: the "Selmi Tower," the "Kressman Ring," and the Kurhessisch Church Administration Building.[1] It instantly establishes that the environment as a whole cannot be immobilized in one go. Expansion and relativization of the term will

1 [The "Selmi Tower" high-rise apartment building in Frankfurt Main hit the headlines when it caught fire in 1973. The "Kressmann Ring," a 1970s high-rise development in the Steglitz district of Berlin, has a scandalous history as a speculation object. The modernist Kurhessen Church Administration Building was likewise built in the early 1970s.]

have an impact on a topic we can only touch upon here, namely the way in which cultural monuments are restored. Just as preservation of the environment proceeds always by adapting the latter to the demands of the day, so too, a building persists by transforming itself. The idealized notion of being able to return a building in its entirety to the style of the (uncertain) day it was first built is as disconcerting to us as the modernist preservationists' so-called creative restoration, which is to say, their harmful interventions in an object. Both methods destroy that which is truly liberating about a monument, that which turns any building we really take a good look at into a lesson in living history, namely traces of the passage of time in combination with the actions of a progressive society intent on gradually adapting its architectural legacy to modern circumstance.

What causes a building to go to rack and ruin? Traditional preservationists would say the culprits are woodworm, rising damp, and those who use the building—and then deploy their usual means of vanquishing these: insecticide, a drying-out period, and, ultimately, a change in use. They turn the old townhouse into a museum of local history, the church into a venue for occasional concerts, and one or the other preservationist may take up residence in some handsome palace ...

If we consider our architectural legacy as a whole, however, then it is clear that neither the passing years nor the users do the damage, but rather the non-users: namely that interplay of state and private players who concern themselves with trade, administration, and the destruction of our architectural legacy in accordance with the current legal framework, institutions, and habits. The public is quick to claim that it is real estate speculators who destroy property. They play a role, certainly, yet they act within a framework set by our state, our society, our credit arrangements, our building regulations, and our system of tenants' rights. Most of these organizational factors foster the destruction of buildings rather than reward their preservation.

Every landmark in INSA (the Inventory of New Swiss Architecture) is under preservation. "We'll all be in the inventory, once we are 60." Drawing: Lucius Burckhardt

That which is invisible destroys the visible environment, namely the rules governing our handling of a building.

Federal and local authorities are major destroyers of property and other aspects of the environment, directly and indirectly. Public corporations are more likely to fund a one-off construction project than maintenance and operational costs. It is easier to acquire subsidies for a new building than for the measures required to preserve an old one. Local authorities are granted federal or regional funding primarily when they build something new: they alone carry the cost of repaving an old road whereas central government assumes most of the cost of widening it. Tenancy laws in their present form penalize any tenant who handles his apartment sensibly, consistently maintaining it and adapting it to his needs. If he moves out, he loses his total investment—and he must count himself lucky if he is not required to return the apartment to its original condition. However, anyone who saves up to buy a property receives subsidies from the state. He is rewarded for moving out of a public housing project and into a home of his own in a new suburban or village development. Our entire housing budget goes into new construction, not into the preservation of existing housing stock.

If we ask why people nowadays are contemplating or calling for a broader definition of the term heritage preservation, we find ourselves facing demands posed by three different bodies. The first comes from the art history field. Given the fundamental shift in conceptions of history, art historians concern themselves increasingly with social history, in particular that of our recent past and our present, the industrial age. Testaments to earlier production methods can be saved for posterity by applying the traditional methods of museology and heritage preservation. However, testaments to the housing patterns of this era can be preserved only by users themselves, that is, by residents who sensibly adapt the original merits of their accommodation to their present needs and thereby facilitate the, if not strictly correct in art historical terms, nonetheless very worthwhile preservation of certain major housing projects of the nineteenth and twentieth centuries.

Architects, for their part, contribute to broadening the definition of the term heritage preservation by introducing the word "environment" to describe the sum total of factors determining the quality of a residential setting. Environment in this sense is not identical with the term "ensemble" now current in modern heritage preservation practice. When used in reference to the "livability" of older neighborhoods or housing projects, the term environment should be taken to mean those qualities that cannot be saved merely by preserving the ensemble—or indeed, that may thereby be destroyed. Let us consider, for example, the problem of urban mixed usage, the popularity of an urban environment in which one can still find a baker's and a bookstore alongside the bank and the savings bank. Such a mix is a sign of its times and as such not preservable. Moreover, the mere preservation of buildings is no guarantee of their continuous, unchanging usage; it just maintains their outer appearance in the stabilization years. The mixed usage of buildings can be assured only by introducing additional economic measures that perhaps go only so far as to ensure that an occasional gap is made in the ensemble; which is indeed the essence of mixed usage.

Thirdly, and finally, it is users and observers who broaden the meaning of the term heritage preservation, namely owing to a phenomenon that I like to describe as the "re-semanticization" (or: change in meaning) of the more recent architectural styles. For one, the meaning of the modern style has shifted. When, in the immediate aftermath of the First World War, a gap was torn in a dismal housing development and a modern house set into it, quasi as a precious gem, then the sight of its façade inspired hope: the rational architectural style put the glimmer of a rational and democratic society on the horizon; the transparency of the façade raised hopes that social institutions too would become transparent and enlightened. The idiom of the modern style forged at that time has since become easy to manipulate. Snatches of this idiom, vestiges of this architectural style, are now common currency in all kinds of construction. In the eyes of today's urban dweller, modern architecture is an expression of the power and the terror that have hounded local residents out of their homes, as well as of that coalition between politics and business which has made our inner cities and ultimately our cities in their entirety both inhospitable and uninhabitable.

It must be said, however, that the nineteenth-century styles have likewise undergone change. Although once intended as an expression of power and dominance, today they evoke in the beholder a sense of familiarity and comfort. Just as a medieval fortress no longer fills us with dread but rather inspires us to visit it one Sunday, nineteenth-century façades feign a sense of security in an orderly everyday life. Even the talmi gold of alleged bourgeois respectability, such as was liberally applied to countless façades in hastily built residential towns in the so-called fin de siècle and Art Nouveau styles, inspires this sense of familiarity. The public is now calling for the restoration of elaborate ornaments that until very recently were considered an affront to so-called good taste.

Our arguments so far have played out in the sphere of aesthetics. But if we are henceforth to regard heritage preservation no longer in the museological sense, as the task of conservation, but rather as a strategic approach to dealing with existing building stock and its administration then we must speak first and foremost about economic, social, and urban development processes. A preservation policy that seeks not to restrict the usage of a building but rather to ensure that its use and users are beneficial to preservation must address architectural and structural problems in their entirety. The restricted usage principle used to date could not be applied to building stock requiring preservation today, even if it were economically viable: for such intervention in the building stock would alter the social situation of the neighborhoods concerned. For example, it would give rise to zones of nocturnal insecurity. Preservation alone does not suffice. It would be too expensive and would bring about destruction. Protected neighborhoods could turn into slums as rapidly as new housing developments on the city margins do.

Now, one might well suppose that there is nothing easier than renovating cherished old apartments and tenement buildings and returning them to the sitting tenants. But as we have pointed out, this is in fact an extraordinarily difficult task for various reasons—first and foremost financial reasons and not by any means structural ones. Our housing policy is nothing but a housing construction policy; and since this has been the case for several decades, it has had, and continues to have, an impact on the terms and conditions of funding programs, on tax and fire-fighting regulations, on the development of the construction industry—particularly the current preference for industrial rather than artisanal construction methods, and the subsequent loss of professional skill sets—and, finally, also on users and tenants themselves, who have been actively discouraged from

"Heritage Preservation Is Social Policy," a conference organized by Lucius Burckhardt and students of the organizational unit 06 (faculty of architecture and urban and landscape planning) at the University of Kassel from 3–8 November 1975. In conclusion, a monument ("Denkmal," in German) bearing the words "Denkmal Nach" (meaning "Think about it") was erected on the downtown square Friedrichsplatz in Kassel. Photo: Annemarie Burckhardt

— What is a typical visual feature of the town of Heimatswyl?
— ...the abundant parking lots
— ...the freeway intersection
— ...the new pedestrian underpass
— All wrong! The old dairy recently restored by the heritage preservationists is typical of Heimatswyl!

Drawings: Lucius Burckhardt

Was ist charakteristisch für das Ortsbild von Heimetswyl?
... die vielen Parkplätze
... der Autobahnanschluss
... die neue Fussgänger-unterführung
alles falsch: charakteristisch für das Ortsbild von Heimetswyl ist das vom Heimatschutz neu aufgebaute alte Milchhüsli.

inhabiting a building with care and a sense of responsibility, and thus from personally contributing to its preservation.

To understand how this complex housing issue came about, this closely interwoven network of state and private players involved in the destruction and construction of housing, one has to look at history. Already in the initial phase of the industrial revolution, the time when railroads were being built and the population density in industrial cities was rapidly rising, it was evident that the construction of housing for the masses could not be left to the so-called free market forces. That which liberal economists liked to preach was patently untrue: the worker's pay packet was not automatically geared to a level of purchasing power that would drive demand for living space and thus the production of housing. It is far truer to say that wage levels and rents were subject to market machinations: an entrepreneur gave low wages and cheap housing to those sections of the working population that he hoped to bind to his business, and abandoned the rest of them to an indecent standard of living and the precarious nomadism of journeymen.

The fact that this proletariat posed a security risk for the state forced the federal and local authorities to intervene in the housing market. So, thanks not to the free market but to the concerted efforts of private entrepreneurs and the state, the housing shortage was kept at a just about tolerable and a just about lucrative level; and this had a considerable impact on the construction industry. Even though concentration of the construction industry appears to have long since been minimal—which is easily explained by the sector's very nature, namely the local distribution of its products—concentration of the businesses involved and the funding behind them was substantial. Today, large parts of the construction industry are geared almost exclusively to the needs of the government and major cooperative business ventures: the sole clients. Minimal changes in the policy of the government or such cooperatives have an enormous impact on employment in the sector and on prices. A potential crisis in the construction industry has a domino effect on the economy as a whole, and so the keys to boom or bust are in the hands of a very few.

Reason enough to keep up the perpetuum mobile of contract acquisition and the continual demolition and replacement of housing stock. Housing was built in the 1960s for a specific population, namely for the rural exodus to the cities, and superfluous housing stock thereby accumulated where it was easily overlooked, in the villages—this too a root of heritage preservation problems of difficult dimensions—whereas housing today is built for a population that no longer exists, and that cannot be quickly generated either in the countryside or the cities; and, in consequence, new housing stock can be filled only by demolishing the old residential towns of the nineteenth century. This is why the current crisis—and not for example the 1960s boom—is the greatest enemy not only of heritage preservation but also of the comfortably and affordably housed population.

So what are the tasks of heritage preservation facing us now, considering the term in its broader sense? I'll illustrate my answer with a few examples:

- The Hellerhof housing estate in Frankfurt Main. This residential development built by Mart Stam in the framework of the "New Frankfurt" movement is still a fairly typical example, one facing the same sort of problems as Otto Haesler's Rothenburg housing estate in Kassel, or that of Hannes Meyer in Freidorf near Basel. The shift in demographics and lifestyle as well as the not yet fully exploited option of adding more stories prompts the property developer to modernize. The backlog of work to be done is considerable, since residents are strictly forbidden to modernize the apartments themselves. The external appearance of the development is largely retained. Intervention by the property developer would entail major changes to the look of the housing estate. But given the prevailing legal constraints and conditions in the construction industry today, it is virtually inconceivable that the property developer would proceed with anything but a necessarily destructive intervention. Anything else currently seems to be a pipedream. Yet if we are permitted to dream on here just for a moment, we'll come up with some organizational measures that would guarantee the long-term preservation both of the present population structure and the original look of the estate. I'm thinking that the property developer could allow the tenants, or tenants' cooperatives, the leeway to carry out certain minor building tasks themselves.

- Second example: the Cité Ouvrière in Mulhouse. Built as a charitable foundation by progressive industrialists at the time of the Second Empire, this residential development comprised of terraced housing and blocks of four gradually passed into the possession of the working-class tenants who had paid rent there continually for the requisite number of years. Since 1860, these working families—some of them meanwhile lower middle-class families—have often modified their houses, barely one of which still looks as it did when first built. Nevertheless—or perhaps for this reason precisely—the development overall is attractive, a desirable place to live, and, simultaneously, a most invaluable social monument. The housing estate does not appear to be endangered: almost all the fortunate owners intend to hang onto their property, so it is highly unlikely that some private entrepreneur can buy up and destroy the whole complex. The real menace to the housing estate is the city's urban planning. By today's standards, the estate is too close to the city center and so is under threat from that which our corrupt language now calls "redevelopment." Friends of the Cité Ouvrière are therefore calling for the estate's protection; but to classify it conventionally as a landmark of historical importance will simultaneously put an end to its maintenance by the inhabitants: and they would probably move out of the settlement, if hampered in their construction initiatives.

- For obvious reasons, the numerous workers' housing developments in the Ruhr District were built on the city outskirts, close to the mines: firstly, to make the most of already hollowed-out sites; secondly, to shorten routes to the workplace. The concentration of major highways and interchanges presently restructuring the Ruhr District is a threat to the small number of settlements that are caught up in the maelstrom of transport hubs and hence obliged to cede to denser agglomerations. However, the majority of the settlements find themselves largely cut off from transport provision and so are suffering the opposite fate, namely that their owner-administrators—the original miners' building societies—are losing interest in their housing stock. Various strategies for its future use are under consideration, the simplest being to sell it off to the sitting tenants. But the prices proposed are inflated given that tenants have already invested in their housing. The value of the location and hence of the properties is falling, since the regions in question are losing not only their transport links but also their infrastructure, schools, centers, etc., which previously enhanced the standard of living there. Will it prove possible to keep the inhabitants in the locality and save the houses from going to ruin?
- Another example: the Vorderer Westen (Upper West End) district of Kassel. This late-nineteenth-century residential district followed on the heels of the founding of the German Empire and the public administration's removal from Berlin to Kassel. The textile manufacturer Aschrott and other businessmen saw their chance and began to systematically plan new residential districts, from the street layout to housing. Their partly aristocratic-looking,

partly solidly upper-middle-class apartment buildings evince ornamental façades either in the style of Historicism, then waning, or of Art Nouveau. Now, in those places where front gardens, cobbled streets, fences, and tree-lined boulevards are still intact, even war-damaged Kassel looks quite the hospitable city. This housing stock is under threat from various factors, but none of a purely technical nature, such as the extreme old age of the buildings. Cases of structural neglect are caused rather by the limited capital of those owners who do not know how to clear the many hurdles to capital acquisition—and whom no one helps. Other property owners do have capital to invest but are ill advised by construction specialists and so make unnecessary investments while neglecting repairs essential to the long-term preservation of a building. And as long as the collective or private construction of new housing is assured far greater state subsidies than the maintenance of existing housing stock, the threat to nineteenth-century residential suburban districts will be unabated.

- Another example is the Henschel premises in Kassel. The Henschel Company's office and factory buildings on Holländischen Platz, now earmarked as the future core of Kassel University, are "worthless," if assessed by the conventional terms of art history. Nonetheless, these factory sheds put their stamp on the northern reaches of Kassel's historical city center; and anyone who wanders unsuspectingly into the five-aisled shed in which until only a few years ago locomotives were assembled gains an impression not unlike that once assured by Paxton's Crystal Palace or Baltard's market halls and slaughterhouses. Now, anyone who believes that these buildings with their until recently fully functional offices, administration tracts, technical drawing rooms, and assembly sheds can be rationally converted into a university that is likewise in need of offices, technical drawing rooms, and experimentation labs, is in for some strange surprises, which demonstrate, in sum, how very much our construction industry is geared to demolition and new-builds, and how very little to dealing with existing buildings. It would take too long to name all the reasons for which the viability of individual buildings is either denied in full or admitted only when the sum to be invested in conversion is virtually equal to the cost of a new-build. The term "fire prevention" plays a major role here; but more important, in my view, is the manpower issue. The specialists employed by the authorities and likewise their professional associates, construction managers, and suppliers are all geared to new-builds, not to renovation. When they do renovate, however, the wood chips *and* the sparks fly, very possibly because of how the state calculates construction costs. Evidently, it prefers one-off investments to phased or recurrent expenditure.

I have specified here some cases typical of today's construction industry, or which fall under the broader heritage preservation concept, outlined above, or overtax conventional heritage preservation. The Henschel Company's sheds and workers' housing in the Ruhr District do not need to be protected and certainly not to be restored; but to maintain and rationally convert them would serve not only the preservation of their traditional appearance but also the economic management of building stock, the most important part of our national assets. For long enough we have allowed ourselves to be frightened off by the claim that demolition and new-builds are cheaper than maintenance; but this theory stands up only under certain circumstances, namely circumstances that hinder a calculation of costs that makes economic sense.

From the protection of the architectural monuments bequeathed us to our handling of our building stock in its entirety—this is how I would characterize the paradigm shift in our understanding of heritage preservation such as has gathered currency in recent discourse, not least in light of the European Year of Heritage Preservation. Art history's daughter is turning into a complex body of organizational and technological knowledge that is unfortunately not yet taught anywhere, except by those users, concerned persons, and citizens now involved actually or empathetically in its practice.

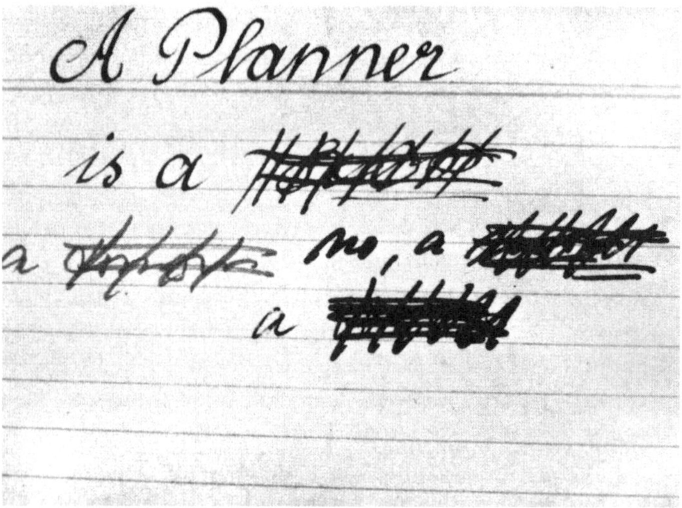

An "index card" by Lucius Burckhardt

The Shortsighted and the Farsighted (1978)

I was still a student in 1949, when I happened upon a copy of the "Greater Basel Correction Plan," a scheme that had not yet come into force but holds still to this day, except in the few city districts meanwhile exempt. Neither professionals nor politicians in Basel like to be reminded of this plan, since many who praised it to the skies back then are still in office. Today, they consider it "shortsighted" and the positions they later adopted as "farsighted." We will try to show that both positions derive from one and the same mistaken view of the city.

"Shortsighted" planning

The core feature of the "Greater Basel Correction Plan" of 1949 was the so-called Valley Relief Road, a three-lane highway that was to run ineffectively and destructively through the historic city center at the foot of St. Leonhard's Mount and Spalen Mount. Nowadays, three-lane downtown traffic can raise only a bland smile from the "farsighted" traffic expert. Nowadays, he has methods at his disposal with which to calculate the circulation area he believes is currently required. But there is a drawback to inner-city roads that fulfill this alleged requirement: they destroy the very destinations to which the urban traffic is headed.

In Zurich, the shortsighted planners' fashion bore another fruit, the subway. Given the seemingly imminent boom in motorcars, attempts were made to clear streetcars out of the motorists' way. It was thereby "overlooked" that the streetcar is the pedestrian's means of transport and that the pedestrian cannot simply be banished beneath the asphalt. Construction of the subway would have substantially accelerated and heightened the sense of devastation and insecurity, the fear of robbery and crime already menacing our cities; but the "shortsighted era," as we call it, ended in Zurich too, in the aftershock of a memorable referendum held in 1961.

Is it permissible for us to so harshly judge the immediate postwar period? Were models or findings available then to demonstrate the shortsightedness of such plans? That widening roads for motorized traffic is no way to improve inner-city access was known before the war, in CIAM circles, for example. And that we must garner new experience by means of cautious experiment was shown us by the New Towns of the considerably more war-battered Brits. And, finally, we must make mention too of our own contribution to common sense: Frisch, Burckhardt, and Kutters' *Achtung—die Schweiz* (Look Out!—Switzerland) proposed a last-ditch alternative to the destruction of our cities. Where did the idea behind *Achtung—die Schweiz* lead?

It too ended in the hands of the shortsighted. Professional planners convinced they had a higher calling than ours snapped up our idea and planned precisely that which should have been avoided: a Zurich suburb in the Furt Valley, a garden city idyll amidst a spaghetti mound of highways with no intersections, one of those dormitory city time bombs that threaten to blow apart the city of Zurich one of these days.

The "farsighted era"

Meanwhile, the 1960s were upon us and the authorities had completed their obligatory trip to America. They had learned two new words there: prognosis and extrapolation. If the apple tree in my garden bore five apples last year but fifteen of them this year, how many apples will it bear in the year 2000? — Millions of tons. Switzerland with its population of ten million ruled the roost in the 1960s. Nowadays, we are happy if we can keep the population from shrinking. The negative impact of the Pill, (the experts' official excuse), does nothing to alter the fact that the prognosis was wrong—and destructive too. Haven't lots of things already been paraded forth for Switzerland and its ten million Swiss? Widening roads, and building car parks, express highways, underpasses, and overpasses for the fictitious population has caused the present urban dwellers to flee the inner city. For farsightedness is not neutral: there is also the "self-fulfilling (and self-destroying) prophecy." The farsighted era was that of the major surveyors: Prof. Jürgensen and Prof. Grabe, who checked the findings of Prof. Leibbrand. The sums paid for their surveyor's reports rivaled those previously allotted to public works. And whoever queried this state of affairs ran risk of being ranked among the shortsighted.

Experts were deployed in a way that suggested urban development issues are technical matters that experts alone can solve. In fact, urban development and regional planning are minefields of social conflict. Behind the ratio of street curves, multistory car parks, and second rows lie decisions with a social dimension: What is a reasonable level of noise? At what speed should one drive? What degree of accident risk is at all permissible? May a busy road intersect a school road? And, first and foremost, how should public funds be spent? In cities with bigger problems than ours, things have ground to a halt because of expert planning. The affected local residents have roundly rejected the Correction Plan for London. Italy is endeavoring to push through the remains of its urban planning projects with grass-roots approval. France has dismissed radical measures of the Pompidou era and is now trying out a new scheme, *urbanisme intègre*, which is to say, urban planning of the structural and organizational sort. And local election results in the Federal Republic of

Germany, in particular the ousting of Frankfurt Main's Socialist Democrat mayor, have signaled change.

What came of that period we called the "farsighted era?" The 60s were a time of massive environmental destruction. Highways headed for the cities and the city fathers did all they could to get the oncoming traffic onto their streets, since this assured them "money from Berne:" inner-city roads, if misused as freeway entrance ramps, could be repeatedly widened, turned into an underpass or an overpass, or rebuilt elsewhere, all thanks to the federal budget. Such providence still costs our cities dearly. For the hypothesis that widening roads brings "relief," that urban traffic can be "channeled" along express highways, proves to be nothing but experts' ideology.

Zurich's subway ranked among the outstanding examples of "farsightedness." It would never have been any use to the then population but certainly to those anticipated suburban masses—the masses that have never arrived. The subway would have taken us another step towards depopulation of the city center and an unwelcome rise in property prices there. It was a part of the sickness that planners were claiming to cure.

So whatever was advocated as a "farsighted" project in the 1960s was merely a large-scale perpetuation of the "shortsighted" measures of the immediate postwar period. "Switzerland 2000," "Timeline Z2," and "Vollausbau" (Total Development) were the slogans of the day. "Vollausbau" in particular showed up the forecasters' mental block: they thought in terms of end states, not processes.

The outlook for the normal-sighted

1. Population growth is stagnant and we believe cities should therefore serve their present urban dwellers, not some fictitious population likely to be here by the year 2000. The present population

has a right to a degree of "livability;" and also certain needs, not least—since it is rapidly graying—an improved system of public transport. Soundproof fencing and windows cannot recreate the complex (and meanwhile demolished) conditions that assured the comfort and livability of our cities twenty years ago. Nor can pedestrian zones bring back inner cities navigable on foot, for they are nothing but the counterpart to the "traffic channeling" that has wrecked our cities.

2. We also recognize that comfort, convenience, and beauty are positive factors in urban policy. In anchoring the population in the city they also obviate overly long journeys to work. To acknowledge that livability and beauty save gas paves the way to further discoveries: urban development evidently consists not only in the construction or conversion of physical elements—walls, streets, parking lots, etc.—but also in invisible things—in wellbeing in one's social context, in well-established social structures in residential neighborhoods, in schemes for road safety, and the prevention of crime. Security on our streets, particularly at night, is directly related to the level of pedestrian traffic.
3. We recognize that existing urban building stock and infrastructures constitute a national asset. Demolishing houses may well go down as profitable in a businessman's books but it is a grave loss to the national economy. The myth that it is cheaper to build than to maintain existing stock must be challenged. If demolition and new build do in fact prove profitable then only due to mistaken urban planning.
4. The appeal of our cities rests not least on the fact that they have a history. This history may on no account be thoroughly erased by new buildings nor brought to an artificial standstill by total heritage preservation. Our aesthetic eye is on the lookout rather for signs of people who actively engage with their past, which is to say, who gradually re-appropriate and restore the architectural

substance of their city. That which we have witnessed in recent years, however, was the destruction of the very framework of our lives; and there are two possible reactions to this: the local population either opposes with more or less success all the changes being wrought on the face of its city (as is presently the case); or—the much worse scenario—it completely loses interest in the city, and regards it henceforth merely as a place to go unhappily about its business, day after day.

5. Authentic planning is not about already conjuring up the year 2000 but about tackling contemporary conditions in a sustainable manner, which is to say, in a manner that mitigates constraints and thus leaves future generations free to live in ways similar or different to our own. This is why planning should first and foremost demonstrate which decisions can be postponed. We get smarter, not dumber, with time. And there is nothing far-sighted about prematurely laying down the future. Planners and local authorities of the 1960s often thought themselves courageous when cementing their far-reaching schemes; yet in reality, they were probably afraid of the deepening insights of the populations concerned, afraid of vocal public participation in urban development.

Quality ... (1967)

“Swiss quality workmanship”—advertising and performance alike have helped make this phrase common currency. It is thereby supposed as a matter of fact that everyone understands the word quality and takes it to mean the same thing. Quality, that is the characteristic of the pocket watch one inherits from one’s father then hands down to one’s son at his high-school graduation; or it’s the pair of shoes that one initially wore “for best,” then for taking a stroll and, lately, since an Italian shoeshine service assured a high-gloss polish, “for best” again.

And yet the very notion of quality itself gives rise to doubts: Does durability actually make sense? One need not fall hook, line, and sinker for disposable products to see that “premium quality” is not always in the consumer’s best interest. Quality may well cost one dearly—as, for example, when the proportion of craftsmanship invested in a product far outweighs that of its industrial manufacture. There is likewise little sense in the quality casing for a product lasting longer than the technology it houses—as when the leather cover on a portable gramophone from the manual-pick-up era remains intact to this day. Or the reverse: when technical durability outlasts design, which is to say, the aforementioned son won’t wear his grandfather’s turnip watch for the world. And this, for hard-liners, is where the “throwaway mentality” comes into play.

Then what is quality? “Appropriate durability?” Very well. But who determines this? Optimistic answer: The designer who fashions the product. And another thing: thanks to “appropriate durability,” many a thing previously not competitive is competitive now. So what remains of “Swiss quality?” Another optimistic answer: Good design, good form.

Here too, there is much to discuss in that vast field between "classic beauty" and "fashionable disposable product." At the latest when the first clay jug was fired and at the very least since publication of David Pye's little book *The Nature of Design* (London and New York 1964), people have been noticing that beauty and utility cannot be simply equated. Things do not look how they look because it was impossible for them to look otherwise but because someone gave them their particular form.

Then what does "quality design" mean? Thanks to their respective new design concepts the English and the Italians have each taken a great step forward, the former in textiles, the latter in furniture manufacture. If one ignores all the marketing hype, then it has to be said that Carnaby Street fashion is a great achievement, one that radically intervenes in the role of clothing in our time, and hence also in our very lifestyle. And the same is true of the way in which Italians are now making use of color and synthetics in furniture. The question is: Is Switzerland progressive enough to be able to make similar achievements in the manufacturing and service sectors it is famed for—in tourism, for example?

On the Production of Counter-productivity (1998)

At last a manufacturer has had the great idea of putting those good old kitchen utensils—the almond grinder, meat grinder, and salad spinner—back into production. How much progress, or more precisely, backwardness has it taken for us to return to where we were one hundred years ago, how much erroneous design, how much counter-productivity?

Inventors are conservative. They devise improvements to objects but fail to alter the founding principles on which such objects rest. Take the transport ticket, for example: the principle when I use public transport is still the same, for I must decide in advance on my destination, purchase the relevant ticket, then have it stamped during my journey. Automated ticket vending and stamping machines have meanwhile been invented; but neither has the principle of selecting one's destination in advance been abandoned (I cannot get out or travel further at will), nor the convenience of passengers constrained to waste time at the ticket counter been improved.

Let's take another simple example and ask what counter-productivity is. Perhaps it obeys a rule of some sort, just as there is an error design formula. Central heating is a broad field of erroneous design and apparent improvement. Some years ago we rented an apartment with oil-fired central heating. At the end of the year, the three tenants in the building each assumed one third of the total heating costs. This was imprecise, since anyone who had turned up the heating paid no more than his neighbor upstairs or down who had been thrifty. How much surplus heat had gone to the neighbor via floors and ceilings could not be measured. But then justice was decreed from on high: radiators were to be fitted with an evaporation meter

"Just sign here, please, on the dotted line."
Drawing: Lucius Burckhardt

and consumers thus encouraged to save money. In consequence the residents turned off the radiators each morning, before they went to work, and turned them back on when they came home between 5 and 6 p.m. The fact that it then took several hours for the apartments to warm up was initially a cause of irritation. But then someone had the idea of setting the central heating overall at a much higher temperature. The house continued to grow cold in the daytime but the basement became burning hot (with an unwelcome side effect: my stock of white wine was ruined). However, the radiators did warm up immediately after 5 p.m. Now everyone paid according to how much he used, but the overall consumption was higher than when costs had simply been divided by three. And as for the justice of it

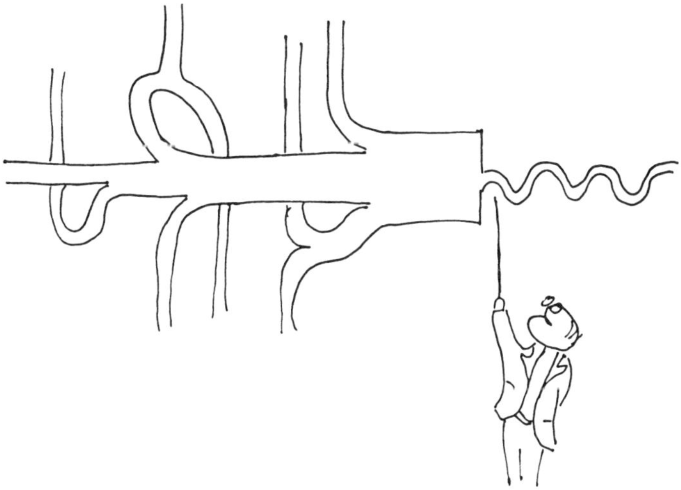

"And this part of the master plan is meant to ensure people understand the need for the highway." Drawing: Lucius Burckhardt.

all, well, it was debatable at the least. Why should the ground floor and the attic floor pay more than the floor in-between?

All of us are familiar with such tales. The question is: Do they have an algorithm in common? I'd like to suggest that our lifestyle is caught up in systems (the system in the above case being the tenant community plus central heating). But our approach to solving problems is not system-appropriate but rather polytechnic (as in: an evaporation meter should encourage thrift). The polytechnic solution intervenes in the system—a system that was hitherto far from perfect but somehow nonetheless balanced—and its effect is counterproductive. Why do we solve problems in polytechnic ways? There are several reasons:

1. We do not make an effort to "completely" understand the system. (How can one optimize the heating of a building?)
2. We name the grievance and its very "name" holds in store a polytechnic strategic solution. (Traffic jam: "jammed streets must be widened.")
3. Our collective decision-making is based not on argument but on authority. ("The state and the plumber determine how savings can be made.")
4. We don't enjoy discussing difficult issues—we just want solutions. ("Saddam Hussein should be bombed.")
5. We want one solution only: the best one—circumstances allow several possible routes, but none that is truly optimal.
6. We want to hold someone responsible, even if that person cannot actually assume the responsibility. ("The surgeon should operate at last!")

Probably even more reasons occur to the reader as to why we alleviate system-type problems using polytechnic solutions and thereby give rise to new problems. But now here come more questions: Do we truly live in systems? And what is a system?

That everything is connected to everything else is a commonplace. If my fountain pen falls to the ground then the moon moves, but admittedly only a fraction. Effective systems are subjectively compiled excerpts from this all-encompassing system: excerpts such as traffic, or the housing system, or care of the sick. Certain relationships are consolidated whenever one cuts another off. But nothing can be isolated: traffic generates people in need of care; care of the sick generates traffic.

Subsystems exist only in our minds. Nonetheless, they are our conceptual toolbox. Rational activity presupposes a concept of rational systems. Systems are rational if they have numerous and strong internal links and can be constituted without more than a few external links needing to be cut.

The system of "heating my apartment," to return to where we began, is not rational since it makes a mental cut in the heating pipes at mid-point within the apartment building. The consequence is: attempts to save money increase overall costs. "To heat the house co-operatively" is a more rational idea and also implies further deliberation: Is our central heating system too old? Should we install a small gas heater in each apartment? Should we improve the insulation of the exterior walls? Or does anyone have some other strategy in mind?

And the transport ticket, this invention that is as old or even older than a rail track. Isn't it high time we resorted to carrying a notebook with us on train journeys, in which ticket inspectors could note where we get on and get off, then automatically bill us accordingly, either monthly or half-yearly? And while we're at it, let's do away with those nerve-wracking special discount offers and reduce prices for everyone instead, all of the time. And as for short trips, I have long since argued that a newspaper should double on its day of issue as a ticket for inner-city travel. That would give a great boost to newspaper sales and transport operators alike.

There's Nothing Simple about Simplicity (1998)

In 1910, Adolf Vetter won enthusiastic acclaim on the annual Deutsche Werkbund Day when he quoted from Justus Möser's *Patriotische Phantasien*:

Child: Mama! Why did the artist paint a garland there, at mid-point above the mirror?

Mother: Can't you see that the mirror is cracked? He evidently wished to hide the crack.

Child: Mama! So wherever there is superfluous ornamentation there are cracks and holes?

Mother: Yes, my child, everywhere. Excess plaster is always a sign that something somewhere is missing, either in people's minds or in the thing itself.[1]

It is as simple as that. Here, we have a pioneer of modernism, telling us about how his mother grabbed a handsaw one day and did away with the ornamental, turned wood fir cones on the arms of her chairs. In our eyes, the armchairs, however ugly they may have been beforehand, were now forever ruined; but the modern family thought itself as progressive as if it had just purchased a dozen tubular steel chairs.

It was a case of *Schein oder Sein*: illusion or being. Hans Cornelius, in his *Elementargesetze der bildenden Kunst* (Elementary Principles

1 [Justus Möser: *Patriotische Phantasien*, (Patriotic Fantasies), Nicolai Berlin 1775, p. 69; "Wozu der Putz diene?" In: id.: *Anwalt des Vaterlandes, Ausgewählte Werke*, Kiepenheuer, Leipzig and Weimar, 1978]

of the Visual Arts), noted optimistically that a talented painter of porcelain may use decoration to make even a somewhat wonky vase look perfect. This of course brought him into disrepute among the guardians of "authentic being:" the porcelain painter was held to be no better than the artist who hides a crack in the mirror with an artful tendril, and so prostitutes his art.

Another aspect of this authentic being is the authenticity of material. It is always difficult for us today to get our heads around a debate that was conducted long before anyone had a clue about linguistic semiotics. For Werkbund members and modernists alike, the object could never "mean" anything but itself; and if ever it purported to do so, then this was quite patently "a lie." All the exquisite sophistication developed in the applied arts in the course of the eighteenth century, in particular the so-called marbling process, fell victim to this simplistic mindset. It is only now that we are beginning to once again appreciate the serenity evoked by a wooden pillar finished in several coats of high gloss paint so as to portray marble of a beauty inexistent in this world—as can be seen, for example, in the church at Zwiefalten. Or what are to say about those faience creations of Niderviller, which were trumped in turn by Nymphenburg porcelain depicting a copperplate engraving hanging on a wooden board? No one is deceived by it. No one mistakes the plate for wood or attempts, with a drawing pin, to correct the ear of the donkey in the copperplate engraving. Gustav Pazaurek, the leading custodian of "good taste" in Germany, uncomprehendingly wrote: "We experience in such cases an illusion that actually isn't one because it is formally suspended; but for this reason precisely, it is regarded with aversion as an abortive joke, a joke without a punchline."[2]

2 [Gustav E. Pazaurek: *Guter und schlechter Geschmack im Kunstgewerbe*, DVA Stuttgart und Berlin, 1912. p. 272]

Somewhat more ingenious than this tired struggle of the modernists for authenticity and simplicity in the applied arts are those recurrent endeavors to "reform" excessive sensuality in favor of the "true nature" of geometric forms. The Neoplatonism that pervaded Christianity took nature to be the simple set of rules hidden behind the scenery of the visible world. Any harking back to true Christianity is inevitably accompanied by strivings to anticipate this extrasensory world of regular bodies in the real appearance. I regard the Cluniac cushion capitals as an example of this, although I am aware of how quickly Cluny itself abandoned them. The Florentine Neoplatonists of the court of the Medicis further elaborated this idea. In numerous tracts penned by that circle, the architectonic endeavor linked in our minds with the style of Bramante or Palladio is described as an imitation of nature. But what are we supposed to make of the fact that the façade of the Cancelleria, say, imitates nature, or of the claim that nature herself could not have made a simpler or more rational job of the place? After all, the apparent simplicity of its façade is sophisticated enough. Two visible structures cover the façade of the building: firstly, the clearly elaborated load-bearing system of cornices and pilasters, and secondly, the system of bosses and joints. Both systems are purely ornamental. So when modernists called for buildings that adopt the proportions of the Cancelleria but not its two ornamental and illusory load-bearing systems they were in for a disappointment: in spite of the golden ratio, such a building would look out of proportion. How come?

The white cubes of concrete Modernism hide load-bearing structures. The Masters' Houses at the Bauhaus Dessau preempted prefabrication at a time when this was still imagined to be a type of seamless construction composed of modules without joints. Thus illusory or actual prefabrication remained simple only as long as an impeccable craft tradition was still on hand to create the illusion. I was able to see what pretend simplicity can be when I paid a visit to

Nervi's field factory during construction of his audience hall for the Pope. Only in Italy, where handicrafts are still intact, is simple prefabrication possible. Of the classical modernist architects, Mies van der Rohe alone, in my view, has grasped what it means to approximate Platonic simplicity, to imitate the true nature hidden behind appearances. For Mies discovered that while such simplicity may indeed not exist it can nonetheless be portrayed. Even if builders and mathematicians say today that Mies's steel girders are merely screwed together and cannot bear a load, their very critique confirms my point. The famous corner of the Seagram Building, which recedes at the point where classical architecture would have foreseen structural support (such as the corner post in Sansovino's library, say) demonstrates that Mies's ideas pursue the same Palladian paths and that this omission (like Serlio's infliction) is unnecessary and extravagant yet vital in terms of the overall appearance of the work. Simplicity cannot be constructed but it can very well be portrayed as the true nature of construction, or as a type of architecture conform to the true nature of the mathematics hidden behind the visible realm.

Here, I'd like to briefly digress on the topic of that by no means simple simplicity generally described as a "purity of style." It was left to the American architect Robert Venturi to liberate us finally from the notion that there exists—quasi as the zenith of each style—the architecture of pure style fulfillment. For a long time the epigone of the great nineteenth century art historians forgot that styles do not "exist per se" but are merely a means, invented in this [the twentieth] century, by which architecture may be discussed. The notion of regarding architectural development in terms of styles is modeled largely on parallel findings made in the light of Darwinism regarding the development of fossils. Accordingly, and whatever the style, one can identify an early phase of nascency and a zenith, as well as a late phase in which elements of the following style epoch are beginning to show. It is in the middle phase, therefore, that stylistic formulae are followed most purely, (i.e. strictly), as it were, and a building hence is "simple" inasmuch as it merely reproduces the formulae of the Romanesque or the Gothic style, or whatever.

Now, however, Venturi has drawn our attention to the fact that it is not simplicity but elements such as "complexity" and "ambiguity" that connote the novelty of a building. Mere simplicity of style is a construct—and a non-artistic one, to boot, derived from the mimetic reading of art history as a history of styles.

We do not know exactly whether there is a Platonic "Nature No. I" behind "Nature No. II." Yet we allow even "Nature II" an ideal quality of simplicity: it is purposive, we say, although we do not know its purpose. And we too, like nature, want to make our products simple and purposive. Unfortunately, we manage to do so only when making very simple artifacts, such as elementary tools: hammers, pliers, and the like. These are actually and by all appearances purposive. For a long time it was believed that the bicycle too belonged in this category and therefore did not need to be further developed—until a few years ago, when much improved specialized bicycles came onto the market. Here too, there is only a sub-optimal range of forms, such as the extra-lightweight model, the mountain bike, the racing bike, and so on. The design of every object results in several sub-optimal forms, but not in the optimally purposive form; and the criteria by which these sub-optima are selected cannot be discussed in technical terms; opinions come into play here, and not everyone finds the end product convincing; and so two circles develop: those who'll buy it and those who won't.

The product should nonetheless at least look purposive. So one reaches helplessly for that quote from Immanuel Kant: beauty is purposiveness without purpose. Is beauty—accordingly—also thrift without thriftiness, or simplicity without being simple? The purposiveness and simplicity of nature also appear to be constructs added after the fact: nature is simple and complicated, thrifty and extravagant. Which of these is simpler: the fern that assures its reproduction by releasing hundreds of thousands of tiny spores into the world, only very few of which will germinate; or the avocado that produces a large fruit with a single seed that will in all probability grow into a young plant? Which of these is simpler: the massive production of pollen, one speck in several millions of which will reach the female pistil thanks to serendipity; or the act of sexual intercourse? So there is obviously a lot to learn from "Nature II," but certainly not simple simplicity.

How can a bee live without the plant that both provides it with honey and thereby passes on pollen to assure its own reproduction? How can the plant reproduce itself without the bee in search of honey? Did the plant have the idea of producing honey until the bee at long last came into being? Or did the bee exist long before the honey? Not even biologists can say for sure. But we can learn from nature, here precisely. We work in preordained, inherited contexts. We design objects in a way such that they are suited to the visible and invisible givens in the environment; and we possibly manage in this way to simplify, to improve this environment. "Design is invisible" was our name for this approach. The simplicity of a design consists not in the fact that it interacts in a simple manner with the givens in its environment. Simple objects that do not interact with the environment are like tropical fruits that taste better than apples, pears, and oranges but cannot be eaten using the tools of our gastronomical culture: the knives, forks, spoons, fingers, and napkins leave one appreciative but stained. The fruit is good but cannot be enjoyed in company.

Transport tickets, for example, are of a seemingly simple design; yet only those for the railroad management are truly simple. (I am not speaking here, by the way, of the exorbitant complications wrought by endless special concessions, which have now made purchasing a ticket a test of one's patience.) The railroad ticket has had a drawback since its inception, namely that it requires one to name one's destination. We have to buy a ticket to our destination; if we leave the train before we reach it, we lose money; if we travel beyond it, we pay a fine. However, railroad tickets are child's play compared to streetcar and bus tickets. Every city has its own system. Is that simple? For the city, certainly, for the tickets sold allow it to gauge usage. For the user, not at all, for when he arrives in a strange city, his first question is: Where can I buy a ticket and how do I get it stamped? How is one to know what zone one's destination is in? Simplicity here means passing on complications to the user. Simplicity for the service provider creates complications for the consumer. Only monopolists can afford this state of affairs. Taxi drivers also benefit from the situation. They get to drive off from the station with helpless strangers on board, all because tickets are badly designed. Improve this? Yes, with pleasure. An off-the-cuff solution: the passenger carries with him a ticket that is stamped not at the start, but at the end of his journey. This sounds to me like simplicity itself in a complex context.

More comprehensive and far-reaching, however, is the realization that technical "neat solutions" lead to more bother and unwelcome complications—mostly for the consumers, not the planners. Design in context has to address inextricable problems for which there is neither a neat nor an optimal solution but only optimized strategies that can provide satisfaction for a while. When it comes to traffic problems, we all know that every neat solution leads directly to traffic jams at other points. In the case of subtle design problems we must first learn that simplicity at all costs does not simplify the situation but merely redistributes the burden of complexity in new ways—at times, more unjustly.

All Over the Place (1994)

Andreas Brandolini: *What do you understand by the term avant-garde, in relation to design?*
Lucius Burckhardt: For me, avant-garde has something similar to modern. Avant-garde connotes an idea of the 1920s, which is to say, a situation when the vanguard saw something new. In the background there was the ruling power and the conservatives. That is not the situation we have today. Today—to continue in the same military vein—one might say that various reconnaissance troops are pushing ahead in search of something to do. There are only groups these days; the avant-garde has splintered into very many small parts.

But the springboard for any talk still going on about the avant-garde today is rooted actually in the recent past. In the 1960s in Italy there was the Radical Design movement, which broke away from established notions of design; and later, in the late 70s, Alchimia; and then Memphis, which emerged in the early 1980s. That was definitely an awakening of sorts.
Yes, but I think that those were already postmodernist movements inasmuch as they were aware of what they were about. Discourse in Italy has been at an ambitious level for quite some time already. These people, Mendini, Superstudio, and so on, have long been addressing the situation. It is a breakthrough, but one that culminates in a different use of the existing language, quasi with a dual code; which is to say that the language brought forth by modernism should be reconsidered and used to describe its own self, as it were. And I personally see Superstudio and this whole movement as second-wave modernism, which is now reflecting on itself in the language of

modernism. I don't see that as an avant-garde gesture, but rather as a sign that the avant-garde has become a part of the culture now, inasmuch as it is intently discussed in these schools and circles.

And what brought it about? What produced it? Has it changed anything?
I think it has. I mean it's the root cause of semiotics becoming accessible. Not only linguists but also ordinary people suddenly knew what semiotics is, talked about it and asked: What is actually available in terms of styles, signs, and tools? What has modernism achieved? And what use can we make of it now?

Hmm.
And this introduces a touch of irony too; it's partly a self-deprecating irony, but equally an attempt to use these tools to say something new.

I have noticed that such irony was often misunderstood; it developed a momentum of its own, as a kind of "design-speak," as it were, or design jargon.
Lots of people then jumped on the bandwagon and harvested the fruits of what the Italians had sown. But I think they really did sow the seed, also given that they reflected —way back in 1968—on Disegno Banale. They were asking: What is banal design? What are the 1950s? The hopes of the 1950s? And the work of that decade?

Hmm.
Later, people all over the world felt they could make fun of the 1950s. Of course, anyone can make cheap jokes about those multi-armed lamps with cone-shaped lampshades but I mean, the Italians and likewise other people in your circles really did reflect on what it was all about, what the 1950s decade was really after, and what it brought

forth. What was it supposed to mean? And how do we embed that, how do we reflect on it?

What status do you think design and artistic production have in society today? Should design take a critical stance on society? Would that be beneficial? Or should it aim merely to produce diversity? The Ulm School of Design, for example, adopted a very clear position on its social role.
I think design now has a different role than the one we envisaged for it at the Ulm School of Design. Our hopes there, in a sense, were to produce the future. But design today is more about dialog, a means of portraying oneself and one's environment so as to able to enter into competition or communication with other people. And as one speaks so too one dresses, or surrounds oneself with objects. Talk alone is not enough. But it's no longer about paradise, about the future, as it was in Ulm. In Ulm we lived provisionally, quasi, while awaiting salvation.

But what was done in Ulm still had something of the classic avant-garde about it, an avant-garde that was of course always focused on the future… On redesigning the world.
Yes, it was still a thoroughly classic approach. We lived in anticipation of the future. We designed the future.

But as a pretty clear picture. Basically, all the classic avant-garde designs speak one and the same language, have a similar way of handling materials, and the materials express a similar economy.
Strangely enough, we didn't speak about appearances, or not officially. We felt we had to design objects themselves, but not their appearance. So we were still completely naive. The future realm no longer had a look. Looks had been abolished. So it was always weird when students presented their objects. We lecturers had to give them a grade. But we weren't allowed to comment on how anything

looked. We couldn't test anything either, since nothing worked. Actually, we just talked about whether it functioned, but not about how it looked—or even about whether it had a look! We all had appearance on the brain, but we never talked about it.

So there was a fashion aspect to all this too?
But we were blind to it. It was only later that we realized modernism is a style, and Ulm a sub-chapter of modernism; but even then we didn't admit it. Instead we claimed that happiness itself, the future itself, would now be designed.

Hmm.
Do you remember how Hans von Klier presented his espresso machine? Espresso machines have a waist, right? But of course, the future looks different. So espresso machines of the future are cylinder-shaped—it stands to reason. So there was just this cylinder. Then he made coffee in it and the lid began to rattle, because he'd not thought about the fact that the steam has to escape. So he then drilled a hole in the lid. Well, we all sat there in embarrassment and you could tell from people's faces what they were thinking: "Well, it's a nice object, but what about that hole?" But no one dared ask, until one of the master craftsmen said: "What happened up top?" And Von Klier replied: "A hole." Of course the master craftsman had a go at him. "So why the hole?" he asked. Well, otherwise the lid rattles. So a hole. Simply a hole. Of course we wanted a totally sleek cylinder with a sleek lid to match. But then there was a hole in it. And somehow we felt that the invention was not thoroughly thought through, since there'd certainly be no hole there in the future. Then Banham paid us a visit in Ulm, and he was the first ever to speak there about appearance. He came from the world of Pop, and Pop made it suddenly permissible to say that things do have a look. From then on, we were able to argue along semiotic or linguistic lines.

So that was quite a turnaround?
Yes. Unlike in Ulm, design today thinks not about the future but about us. Today, we style ourselves; but in Ulm in 1959, today meant nothing. Badly dressed, hungry, and freezing cold, we sat around on Cow Mountain [the Kuhberg District] and thought about how fabulous everything would be in the year 2000. Whereas no one these days sits there thinking: "In the year 2020 …"

They're more afraid.
We want to be warm here and now. Paradise is no longer in the future. If a slice of paradise is at all possible, we want it now.

We have now realized that now is what matters. And now, things are allowed to tell a story, or even have to: things must speak. That reminds me of an article you wrote in 1980 for the Forum Design *exhibition in Linz: "Design Is Invisible." But there you described something else entirely.*
Yes, I expanded the meaning of design to include organizational and invisible factors. And I said things have a look as well as invisible parts, as in: the bus has a schedule.

How do you see that now, ten years on? It was a programmatic exhibition that hoped to have an impact—and indeed did, as far as I can tell. Do you think that the last ten years have redeemed or confirmed its promise?
The intention back then was different. Back then, we hoped to broaden the scope of design, because it was actually restricted to a very few objects. Many things were always subject to design, others not at all. At the very least we wanted to convey how vital it is to address the whole as well as system-type objects, to look at transit systems rather than design individual cars, for example. Buses don't only need doors that allow for easy access but must also operate at circa five-minute intervals—otherwise they won't be used. That was our

intention at the time. Today we want design to be communication—this too, in contrast to the avant-garde era. The future is not in the future, but now. We want to make our environment, our setting, rich in information. What we achieved until now through fashion alone—showing who we are by the way we dress—now extends to a broad range of topics, groups, and institutions.

Yet this information has to be sourced somewhere or other. There are those regionalism theories but they contradict how things are produced today, on the whole—starting with the cassette recorder I'm using here. It actually comes from Japan, but it's everywhere.

It's certainly a crisis of design when things such as cassette recorders disappear into boxes and the "function is visible" thesis falls apart. In the case of electronic gadgets, purpose, function, is not visible, and we therefore have to invent a second language for them, namely a console. But that's the minor problem, in my view. The other one is that the language of representation—if that is what it wants to be—needs material to feed on, to renew itself, which it can draw from the past or possibly from the regions. Now, the regions underwent an interesting revival at the start of this century. These groups, such as François Burkhardt portrayed, for example, be it Czech Cubism, Pleçnik, Asplund, the Hungarian applied arts movement around Ödön Lechner, Italian Art Nouveau in Italy, which then caught on in Istanbul, because D'Aronco created the new Turkish style, as it were; or then Gaudí, this entire "Young Spain" complex which was of art historical origin—some of these architects in fact delved straight back into Spanish Romanesque architecture: Puig i Cadafalch and Domènech i Montaner derived their Art Nouveau directly from Romanesque architecture. Gaudí ranks among those too, although he more than anyone brought forth new forms while the others tended to botch Spain's Early Romanesque style. And what else? The Belgians ...

I'm just off to buy cigarettes . . .
. . . Horta, Mackintosh in Scotland, and then Asplund up north.

But one could say these regional distinctions ensued from a dearth of information.
Yes, that is the major difference. A man like Pleçnik really hadn't a clue what Corbusier was up to. From 1925 until the war broke out, he had no idea that modernism existed—and nor did he want to know. That was possible too. Regionalism was therefore still regional. Today, by contrast, everyone knows everything. I think "global village" is a good expression. The world is a village. We do our village gossip but everyone knows everything. And this is why all forms are universally available. Of course there is such a thing as Italian design, because the people are there; but there is nothing Italian about it. The traditions are at our disposal.

That was evident in the case of Memphis. It was no accident that Sottsass was always referring to his travels in India. Or now, to see the amazing palette of colors people are suddenly drawing on. Well, that started off in London actually—a few years ago, in fact, thanks to Punk. They didn't design; they just painted stuff. There'd suddenly be pink-painted tables in apartments.
Even earlier, when Pop took off. I think the English changed the color range, which was also a way of putting language at people's disposal. Color theory used to be taught in school as something fixed and unchanging. Or it was said that this tie doesn't go with that shirt. In my view, Carnaby Street blew all of that apart and made color available again as a language. Now we can use it again; even clashes hold a message. People used to say: get rid of that; that's awful and this is correct. We were talking earlier about where language gets its sustenance. One dimension is regionalism, I think; another is the past; and one is rooted in the fact that people have thrown rules such as color theory overboard.

Yet regionalism also implies history. I am thinking now of local history classes, as in: these types of architecture have been here for three centuries. But that is not what Andrea Branzi and François Burkhardt mean. They have in mind another kind of regionalism that feeds on other information.

Well, I do think that the regionalism of around 1900, as described by François Burkhardt, has a historical dimension inasmuch as it represents young nations. The Hungarians, Ödön Lechner's circle, wanted to say to Vienna: We are different. We have a particular craft tradition, and ceramics is a part of that. The use of glazed ceramics in Hungarian architecture is a regionalism that draws on history; it is not so much modernism as an Arts & Crafts movement, one that stands up to the Viennese Arts & Crafts movement and says: We are Hungarian, not Viennese. Insofar it was all tied up at the time with the emerging nations. Hungary was liberating itself, Yugoslavia was coming into being, and Slovenia was taking shape in Yugoslavia …

Regionalism today is dictated more by industry. It seems to me that the industrial north of Italy is typically Italian; and it is honing a design profile. Industry there works differently than its German or Japanese counterpart.

That's what makes it stand out, in our eyes, but there is nothing Italian about it. The difference is structural: they have different people, different schools, another type of industry, and the relationships between designers and industry are a bit different. Sure, it's local, but it's not rooted in a local supply of forms; rather it's the manifestation of Italian society, in which people talk more to each other, and develop things. We design perhaps in total silence, and then we say: Take it or leave it. The industrialists there have an ear to the ground. Here they just say: I'll buy this, but I won't buy that. Those are the differences.

If, as you say, it is now accepted that forms communicate, could you predict where design will go next?
My outlook at the moment is pessimistic. I say, yes, we no longer work for the future, we work for the here and now. This also means, that paradise no longer exists, or only for the limited few. What scares me is that paradise is here now, but people have been left behind. I have the feeling that different levels are taking shape: there's the society of those who have made it, and the broken society of those who have not; and I find it difficult to say how the latter will develop.

But that in itself is a new incubator for a new avant-garde.
It may well prove to be a source of inspiration, and people may well make themselves heard; it could be stimulating, what with their linguistic creations—or linguistic pilferings, since they too, like young fashion, tend to steal. That's conceivable. But when it comes to society and social developments, my outlook right now is pessimistic.

It's giving rise to conflicts already.
Conflicts cannot be resolved simply by saying, wait awhile, one day we will all walk through the golden gates of socialism. No one believes that any longer. Now it's a simple case of sink or swim. And I find that loathsome.

It's also difficult, as in the 1920s, to say, we'll work for the minimum living wage; we'll create an equal basis for all. One need only drive to the border to see how much more the others have.
Or how much less. I think it's difficult too. And it doesn't work any more to go on at people about how we are working together for something. There are people who work like crazy, but in vain, and with no future prospects. Or at least that's my pessimistic outlook for the moment.

Do you have an optimistic one too?
Splintering into small tribes will continue, I think, in design terms. That which manifested for a while as young fashion and youth lifestyles is no longer youth lifestyles, just lifestyles. So: some people live this way and some people that. Some people wear jeans their whole life long, or ties. Or they switch from time to time; but it's not like young people have a certain lifestyle and then switch to an adult lifestyle at the age of twenty-five, as they used to; rather, the youth lifestyles around from 1955 to 1980 have meanwhile, in the 1980s and 90s, turned into what I call tribes. In England there are hooligan dynasties: the son, father, and grandfather go off to a football match to get into a fight. It is not like the sons get into a fight while the father and grandfather sit in the stands. There are hooligan families now in their third generation. And that, in my opinion, gives pause for thought. It's possible that dialog or non-dialog between tribes is the lifestyle of the future.

Does that mean a designer has to decide which tribe he belongs to?
The paradox is, there's still a kind of super-language on this topic. And funnily enough, everyone understands it. Even CEOs in ties know the good jeans brands, and even people in fraying jeans know which tie is the right one to wear. There is the language of the group itself, and then there is the super-language. Probably that is the game of the future: that everyone understands everyone else and likewise enjoys it when something is good. Which is to say, the CEO takes pleasure in the excellent punk. And the excellent punk takes pleasure in the immaculately dressed CEO. And this way, everything still hangs together.

So the designer becomes a linguist.
If the language analogy still works. It's not a one-hundred-percent analogy … Have we been talking nonsense?

I've no idea.
People now, in part, are trying to profit from the fact that contradictory things always look very informative. But they are not. The old rule for horoscopes: You must be cautious next week, but also courageous at just the right moment. Or: You are basically an extremely thrifty person but also generous when it comes down to it. I feel then that someone has really hit the nail on the head and described my character to a T. It doesn't mean a thing and yet I feel somehow flattered, because I like to believe I am thrifty or generous at the exact right moment. Fashion has been on this path for some time now, mixing leather jackets with silk lace; fashion has been working for some time with things that are inherently contradictory, and I think it's a dirty trick that things are as swanky as hell yet could be perfect for a jungle expedition.

I noticed that in France. I had a conversation with Elizabeth Garouste, who in partnership with Mattia Bonetti makes ornamental furniture that draws in part very heavily on African history and this entire formal repertoire—in order to create luxury, they say, but the materials are cheap. It only looks like gold. But ultimately, this furniture ends up in designer galleries and boutique stores and is incredibly expensive. It's like the CEO in jeans.
Or there are those elegant jeeps ... One can tell just from looking at them that they're not really fit for the jungle, even though they have all the features of a military vehicle. This again is an attempt to mix idioms and make a fortune from doing so. It is amusing at times, but it's also a rubber check. A fortune is created from thin air. As in: "You are very thrifty ..." This bag is actually for the salon, but can also be taken to the jungle. This of course is rich, but also flimsy. More precise information is required.

Nowadays, given the very major differences—some people have everything and make a show of it, others have a vision of wealth but nothing else—it's possible to imagine a future in which people say, ok, we promise to advocate a new modesty and to endeavor, with all the means at our disposal, to create a certain balance for everyone.
Objects would then have to be sufficiently rich in information. Also because the rich are so rich that they can no longer dispose of all their money. As a rich guy you cannot effectively get rid of your money: even if you buy ridiculously overpriced artworks, you will not manage to spend it all on luxury alone. No one can spend a million on luxury—not without landing in hospital. So the question is whether an era of superfluity is possible, when to save creates an impression, when no longer the product itself really counts, but what the product means. Now, that would be a vision of the future, if things were no longer bound up with paid labor and purchasing power, and everyone had enough; and one cannot—should not, alone for ecological reasons—ever use more than is there. Then it would be matter of making the few things we really do need somehow entertaining and clever. Just as we don't always eat more—because we're really not so hungry—but eat better, so too we should strive to make better the things we really need. One used to be able to spend a fortune on castles and horses. But there are limits to that now.

Hmm.
It would be interesting to find a refinement that doesn't cost much, is accessible to all, and does not use up too many resources.

But then it would have to be available too. There are some designers, especially among the younger generation, who are already working in that direction, but society hasn't yet recognized the value of what they are doing. It is sold as fashion or chic.

But that's what's good about the failure of mass-produced products. In Ulm we believed in the mass-produced product: we saw Hans von Klier's espresso machine and said that is *the* coffee maker, so let's produce it twenty million times over. But that's not the way it goes.

It is telling how much industry is doing now to frequently change its product lines and no longer treat large batches as the be-all and end-all of production.
Even if things look like there's a million of them, in fact there's only a thousand.

Hmm.

An Ecological Innovation (1994)

It must have featured in some hospitality trade magazine or other, namely that a lettuce leaf garnished with a slice of tomato should enliven any dish. Ever since, whether you order salted pork and sauerkraut, pike dumplings and pilau rice, or Westphalian "Pfefferpothast" braised beef and vegetables, you inevitably get the lettuce leaf and tomato trim. Even a tomato salad on the side comes with a lettuce leaf garnished with a slice of tomato.

In and of itself, that isn't a problem at all, at least as long as the lettuce leaf doesn't come into contact with the dish you intend to eat. For I don't want the pesticide sprayed in the greenhouse to end up on my steak. But it's annoying to add up how many lettuce leaves and tomato slices are used in this way. — Let's assume that ten million plates of food are dished up each day in the Federal German Republic. To garnish each of them with a lettuce leaf requires, say, some 500.000 heads of lettuce, plus two million tomatoes cut each into six slices. I'll calculate some more: the two million daily tomatoes grown without earth and under glass require some 400.000 square meters of glasshouse. Plus, circa 80.000 square meters more for the salad likewise grown without earth. That makes—it makes me woozy—how many liters of fertilizer? How many liters of pesticides? How much packaging? How many trucks to transport it from Ostelijk Flevoland to Steinau an der Straße?

Forget it. For salvation is nigh. We have now designed a recyclable lettuce leaf with a tomato slice that can be stuck in a dish every day. The new product will obviate the need for all the aforementioned resources and has the added advantage that it will poison no one.

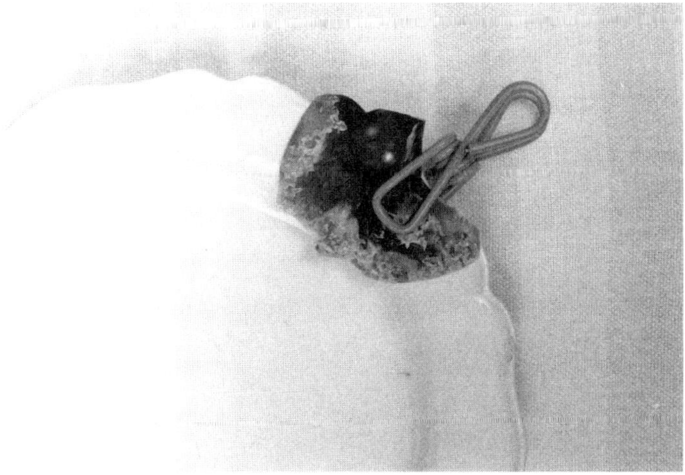

Photo: Annemarie Burckhardt

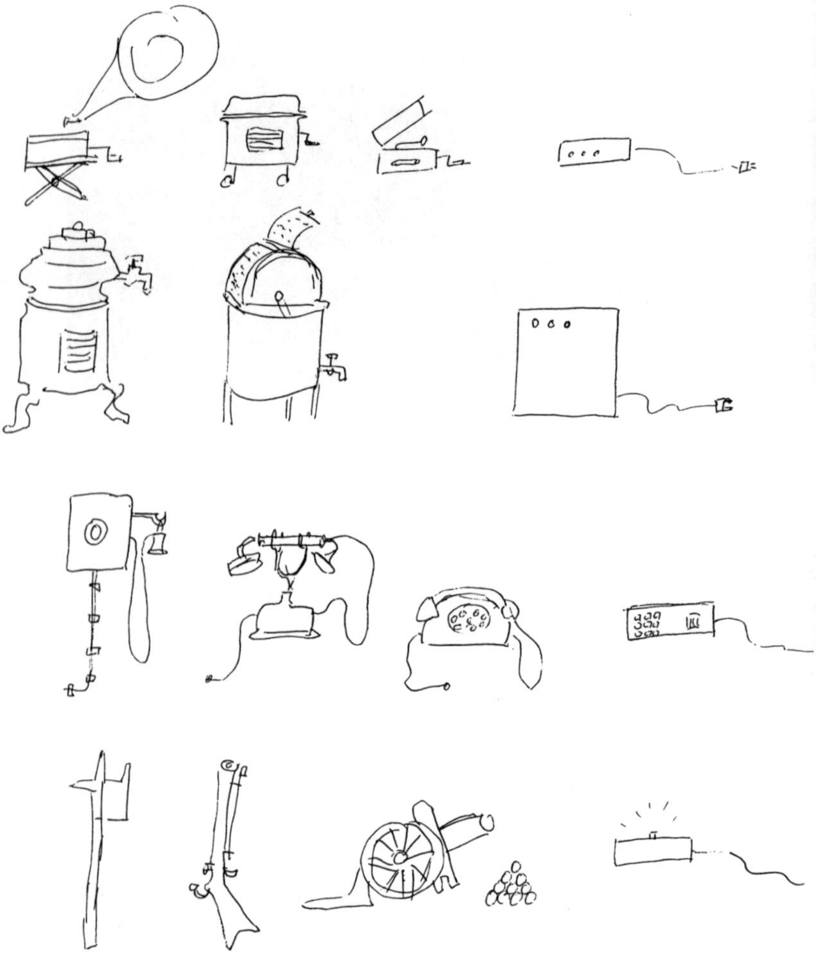

The Triumph of Good Form. Drawing: Lucius Burckhardt

Landscape-theoretical watercolor drawing by Lucius Burckhardt, untitled. The atomic power station becomes part of an idyllic landscape. Lucius Burckhardt drew on a great variety of media to communicate his thoughts and intentions.

SOCIETY

Good Taste (1986)

Today, we want to find the time to squeeze in a little think about good taste and thereby posit that good taste belongs to a long since bygone era. However, we must also note that the era is perhaps not completely over and done with. I ripped an ad out of a magazine, an IKEA ad, featuring a brief text in which the word taste occurred no less than three times. At the first mention, taste is claimed to be more important than money; at the second, you decorate your home completely in line with your taste; and by the third, IKEA has more money than taste.

It is a strange text given that it offers two interpretations of taste. The second quote—You decorate your home completely in line with your taste—means "What you buy here at IKEA is unimportant, since we are only a furniture store. You can choose whatever you like, as long as you pay for it. You are free to choose according to your taste." And this is where the subjectivity of personal taste comes into play: each to his own. We [at IKEA] bear no responsibility. You can collect whatever you like from our furniture store, since everyone creates a home for himself according to personal taste.

The first and, above all, the third quote (more taste than money) demonstrate a contradictory use of the word taste. The phrasing presupposes some background knowledge on the part of readers: We [readers] know what taste is and can measure it against money; and evidently, we all do so in the exact same way. We then all come to the same conclusion: Go to IKEA, because there one has more taste than money. That is a normative use of the word taste.

These two levels, the subjective and the normative, together bring forth that famous antimony: everyone has his own taste and there is no disputing taste. Both statements are correct. "There is no

We at IKEA thrive on an idea.

This idea is very simple. As many people as possible should be able to furnish their home just as they wish. Taste should be more important than money.

In order to be able to sell good design and good quality at affordable prices we need your help.

At IKEA you have to pick up your furniture from the store yourself, transport it home yourself, and assemble it yourself.

After all this effort you have a home completely to your taste. At a price that benefits you and us.

Us, because we now have sufficient money to further develop our idea.

You, because you still have enough money left to enjoy life in your lovely new home. Perhaps by throwing a small party for good friends.

For furniture is not all life has to offer. There is also champagne.

IKEA: More taste than money.

disputing taste" is expressed by IKEA's claim "You get a home completely in keeping with your taste." No one will argue with you. You have your taste, and that's it. Each to his own. The second sentence, "One can argue about taste," says: If anyone claims he has more taste than IKEA we [at IKEA] are in a position to dispute it. He should bring proof of his claim and we will provide evidence to the contrary. This antimony was discovered by Immanuel Kant and can be found in Paragraph 58 of his *Critique of Judgment*. There, Kant juxtaposed these two statements: everyone has his own taste and there is no disputing taste. I would first like to reflect on why this significant position was formulated precisely at the moment when Kant was seeking to define the criteria of judgment, and also to consider to what extent there is a before and after to this historic moment. If there is, it would amount to something akin to post-taste.

The surge in use of the word taste in the eighteenth century appears to have been no accident. It is not as if the German language alone was in such dire need of a word as to borrow one from the culinary realm, since the simile occurs in all West European languages: *le goût, il gusto, taste*. The word evidently speaks of a uniform need: something came about for which a metaphor was coined, and not only in our language.

That this by no means new word found itself suddenly in frequent use is evident also from literature. Herder warns against use of this word. Klopstock writes that a word he doesn't like has come into being, and that is taste. Evidently, some people are afraid of the subjectivity of this word. Others use it liberally. I already mentioned Kant. Goethe used it incessantly—he would have been totally at a loss without it. And Novalis then used it in a somewhat malicious reference to Goethe, inasmuch as he opined that Goethe, like English Wedgwood porcelain, is of noble taste. Patently, the elegance of Goethe's taste is thereby called into question.

My limited and wholly subjective survey of the historic turn merely offers a framework for historical reflection. This turn begins with the academics who are incapable of using the word taste in the subjective sense, since they already know what is beautiful, namely the imitation of antiquity. The famous dispute between Blondel and Perrault flares up in French academia: *la querelle des anciens et des modernes*. This dispute between traditionalists and modernists concerns the question of whether antiquity can ever be outdone. Must we, in order to attain beauty, do nothing but improve our knowledge of how the ancients went about things? Is beauty a science that we can learn from our forefathers, or can we achieve more than they did? This dispute flared up about the colonnades on the west side of the Louvre, where Perrault raised his columns in pairs. To support a beam one must raise columns at regular intervals whereas to raise columns close to each other, in pairs, and leave a greater distance between each pair is to admit that a beam does not actually require quite so many columns. Statics experts alone surmise that an iron beam is concealed behind the stone architrave in the section where the columns are more widely spaced. Does this "outdo the ancients," or has Perrault failed to attain their level because he didn't pay enough attention in school? This is a very complicated dispute. As an advocate of academicism, Blondel claims that beauty is a gift of nature. An architect who learns from the ancients learns natural laws. And now something remarkable: the proof of this (Blondel continues) is the judgment of taste. Ultimately, the tools of taste judge the wisdom we gain from studying laws that can be verified. Perrault, for his part, says that architecture is a system one can incessantly reinvent. The architect is a man ahead of his time, an inventor. And even if onlookers initially think something ugly—the wide gaps between columns, for example—they will grow used to it in the end. The architect is ahead of his time and other people's sense of beauty will slowly acclimatize.

This remarkable dispute put an end to the tenets of academicism and marked the start of an era that we might well describe as dilettantish, since people begin to pop up and pass judgment without any legitimacy at all, without ever having pursued academic studies. Winckelmann is a dilettante in this sense, in my view. He discovers antiquity with a different eye than that of the academics whom he calls pedants. He speaks of antiquity without first verifying whether or not the columns evince proportional entasis. He simply looks, and says what he thinks.

The word taste is apt for such people. To judge according to one's taste has been of social import too: it establishes equality. Society was still divided then, on the one hand between the learned and the laypeople, and on the other between the aristocrats one cannot question and the bourgeoisie who in any case say only things one must laugh at because they are funny. At this level, where new aesthetic judgments are based on taste, everyone is equal. And what counts is whether someone has a good eye, whether he can clearly justify his taste-based judgment—not justify it academically, but subjectively, on account of a gut feeling, so to speak, a medium that his peers too can understand and that Kant, remarkably, called mystical: the interpersonal substrate.

The taste-based judgment is therefore the first springboard for the emancipation of this new class. Here, we are all equal. The social institutions of this era likewise highlight the importance of such equality and debate. One example is the rise of the café. In a café, everyone is equal and can debate an issue, without someone announcing that the person speaking happens to be Lord What's-his-name or that only Mr. X ever says this or that. Signs in London's first ever cafés proclaimed, "No one here stands in the presence of persons of high rank." Even a lord has to wait until a seat is free. To establish equality in this way was to demonstrate that we all have taste and that everyone's judgment carries weight.

However, this weight depends on how plausibly we are able to justify our judgment in others' eyes. And this plausibility does not depend on being able to state "I studied namely for ten years" or "I am Lord What's-his-name." Passing judgment was hence a means to put equality into practice.

Two literary intermezzos: firstly, *The Sorrows of Young Werther*. It is always said that Werther killed himself because his heart had been broken. Werther killed himself after he had begun discussing art with his friend, the Count, at the castle. They debated and debated, then suddenly the ladies arrived, the Countesses; so the Count then had to tell his friend: This is an aristocratic gathering, actually, so you must leave. The suicide note followed on this rejection. Werther did not grasp the rules of his day: he may well be everyman's equal in a debate about taste, but not at aristocratic family festivities.

Debate of matters of taste is simultaneously an education in political equality. On this, Schiller's remark in his *Ästhetische Erziehung:* "To bring the aesthetic man to profound views, to elevated sentiments, requires nothing more than important occasions; to obtain the same thing from the sensuous man, his nature must at first be changed. To make of the former a hero, a sage, it is often only necessary to meet with a sublime situation."[1] It is not difficult to see that the sublime situation is the French Revolution, in the course of which people who were already practiced in passing judgment according to their sense of taste had seized the moment and become heroes. I find this of great significance for the moment when the bourgeois class rose up as a political power as well as for the role of taste-based judgments in this process.

1 [J.C. Friedrich von Schiller, *Letters Upon The Aesthetic Education of Man,* Part V. Letter XXIII, 1794, http://public-library.uk/ebooks/55/76.pdf, accessed 09.08.2016, p. 31]

Taste is a natural ally of simplicity. Whoever sets up home simply shows good taste. It is controversial to say so, of course, since aristocrats have always set up home in splendor. Beauty initially was splendid. So if a social class now comes along and says "Whoever sets up home simply shows good taste," and thereby thinks, moreover, "The nobility sets itself up in splendor at our expense," then this is a politically loaded judgment. To see splendor as a show of a lack of taste now means: They take our money and, moreover, they have no idea how to spend it in style on tasteful things. This is the bourgeois' verdict on the nobility at the time of the Revolution.

According to Kant, a taste-based judgment is the ability to recognize purposiveness in things that have no purpose. Naturally, we in the Werkbund smile when we read this. But then again, one can likewise read in *Critique of Judgment* that beauty is purposiveness without purpose. Might not this—to recognize the illusion of utility, without use—be the best ever definition of design? That is good taste. With this "without purpose" the bourgeoisie takes its place on the established side of history, the side that Bourdieu so strongly elaborated in his book about distinctions. The nouveau riche bourgeoisie simply turns around the instrument of taste: it used to serve to distinguish those one saw when looking up, because the upper class spent lots of money on living out its splendor; and now taste serves downwards distinction. Bourdieu says: "Le goût, c'est le dégout."[2] In order to arrive at an understanding of what taste is we firstly need to know what exactly is the object of rejection. And what

2 [Pierre Bourdieu, *Distinctions. A Social Critique of the Judgment of Taste* (1979). trans. Richard Nice, Harvard University Press, 1984. "Le bon goût, c'est le dégoût du goût des autres," meaning "Taste is first and foremost the distaste of the tastes of others."]

is being rejected today is the upcoming class, from which one can distinguish oneself by resorting to the taste-based judgment.

This happens now with the very convenient formula discovered by Kant: everyone has his own taste and there is no disputing taste. Both are equally mean with regard to whatever it is one hopes to distinguish oneself from. You are completely free in matters of taste. Set up home however you like. But basically you are completely lacking in taste, because you do not share my taste. Firstly, this seeming indifference to which the second IKEA sentence gives expression: "After all this effort"—namely that of going to IKEA—"you have a home completely in keeping with your taste." Even if someone were now to say, it wasn't so great in the end, all that stuff you brought home, it was nonetheless to your taste. Or do you perhaps have no taste at all? — That would be bad, since "Taste is meant to be more important than money" (Quotes Nos. 1 & 3).

That is not the end of the story. And certainly not the end of my lecture. For now we are witnessing the comeback of the era of those who know what taste is. I mean by this the era in which the Werkbund came into being, when people who discovered craftsmanship laid claim to be in the know again — "It is impossible to argue about taste." — They drew a stroke through that sentence. They did argue about taste, and they were right to do so. Instead of setting out this position I will just present a somewhat lengthy quote. I found it in Gustav E. Pazaurek's book, *Guter und schlechter Geschmack im Kunstgewerbe* (Stuttgart and Berlin 1912). The book begins as follows: "To promote and disseminate good taste in all realms and not least in the applied arts is one of our most sublime cultural challenges, both in terms of aesthetics and the national economy. Even if no difference of opinion prevails regarding this topic, clarity as to the nature of good taste is often lacking, since very many people describe only their own taste as good taste. The following represents an endeavor to liberate questions of taste from the straitjacket of all too subjective and arbitrary views, and to create tools rooted in practical aesthetics, which can serve to sharpen our often atrophied senses and make us more receptive to finer differences in quality, which are after all so very important."

And further: "We first of all want to clean the construction site and put aside everything that doesn't belong there. If we want to recognize what good taste is then we first must rid ourselves of bad taste." (Parenthesis: "Le goût, c'est le dégoût.")

Further: "This is why I opened the Cabinet of Bad Taste in the Landesmuseum in Stuttgart on 11 February 1909, and have added to it ever since, introducing a three-part system: ... lined up there are lapses in taste regarding material, construction, and ornament. ... If we were to make a thorough study of all the indiscriminate serious crimes against good taste that are to be found in these three categories then it would be relatively easy for us to lend considerably more backbone to labile judgments of taste."— Mr. Pazaurek's formula is: One simply does away with everything that is in bad taste so then only things in good taste remain. Anyone of that opinion spends no time wondering about changes in taste. People who know what beauty is, be it the academics at the start of our era, or the turn-of-the-century Werkbundians, know what is forever good: things authentic, honest, plain, and permanent. That is, they banish the matter of fashion. And the modernists of the 1920s, the classical modernists, did precisely that too. For them, to aestheticize things was in and of itself a revolution. The revolution must not, as Schiller claimed, be brought about. Today, modernism creates happiness simply by fulfilling needs. It recognizes needs, does research into them, meets them; and in so doing, it expects some reconciliation with the object. Lasting design solutions overcome alienation.

The paradox of the modernist movement lies in the fact that the formal idiom born of it was once again a language of the elite. Reconciliation with the product, which was proposed as a means of overcoming alienation, failed to reconcile the masses, because it failed to overcome the language barrier. The allegedly direct relationship between need and meeting need actually took the form of an elite language that had to be learned—the language of modernism.

Let us return to the matter in hand, namely the change in tastes. Let me tell you—while we are on the subject of the early Werkbund's arguments against all that is fashionable or classic—that there is, in my opinion, no difference between fashion and a shift in taste. The ambivalence of the term taste reveals itself, here too. The term taste apparently is anti-fashion. I don't dress according to the current dictates of fashion. I follow my personal taste. But then, the ability to create fashion requires taste above all. Both statements sound plausible. For me, the problem of changing tastes is the problem of shifts in fashion.

Therefore, one example among many: Schultze-Naumburg and Mohrbutter have each written a book condemning the corset, condemning that lacing of the female body, which was once the symbol of a bygone age. To restrict the body is virtually to restrict the mind, i.e. it is narrow-mindedness. The nineteenth century was narrow-minded. The role of women was restricted by society. — When one reads about all this, one asks oneself why for heaven's sake did women back then wear such restrictive clothing? And if one inquires into the matter further then one finds that it was at the time of Napoleon III that they all began lacing themselves up—that sort of wasp waist plus a bustle—because to be corseted that way was supposed to be elegant. Which is to say, women didn't lace themselves into tight clothing against their will. No man said to them, "Kindly get yourself all laced up—Put on your corset." No, women actually got themselves laced up by their seamstress or tailor, and thereupon mingled in society with more self-assurance. The elegant, today one would say liberated woman who wanted to look self-assured and confident in society and not always merely follow in her husband's footsteps—that was the woman in corsets.

How is it that a shift takes place, that people suddenly say the corset is an imposition, a compulsion, that it is society's mistaken view of women's role that leads women to put up with corsets? That happened some thirty years later, by which time the liberated women who had once stepped out so elegantly had turned into Aunt Lieschen and Aunt Rose, who still wore a bustle, whereas women of the next generation no longer laced themselves up. Lacing up nowadays smacks of "behind the times;" with hindsight, lacing up looks like the height of conservatism. For these old ladies espoused the views of their day, and harped on at the youngsters about things no longer up-to-date, and this became associated in people's minds with their laced-up look.

It is equally mistaken to say that lacing up the female body, nineteenth-century narrow-mindedness, and the lifestyle of that era were all one and the same thing. The shift in taste consists in the fact that we initially look forwards in time and then later backwards in time, and one and the same phenomenon, seen retrospectively, has a contrary meaning, the opposite connotation. This process of fashion can be described as follows: a leading group, possibly even a social elite, starts something, and other people throw up their hands in horror and say, "O Lord, how indecent, that she dares go out on the street dressed like that!" But the story ends with people saying, "O Lord, how conservative, that the frump is still running around in that old garb." The meaning of a form has meanwhile morphed into its opposite.

And now I'd like to present my final hypothesis, namely that the era of fashion, the era of taste, is a bygone era. By this I mean that the fashion pyramid—the elite starts, the masses follow and, finally, only the old aunts remain—this pyramid no longer exists. And perhaps this arguably characterizes the post-taste era. I refuse to accept a concept of postmodernism that argues simply: "After the Stone Age comes the Bronze Age, and after the Bronze Age comes the What's-its-name Age, and after the Gothic comes the Renaissance, and after Modernism comes Postmodernism." It is not as simple as that. We cannot simply take the retrospective view elaborated by art history and project it onto the future.

The so-called young fashions are not fashions at all. They are a new phenomenon. Because, for the very people whom we claim follow youthful fashion, fashion is dead. That sounds a little strange given that more money is earned today from fashion than ever before. Fashion stores are mushrooming. They are over the shock of 1968, when no one wanted to dress up any more, and now money is being spent on so-called fashion again. But this fashion is not fashion in the old sense of the term. It is anti-fashion.

All previous "fashions" to date are reinterpretations of older forms of dress, be these fashions or uniforms. People adopted the Palestinian scarf, adopted blue jeans, and delved into the world of labor, the world of the marines, of uniforms, of revolutions, of the Third World, and appropriated the symbols available there, and used them to express a different meaning or, initially, to mean nothing at all. Someone who dresses as a worker doesn't necessarily want to go to work, just as someone who dons a uniform doesn't want to sign up to the military. The signs used are existing agents of meaning but the meaning is suspended. This can lead to misunderstandings. Most people realize straight away that something else is meant. But my old professor once said to me, on his return from Paris, how immediately obvious it is, in Paris, that the solid bourgeoisie studies at university, because female undergraduates there still have very long hair.

New meaning arises out of the tension with older meanings, and one can ask oneself, why don't these young folk dress in something novel? Why are they lacking in new ideas? Fashion designers have new ideas—so it's not hard to imagine that those in the anti-fashion camp may have some too. Yet in order to invest a thing with meaning one has to take away a signifier and introduce another meaning. This happens on several levels. Probably the most taboo symbol known to us is the swastika. Hell's Angels and other groups have adopted this symbol precisely, a symbol that hurts so much when we see it, because we have so much stored up in our minds about the meaning of the swastika. And they want to confront us with this symbol and give it a positive meaning. But it is not only the Hell's Angels who do so. Recently, Helmut Federle made a painting that depicts the swastika and I believe he even sold it to Basel Museum. It was called "Oriental Symbol." It hung there for some time, apparently. But then suddenly it was there no longer, owing to public protest. Existing symbols are accordingly used and invested with new meaning at the level of high art and, if we want to take young fashion into account, also at the level of popular art. Existing symbols alone are understood. A newly invented symbol initially means nothing at all. We have to draw on the store of existing symbols. We can only ever really communicate with these alone. Which is why people take existing symbols and give them new meaning.

In the course of this process we must take a look at subcultures' fashion trends. On this point, two deductions: in the course of this process, high culture becomes just one more subculture among all the rest. And note this too: the young fashions with which a subculture begins are no longer only young fashions but cultural groupings of certain stability. The young people of Zurich who picketed the opera a few years back in hope of preventing the old folk in their evening dress from attending the premiere, cannot be told: Just wait a few years and then you too will enjoy a night at the opera. Some of them may well do so. However, abstention from nights at the opera is not a problem of youth, but rather of cultural groups who have taken different paths in life. Cultural belonging can sometimes go topsy-turvy generationally speaking too: the father may listen to rock music while the daughter practices at the spinet or goes to the opera. It is not a problem of youth but rather a problem of cultural, subcultural groups who part company, whereby within this spectrum, for a neutral onlooker, high culture too is a subculture. There are those who talk about whether or not one should stick swastikas on one's sweater, and those who want, or don't want, to see them in an art museum. But they are subcultural groups, up to and including highbrow culture.

And now an unresolved problem crops up. I'll just simply spell it out and ask you to think about it. Where does comprehensibility come from? Is there, so to speak, a super-language from which we recurrently derive symbols and then invest them with new meaning? What resources does the symbol war draw on? I take your uniform and wear it in order to demonstrate that I refuse to do military service. Which is the super-language that succeeds still in winding others up? Evidently, there is still the whole language, and individual groups can take the symbols of others and change their meaning. Just as fashion designers today take away the symbols of youth. Every revolutionary symbol lasts for six months and then elegant ladies start wearing it. I wouldn't be surprised to see everyone soon running around sporting a swastika.

We assert therefore that the shift in taste so longer moves down through the pyramid, from the elite at the top to the lower levels, but rather that we are a society that has gone to pieces, each piece being a subculture with its own symbols. And this now brings us to the final question: How come one group understands the symbols of the rest? And the great thing is, we understand other people's symbol systems so well that we are even able to judge their application within the alien group. We can say: "I in any case dress quite differently than Mrs. Thatcher, but if ever I were to dress as she does then I'd dye my hair a little more discreetly." Owing to the fact that we understand the languages of others, the application of borrowed symbols within our subculture is rich in meaning, and ambiguous. Here, at the level of established culture, lies the fun in postmodernism: in this new context, historically charged symbols, the column, the keystone, become a multiple code. And this is what's dynamic about the young people's style war (a war that is no longer a fashion and no longer related only to youth): the fact that subcultures communicate with each other in a kind of super-language. — Is there a super-language?

Can A Shift In Tastes Be Planned? (1984)

After the Romanesque comes the Gothic, after the Gothic the Renaissance, after the Renaissance the Baroque: so say all the school textbooks, so say all good schoolchildren, and possibly even publishers themselves believe that this is indeed a fact of nature, like the evolution of the Jura mountain range, or the Ice Age.

But no one tells us how it really happens. Perhaps the client says to his carpenter: "Please don't make any more round windows for me. I'm sick of seeing them. What I urgently need now is a pointed arch." Or does the craftsman say to his client: "Do you really want to be known as the last person ever to have rounded arches?" Is change wrought by a shift in tastes, by the fact namely that the public opens up to new forms, or feels a need for them? Or does it happen by product modification, which is to say, through newly invented forms that must gradually win the favor of a resistant public? Is it even possible to say?

In his book *Produktwahrnehmung und stilistischer Wandel*,[1] Thomas Jaspersen posits that we are constantly witnessing such changes. "Styles" is art history's term for that which we today regard simply as fashion trends, at least six of which have washed over us only recently. We hardly notice, however, because such fashions do not follow on from one another in single file like the styles in a school textbook. I can simultaneously purchase a radio receiver with a hi-tech trim and an icebox with an old-fashioned chrome trim. Shifts in fashion are abrupt and continual at one and the same time. From one day to the next, a wallpaper factory dreams up combinations of

1 ["Product Perception and Changes in Style," Campus Verlag, Frankfurt Main, 1985]

colors previously believed to "clash"—yet this by no means alters the fact that 99 percent of all the wallpaper patterns presently on the market are designed with older harmonies in mind.

"Good Form" is a quite meaningless term

A shift appears to be gradual if we bear in mind a product range in its entirety, and to be sudden if we are on the lookout for pioneers with novel ideas. Styles are hence simultaneously present, in a greater or lesser quantity, but they are visible to us to varying degrees. New phenomena are highly likely to catch our eye. We adore or fiercely reject them. Not-so-new features are less striking. The chrome trim on my icebox no longer really does anything for me, but I can live with it. Only in retrospective do such shifts look like discrete leaps: the new look, mini-skirts, The Beatles, the hippies seem almost to pass by in single file, textbook-style.

Shifting trends and product perception or, in other words, designers' new ideas and the public's willingness to understand them, or even its urgent need to possess them, are like the chicken and the egg. It's impossible to say which comes first. Can anything be said about them with any accuracy? Probably not, for in this matter we are simultaneously onlookers and guinea pigs. Were we able to soar above the pedestrian trot of the rest of humankind we'd be able to describe the mechanism behind shifts in taste and so easily come up with new styles and fashions. We would know whether heads will be covered again by the 1990s, and with what, whether going bareheaded will make a comeback around the millennium, and what hairstyles will be "in" around then. Thomas Jaspersen's book declares such predictions impossible.

However, certain findings were brought to light by Jaspersen's series of experiments with students of design, which were based on product ads in the German weekly news magazine *Stern*. So far, semioticians have attempted to explain shifts in taste in terms of signs and their meanings, as in: a form no longer speaks to us, either because that which it claims is no longer consistent with the signal it emits, or because we have forgotten how to read it. Jaspersen's guinea pigs introduce affectivity—an emotional response—into this cool relationship between a sign and its meaning. They "get" the signs when they love or hate the products; and this is the case if the products are new on the market. When it comes to older products still knocking around, the icebox with a chrome trim, for example, the guinea pigs are not so sure, and cannot reach unanimous agreement. The drop in affectivity means that they no longer want to possess the form and hence also no longer understand it (or: "get it"). This was evident during the series of experiments from their inability to reach agreement on where a form belongs.

Jaspersen's research also brought a second matter to light: we will not understand our era if we limit ourselves to describing those products we classify as good, i.e., those which are exhibited at design fairs, win the "Good Form" design award, are shown in museums, and fill museum catalogs. All such collections are tautological inasmuch as they merely prove that products selected according to certain criteria necessarily evince all the said criteria. They say very little, however, about that which is really going on in the design field in our day. Coming generations will therefore not go to museums in order to learn about our era but rather to trash dumps, the last resting place of the products Mr. Museum Curator scorns to buy.

Trash outlives all the rest

And this brings us to Michael Thompson's trash theory, on which Jaspersen too drew as explanation. The theory is—roughly speaking—that the only products to acquire eternal value are those that survive the being-discarded-as-trash phase. Or, in more scientific terms, it posits that styles are not inherent to the forms that products take but, rather, exist in onlookers' minds; and hence that every generation has to write its own new history of style. And indeed, the worm has been gnawing for some time at classic concepts such as the Romanesque or Gothic, and new concepts are pushing their way in, allegedly as complements, but in reality as competitors. At the least in reference to the past, we can make the mechanism visible: it is today's artists and designers who enable us to see forms of the past from a new angle. Styles are not created by the artists of yore, but by the work of those whom Bazon Brock has dubbed the "high-octane avant-garde" of each and every contemporary era.

Beyond Utility Value (1986)

People have grown far too accustomed to following in the footsteps of established art history and regarding fashion phenomena and shifts in taste in chronological order, as in: after the Romanesque comes the Gothic, after the Gothic the Renaissance, after that the Baroque, and so forth. Far less attention is paid the fact that styles in advanced civilizations coexist: in Tuscan tombs one finds artifacts both from the Classical and the Etruscan tradition; Baroque and Palladian Classicism may be deployed simultaneously, or with variations.

To understand the situation today, one must bear in mind that various styles occur in parallel and at times become the hallmark of diverse types of expression or diverse groups. A quantitative predominance of any one stylistic trend in an era can leave the impression that "style" has changed; but we prudently act on the premise that "nothing dies." Perhaps the group that is now on the outer margins will prove the most fruitful for what comes next. To vow allegiance to some style crowd or other, or some fashion trend, is to manufacture fictitious pasts: differentiation in society depends on people referencing other predecessors or antecedents.

The perfect example of this overall social trend in the aesthetic dimension is so-called young fashion and the "post-history" group has accordingly paid it particular attention. However, our example proves to be of relevance in two respects, above and beyond youth itself; firstly, inasmuch as similar phenomena occur also in the adult realm; and secondly, because one can no longer really speak of young fashion, i.e. of a fashion discarded at a certain age, because carrying characteristics of one's "peer group" over into adult life—as in the case of the lifelong football fan, for example—is now a notable trend.

Parallel styles exist yet each style is a world unto itself. Within any style group, only one particular style is held to be right and proper. However, given that even the most fervent fans of whatever individual group can no longer overlook the proliferation of groups devoted to multiple-styledom—and hence the relative nature of styles—this universalism too has become a relative matter. Nevertheless, or perhaps for precisely this reason, loyalty to a certain style is upheld. The fashion of one's own group becomes a rite, a game, a celebration; and the more absurd it seems, the stronger the loyalty grows. When everything is relative, one's own personal style within the group is taken seriously yet nevertheless regarded at a certain remove. Wearing insignia attests a dual consciousness: on the one hand, one belongs to a specific group but, on the other, one by no means belongs to the one and only right group.

This consciousness of one's own relativity is admittedly undermining yet it simultaneously allows a style to be taken to extremes and even to its most consummate expression. It is precisely the non-binding nature of any society that is open to different views that paves the way to free expression; no one is made an example of; there is no instance of having to stand for the correctness of this or that group's assertions. As the "revolutionary circumstances" of radical left-wing or radical right-wing groups are in any case bogus, the portrayal of a society in a state of civil war can be excessively indulged without fear of retribution.

Sociologically or statistically speaking, such absolute manifestations of style are marginal occurrences. Thus we note on the one hand that the punk wave has left no city untouched and has influenced young fashion everywhere; but on the other that there is only ever a tiny group of less than a dozen punks, or skinheads, or whatever, even in the major cities … Yet they still make a big public splash. This to some extent representative portrayal of absolute devotion to style hence follows the "art" model; the extreme participants assume the art producers' functions—but we will return to that later.

Whatever we say about youth cultures applies increasingly also to society as a whole. Under certain circumstances the group persists: distinctions between youth and adulthood are toned down. Adults split into their former youth groups. The young adult faced with permanent unemployment or marginal jobs never leaves his youth culture behind, because he doesn't ever become an adult in the traditional sense, in career terms.

In this case, all that is left him is identity. The desire for recognition predominates. Self-expression becomes a means to make a statement, to lay claim to something, however groundless that statement or claim might be. In this striving for a group identity, for recognition, we note the two contrary trends inherent to every type of fashion: the drive both to be the same (i.e. to belong to the group) and to be an individual (i.e. to stand out from the group). Likewise the fashionably dressed fin-de-siècle lady used to ask her seamstress: "What are people wearing this year?" Only then to add, "But don't even think about sewing the same dress for me as for my friend."

Identity and recognition are fundamental also to architecture and design. For anyone whose subjective take on the world is of a confusing place that has fallen to pieces identity becomes the final remainder, the linchpin of whatever he perceives to be his environment. To be recognized, to have a clear identity, is all the easier given that whatever one lays claim to is never put to the test. While in modernism the major themes were still hygiene, urban planning, and rationalization, we restrict ourselves nowadays to recognizable models: urban planning cedes to the perfect single-family residence or perhaps to the small, well-configured urban ensemble, which is nothing but a patch in the wider urban fabric. The isolated object or, at most, the limited serial edition is characteristic of contemporary design.

Past styles and regional specialties are excellent means of forging a recognizable profile. Representation acquires something confessional this way: to manufacture the past and all the relevant proofs, forefathers, patriarchs, and fake traditions, similarly to that fictitious-yet-faithful sense of belonging one finds in football clubs. Modern regionalism creates regions that actually never before existed in the said form; or did, at best, but elsewhere. This is how the fake becomes authentic: the imitation becomes the original because the original it is imitating does not exist. Attention has been drawn to a prototype of this phenomenon: architect Ricardo Bofill's Palado de Abraxas in Marne-la-Vallée.

The bogus claim put forward in the service of recognizability remains consistently and patently a fake. The discussion group drew here on the concept of "glamor." Regionalism without a region cannot restrict itself to imitation but must take a leaf out of Hollywood's book and style the region until it can be easily recognized. Vattimo called attention here to Nietzsche's "God is dead," his suggestion being that this key phrase heralds an interim period when *anything goes* as long as it assures distinction and recognizability. The absent antagonist must always be created simultaneously and the fake emergency, the outbreak of conflict, is imagined too, but does not come about. The "Storming of the Winter Palace" becomes a mere staged spectacle.

All this has consequences also for design. The utility value of a thing recedes in the face of its ideal value. The form of the portrayal once again becomes the real thing but in the sense of a spectacle that no one believes in but that everyone takes seriously nonetheless. This dual consciousness can be observed particularly in TV viewers, who take the spectacle seriously yet know it to be fake. As was said at the beginning, the marginality of the extreme case approximates the "art" model. Therein lies the producer's problem. For him, any consciousness of irony must be ruled out. He must shrink his horizon and believe in the character he himself created. He must consciously forget, above all forget, that anything goes. He must contrive to maneuver himself into the delusion and resolutely confront the situation of his own invention.

The situation is different for the viewer. Even once ideologies have been exposed, the pious pose of ironic belief remains an option, and the thwarted aspiration [to recognizability] is still present albeit unfortunately impossible to justify. The argumentation therefore relies on borrowed formulas. Sociologically speaking, we might compare this attitude with the "Pietas" of antiquity, an era when kinship with the gods was acknowledged to be fictitious yet posited nonetheless. From this might be deduced a possible definition of "postmodernism:" the paradoxical confirmation that the thwarted aspiration is still present, the justification thereof however no longer to be deduced from the logical realm but only from mementos, from etymological layers. It is this, which lends design today an important role in the sublimation of conflicts, in the hygienic, orderly enactment of artificially generated enmities. While one of the major goals of early modernism was hygiene, the bathroom, the new goal of design must be to formalize differentiation while retaining a sense of humanity. Design creates, in a sense, "the conflictual bathroom."

To trigger and resolve the artificial conflict requires ironic fanaticism, devotion without the highest values. It requires the division of roles: the producer as fanatic, and for the inessential the recipient as the distanced fan.

The communication society must have something to communicate—content, in a word. Content cannot consist only in revivals excerpted from a past of one's own invention or from the fictitious region. If recognizability is the final remainder then we must also emphasize the right to preserve elementary environmental values. This explains the growing aspiration to ecologically sound practice, a trend that even people's attempts to debunk ecology as a new aesthetic cannot diminish.

The realm of alleged recognizability was complemented in the discussion group by three rules. The first is: nothing dies. All movements coexist, for even if their importance may lessen from time to time this only ups the chance that they will regain importance in the future. Obsolete technologies still have their fans who band together, for example, to keep alive the last steam engines; and the public is happy then to hop aboard for an entertaining ride.

Rule Two: limit understanding. Every group has both an immediate and a distant environment. The symbols used must therefore have a simplified impact at a distance and a more informative effect from up close, whereby these more complicated types of information serve as camouflage, as mantling, with regard to the distanced observers. This explains the apparent style contradictions in contemporary fashion: hard stuff is combined with soft, leopard skin with silk, knitwear with little lace collars. The result is a rough, partial statement for everyone, plus coded information for insiders.

Rule Three: the impossible order. Just as those styles set up by art history can in reality never be found in pure form, it is equally untrue to say that the aficionados of certain fashion groups consume nothing but those groups' products. Were they to do so, it would bring about the collapse of culture overall, of the supra-cultural context of subcultures. Only when the punk listens to jazz, and enjoys doing so, does he come to understand the "antagonistic group;" only then does he learn to differentiate. Last of all comes the question of evaluation, of critical judgment: How can I criticize a work without knowing the norm? — For the "Good Form" design award the norm meant fulfillment of purpose. But how might the effective deployment of a thing look under conditions that are shaped by the relative unimportance of its utility value, its functionality? Efficiency cannot be measured solely in terms of communication. To see communication society itself as the ultimate goal is absurd. We communicate content derived from our cultures. What must be judged, therefore, is the efficiency of the role model, the source material, the historical or regional pseudo-revival—as it really exists or in its fictitious yet accepted dimension.

... In Our Minds (1987)

To write about the future, to speak about the year 2000: that was the favorite pastime of technicians and scientists in the early 1960s. Yet the quarter century that has slipped by in the meantime has taught us that which we always knew to be true, namely that the future never does us the favor of turning out as we predicted. Is the future therefore no longer an issue?

Anyone who closely examines our theme will note that it evinces two instances of food for thought, which stand in contrast to the primitivisms of the 1960s. "Design of the Future" is ambiguous. For one, it could lead one to discuss how designers will shape apparatuses for us in the future. Yet it could equally be taken to mean that our future is designed, that someone designs it and seeks to realize his design. Our politicians too are designers, in this sense, although they least of all manage to realize their designs. Yet through their actions, which are steered by the design in their mind's eye, politicians do influence the future, at least as much as the billiard player influences the course of his game. This brings us to our title: "... In Our Minds." Our deliberations are premised on the fact that, even if it is impossible to predict the future, it can be instructive to know what is going on in the minds of those who wish to produce a new future.

The future is unknown and cannot be predicted. The reason for this is not that witchcraft or a spell of some sort has been cast on our future in a way such as to disrupt its clear and causal course. What cannot be predicted, rather, is when and how and with which intentions those who wish to make their image of the future a reality will intervene. The sum of these rationally intended interventions results in the confused reality of the future. People have always wondered what kind of career is that: to be a prophet. Prophets were around at the start of our culture and people have always taken prophets to be those who speak about the future. It was the theologian Bernhard Duhm who first corrected this erroneous notion, by pointing out that prophets speak of the present. Or, in more modern terms, one might say that they analyze and investigate the status quo (how things are now) and ascertain how far it has moved away from the target state (how things should be).

In the early 1960s, we were faced ad nauseous with another kind of prophet, namely those who were into extrapolation. They were so-called scientists who believed the future consists in everything staying the same; yet what they meant by "staying the same" was that growth respectively contraction rates would stay the same. And this standstill state of growth or contraction would occur not on the same steady level but on exponential curves: growth grows and contraction contracts. Because I ate one apple today and eat two tomorrow, I will eat four apples the day after tomorrow, and several tons of them daily by the end of the month. Every slightly rising curve was extrapolated exponentially upwards, and every sinking curve downwards, and people actually believed this was the future. Who doesn't remember the experts' reports of that time? They said: because the number of bicycles has decreased by this or that amount between 1960 and 1962 there will be no bicycles left at all by 1975. Or: because the number of purchases made has increased by this or that amount between 1960 and 1962, the surface area of the entire city will no longer suffice, in 1980, to accommodate the sales area required for provision of the population.

It was overlooked at the time that this assertion—that growth and contraction rates would stay the same—rapidly spiraled ad absurdum. It led to the realm of absurdity, but by no means to that of ineffectiveness, not as long as someone believed in it. For this is the reason we are speaking now about what people have in mind, how things are planned, built, and decided upon. They not only believe there will be no bicycles left. They also get rid of the bicycle stands. They not only believe they will require this or that amount of sales area. They also build it. And their prophecies hence, at least in part, become self-fulfilling.

It was predicted there would be this or that many more cars in the future, and so cities were altered in a way such that now motorists alone can survive in them. There's a self-fulfilling prophecy for you. Or it was anticipated that the city center population would grow by this or that much, and the moves made to provide sufficient public transport for these future inhabitants actually drove out the present inhabitants. This is a self-destroying prophecy. It is this type of prophecy that we need to address, because those experts who influence our future have precisely this in mind. The experts' supposedly clever future forecasts are basically conservative. In fact, the experts are dazzled by the status quo. There's a federal railroad poster that tells us: "In cold and icy weather, the federal railroad [is] your second car." The federal railroad, a gigantic enterprise, isn't thinking about its own future performance. No, it falls instead for the experts' universal faith in the fact that the future belongs to motorists, that anyone who is anyone will have to own a car. In the eyes of the federal railroad's management, the federal railroad just about makes the grade of second car. The railroad's pricing policy follows the same logic: reduction in ticket prices for those traveling in groups of two or three. Yes, but why just for them? Because most cars are four-seaters and so one passenger rides for free, so to speak. And one has to keep pace with that. But to truly compete with motorized traffic one would have to reduce the price of all tickets for everyone: for this alone would persuade the, in general, sole occupant of the private car to take the train.

By the late 1960s, anyone who was keeping up with current discourse could see that the extrapolator era was over. The student protests, the most important intellectual movement of the postwar period, introduced some doubt as to the benefits of a naively technocratic view of the future. Since then the prophets have fallen into three distinct groups: the "incompletes," the "posties," and the "scenario set."

Whether things are still incomplete, whether some aspect of them still has to be finished, is a matter of definition. Yet the idea that whatever has been started must be finished tends to prompt strong agreement and is one of the most persuasive arguments of all in decision-making processes. If a freeway is to be built in a city yet the plans for it are fiercely opposed, it is generally claimed that the matter in hand is to complete the freeway network already under construction. Naturally, this section of freeway too will do nothing but increase the incidence of traffic and gridlocks, but the assertion that it is a matter of completing a whole network fosters the belief that seeing the project through to the end will solve the traffic problem. However, not only the freeway but also the entire modern era is regarded as an "unfinished project;" and, oh yes, of course, that is why it doesn't yet function properly. Then let's rush to get it finished!

The second prophets we meet are posties. They thrive on the interesting insight that everything is followed by something else. The posties are generally art historians and their mantra goes like this: after the Gothic comes the Renaissance, after the Renaissance the Baroque, after the Baroque Classicism, then Historicism, then Modernism and then, as we know, Postmodernism. There is one thing that the posties have noticed however: perhaps the same does not always stay the same. But they have overlooked a second point, namely that styles, epochs, cultures, or whatever else they use as caesura are terms that were coined only retrospectively in order to describe reality as found. Romanesque architects did not set out to build Romanesque structures, nor did they decide one day to abandon those and build Gothic ones instead. Rather, it was art historians of the nineteenth century who decided to classify certain features as Romanesque and certain later ones as Gothic. But as we do not know how our own products may be classified one fine day we are hardly in a position to predict from when exactly we should reckon with the next decisively different sort of product.

As one often enough makes a fool of oneself, particular by prophesying that things will change, there is a third species of prophet: the scenario set. The scenario set offers several potential futures and is therefore always right, at least in part. The odds that one of its proposed scenarios will come about more or less as predicted are fairly good; what is annoying is simply that the other scenarios, those that don't come about, are the ones one predicted oneself.

For this reason we now must consider the question we touched upon at the start of this paper, namely why it is so difficult to make a precise and correct prediction. — The answer lies in that which, for want of a less pathetic word, can be called historicity. I would like to define this thus: events, the eventually newly arising phenomena, do not have a causal effect on society but they are perceived by society nonetheless. In our minds they take the form of images accompanied by explanations proffered by society's opinion makers, and they lead us to take actions in ways that are not objectively and rationally focused on this or that event or phenomenon, but on the visual and mental processing of it. Take this banal example: the economic crisis of 1929/30 was perceived in Germany not as a crisis of capitalism but as a lack of agricultural land, as a nation lacking in space. Therefore, the solution people chose was not to take appropriate economic and social measures, but to wage war against nations who still had space at their disposal or allegedly needed less space.

And it is this, in my opinion, which gives rise to the specifically unpredictable nature of the future: the fact that the reactions of people, of society, are not reactions to facts but to the image they have in their minds of fact. Our actions are shaped by images, by notions that are indeed prompted by our perceptions yet the precise manifestation of which it is almost impossible to predict.

These images naturally vary from one person to the next. We cannot even fall back on classic sociology and say they differ according to social class. Nowadays the various images cut through the entire population and its groups. Events are interpreted not in line with a person's social class, or age group, or gender, but rather with the subcultural preconditions of their sense of belonging to a group. To track these down is perhaps a part of the task we are faced with. In any case we should not lose sight of the title of this paper, namely "... In Our Minds."

It is a matter therefore of this: Who produces the pictures, the images? Who is so potent as to be able to impose images on others? Where are the gurus to be found? Who is in a position to inscribe the present with names in a way such that it gives rise to specific behavior, behavior that shapes the future? Because such behavior and activities do indeed produce the future.

Some years have passed since we coined the catchphrase "Design is invisible." Our aim was to draw attention to the fact that "future" is a design, a set of drafted forms. That this design is invisible is something we added in order to highlight the fact, that design encompasses the design of organizations too. It is not the new design of the streetcar itself which helps us travel faster from *a* to *b* but the improved timetable. The most beautiful bus is no use to us if it runs only every half-hour instead of every five minutes. Design is always immediately bound up with invisible factors, and hence it is bound up likewise with problems of perception, with signs and interpretations. The way we interpret reality is invisible, and our interpretation is the precondition of how we make use of reality. Of course, this invisible dimension is always tied up with visible components. The bus is visible, the schedule is invisible, and the esteem or self-image that we allow ourselves or that we believe other people attribute to us whenever (or not) we use the bus is completely invisible. Design is insofar visible and invisible at one and the same time, and there was actually no need for a congress with the title "Design Is Visible" to be held in Stuttgart in 1986.

Take genetic engineering, for example: no one knows what new findings and technical advances in the field of gene transfer will bring, nor where they will lead. Nonetheless, everyone has his own image of the subject and forms his opinion accordingly. One man trusts in scientific progress and believes that this technology can help us eliminate nature's noxious aspects, the bacterial diseases of mankind, animals, and vegetation. The next man takes stock of his previous experience of the Challenger, Chernobyl, and Schweizerhalle disasters and regards genetic engineering as the latest criminal attack by unconscionable experts. The consequences, the acts this may prompt in society or in individual groups, and how other groups or science may respond, cannot be foreseen.

Dirt (1980)

Dirty and clean, as you can read in the work of Mary Douglas, are anthropologically determined values. We find cats cute, rats disgusting. Gypsies eat hedgehog meat while other ethnic groups shudder at the thought of roast rabbit. Would you enjoy the taste of roast fox, a favorite dish of alpine farmers? Why did people bury horsemeat for centuries then begin in the nineteenth century to process it in specially built slaughterhouses? What makes butterflies appetizing and flies repulsive? Opinions regarding spiders diverge, and an earwig too, depending on where one encounters it, may provoke outrage or indifference. During the First World War, the zoologist Auguste Forel tried to eat earthworms but ultimately failed to slip them down his throat.

And how do things stand with dirt per se? Drat! There's a grease spot on my tie and my shoes could urgently use some polish. And what about feces? In the case of cats, it is hardly worth a mention while dogs have free reign outdoors, and human beings nowhere. Italians are a dirty nation; our housekeeper is Italian. White linen needs to be laundered more frequently than colored does.

Dirt, which we believe we recognize precisely on account of the disgust it prompts, is evidently a relative and, moreover, contradictory matter. The social system, the upper classes, and majorities dictate standards as to what is dirty and what is clean. In consequence, the lower classes and minorities are dirty—or squeamish; for the standards set and the form discrimination takes may also be reversed. "We are not so squeamish," says the Count, and personally guts the rabbit that so disgusts the cook.

Dirt is not something we can dispose of completely, however. The endeavor to impose increasingly high mandatory standards of cleanliness is a brainchild of the detergents industry—and it is polluting our environment. The fact that standards of cleanliness are relative creates some leeway in the design process. We must each regain a clearer sense of cleanliness, one that will not lead us to socialize disgust at the expense of air and water.

People always cleaned, even long before they knew the reason why. Today, any child knows that dirt contains bacteria and can therefore cause sickness. Yet long before this discovery, certain aspects of the material world were treated as inferior, as dirt, in particular when they cropped up in places other than those reserved for them.

However, knowledge of bacteria turned the spotlight on the invisible dimension of dirt; dirt is visible only as the basis on which bacteria apparently become active. So, can we be sure there are no bacteria lurking on the freshly waxed and polished floors of hospital corridors? In any event, we continue to fight dirt only in its visible dimension.

"And so, was the water that drained away dirty?"—"Of course it was dirty, that day. But the worst of it is that the water was never completely clean." Just who is talking here? You guessed it. The water in question is that used to cool down a nuclear power plant, and what is called dirt here can be measured only with a Geiger counter. New dirt is clean dirt therefore; dirt that can pass through every kind of filter, and resist every attempt to clean it up; dirt, moreover, that is often actually a by-product of pollution control. "Once nuclear power generates sufficient electricity," we are told, "we will be able to afford to treat all our sewage, and our rivers will be clean again."

Standards exist also for invisible dirt, and somebody sets them: not the upper classes, in this case, but an anonymous band of officials, experts, professional associations, and lobby groups. Just what level of lead ions is permissible in the air, in vegetables, and in milk? How close to the highways may our cattle be put out to pasture?

What level of radiation can a person withstand? — Some authority or other always claims to have the right answer. And the manufacturers never wait to be told it twice over; they just hit whatever level of pollution is permitted. To produce less pollution than permissible would not make economic sense. Yet to produce more pollution than permissible is permissible too. It is written off as an incident, a malfunction. Accidents happen. Invisible dirt is somehow like social housing programs: the maximum is also the minimum, and the norms set ensure that better than the norm is never an option.

Let us return now to the issue of visible dirt, to waste and remainders. Do you recall sitting in the streetcar on the way to school, mulling over the previous evening's homework, that long equation you deduced had a remainder? And then a schoolmate boards the streetcar and you shout: "Hey, did you solve the equation? I had a remainder of seven." "Then you are wrong. I had no remainder." But how can we be so sure the outcome without a remainder is correct, and the outcome with a remainder wrong? Surely the opposite might be true. However, the equations in our math books in school were always doctored. For schools are supposed to impart a picture of a world in which everything works out precisely. Students are supposed to grow up to become something sensible, and to achieve a lot in their career: a career as a traffic engineer, for instance. A sensible road width is one that can be divided by the number of traffic lanes; any remainder, a half-lane, would not make sense. Admittedly, a half-lane would make cyclists' lives a lot easier. But cyclists are dirt, as far as traffic engineers are concerned: a remainder that somehow refuses to disappear.

Problems can be solved without a remainder in college too. A professor of architecture in Zurich sets an exercise: build a youth center on the city's Paradeplatz. The proposed plan could be realized on that vacant lot. In reality, however, an insurance company has already begun to build its headquarters on the same site; and besides, young people rarely hang out on Paradeplatz. Yet because the professor's assistants had carried out a preliminary study during summer vacation, everything looks just fine on paper.

So we actually never learn how to solve problems in a way that leaves a remainder, which is to say, we never learn how to deal with reality. And that is why the world is full of remainders, of odd ends of lots and the like. The road built to accommodate cars curves at a weird angle to pass between two right-angled cubic buildings. Fortunately for us, there are gardeners skilled in landscaping such trigonometric clothoids. Yet curiously, accidents continue to happen even on roads purpose-built for traffic; and because such roads are purpose-built correctly, at least one guilty party must exist for each accident. Accidents are put down to human error, which is the remainder in an utterly perfect system.

Even an individual project planned without a remainder will give rise to a remainder when realized alongside another, likewise perfectly planned project. To plan for reality therefore means to plan projects that cater to the existence of such remainders, and that anticipate human behavior. With a stroke of luck, this type of planning might then also reap the beauty once inherent to the older towns and villages in our traditional cultural landscape. Does this imply a return to a perfect world, you ask? On the contrary: it means we renounce the very idea of the possibility of an utterly perfect world.

The Night Is Man-made (1989)

Initially, it seems as clear as day that the night is not a man-made but a natural phenomenon: the sun goes down, dusk casts its spell for a while then, unless the moon musters a meager light to help us on our way, finally darkness falls. Many animals—owls, bats and moths—are experts at locating their food by night while man has driven others, such as foxes, deer, and rats, into the nocturnal realm. Man himself, who is doubtless a diurnal creature, has increasingly laid claim to the world in spatial terms as well as to the hours that are not rightly his: the nighttime hours. According to Murray Melbin,[1] to whom we shall return later, the night is "the last frontier," the last remaining area we have yet to colonize. When emigration is no longer an option, the fact that not all people are awake at the same time may still mitigate the rise in population density in urban areas.

Colonization of the night by the diurnal creature man has a technical dimension: lighting. Yet this interesting strand in the history of technology and design is not the issue here. Our concern rather, is to address that which I call "invisible design," namely those social and legal resolutions, decisions, decrees, ordinances, timetables, schedules, and tariffs that together determine the manner by which man colonizes the night. The term "invisible design" hence denotes those human accomplishments that do not shape actual materials

1 [Murray Melbin, "Night As Frontier" in: *American Sociological Review*, Vol. 43, Nr. 1, February 1978; id., "The Colonization of Time" in: Tommy Carlstein, Don Parkes, Nigel Thrift, (eds.): *Timing Space and Spacing Time*, Vol. 2, Edward Arnold, London 1978]

yet nonetheless have a decisive impact on our lives and our environment. When public transport operates at night, that changes our habits; and even someone who chooses not to leave the house after nightfall may still fall victim to nocturnal visitors. When the post office introduced a cheaper rate for telephone calls made after 10 p.m., lines tended for a time to be overly busy for an hour, then a cheerful chitchat set in and lasted until one in the morning; and even those who chose not to make a call were unable to evade it. The opening hours of stores, cinemas, and theaters, the extended opening hours of restaurants, pubs, and wine and cocktail bars, along with their voluntary or officially imposed closing times determine not only our personal habits but also urban life in general. Where can one go after an evening at the theater? When does the last streetcar leave? And what does a taxi cost after the streetcar has left, when the nighttime rate applies?

We echo Melbin in calling man's encroachment and impact on the night a form of colonization. No such thing was necessary in feudal society, for peasants were tired by nightfall and aristocrats had leisure enough for daytime amusements. The latter welcomed nightfall as an opportunity to pursue their pleasure by other, more flirtatious means. Apart from certain rituals of repentance demanded of monastic communities, worship too is largely a daytime activity. Our only record of the "agape" (love feast) passing for a Eucharist or Holy Communion dates from the Early Christian era in Rome, when religion was still a pleasure and a raison d'être. As a new doctrine free of class distinctions, Christianity had appealed to the working classes, who congregated when they had time, in the evening. To this day we tell the friends we invite home: Do not eat beforehand. This imperative evolved perversely as the dictate: whoever celebrates the Eucharist in the early morning must not break fast beforehand.

"Every day has its own vexations" while—so Goethe claims twice in his work—"Night is the better half of life."[2] Philine says so in Goethe's *Apprenticeship,* after her mother has already said "And the night its joys will bring" to her son Hermann, who wishes to marry Dorothea. The latter verse was omitted from several editions published in the late nineteenth century. Connoisseurs of Goethe at the time, including Friedrich Theodor Vischer, found the verse so indecent, they seriously suspected some malevolent typesetter had smuggled it into the text. Literary historians belonged namely to that species whose nights are spent with bloodshot eyes amid books and manuscripts. This too is a form of colonizing the night: in the daytime one plays the role of professor and privy councilor, and at night one must pay the price.

But let us return to colonization of the night in the industrial era. It was no accident that new discoveries in the field of lighting primarily affected the workplace. Cambacérès invented that for which Goethe had yearned, the candlewick that need not be snuffed out; yet he invented it initially, one must add, in the framework of optical research directed at stabilizing the light source.

Then followed those discoveries, however, which strengthened the light source: gaslight first of all, with which a factory was lit for the first time in 1803; later, Auer von Welsbach invented the gas mantle, which considerably improved the efficacy of the illuminating gas used in the workplace. Finally, Davy invented the arc lamp and, later, Edison the light bulb. Like Cambacérès's candlewick, the light bulb had a major impact on private households too.

2 [J.W. von Goethe, *Master Wilhelm's Apprenticeship,* Book V, Chapter X; as cited by Peter von Matt in: "Die Nacht, die Frauenzeit," *Frankfurter Allgemeine Zeitung, Bilder und Zeiten,* 1.04.1989.]

The means to light factories by night, combined with the high cost of fixed capital, which is to say, of the machines installed in factories for the purpose of gainful exploitation, paved the way for nighttime work.

The latter is determined by tariffs, wage levels, the cost of transport, and legislation; and by the absence of legislation too, of course. In 1803, when the powers that be first allowed factories to be artificially lit, this novel phenomenon had not yet been regulated and consequently the night was open to exploitation. Some time passed before protective legislation came into force, to the benefit of children initially, then of all workers. But shiftwork has never been abolished. It has become less widespread yet even today it is not restricted to vital nighttime provision, such as public transport, health care, and emergency services, but still facilitates full capacity exploitation of the means of production; of chemical plants, for example, which would have to be a great deal bigger than they are now, if they were permitted to operate only eight hours a day and had to shut down for sixteen.

Shiftwork and nighttime work is the fate of a large section of the working population, and nighttime work has never become truly equal to daytime work. There has been remarkably little research done on shiftwork. Several empirical studies do exist, but none of the major critiques of industrial labor makes much of the fact that two-thirds of such work is done at a time of night when the bourgeois class is at leisure. Marx had identified shiftwork, a relatively new phenomenon in his day, as a novel form of exploitation yet it appears to have interested his successors only with regard to tariff policy or medical issues. However, the cultural and social repercussions of shiftwork are considerable. Can a life in which one's waking hours never or only rarely coincide with those of the majority population even be called a social life? Most shiftwork schedules experiment with a week-by-week reversal of the circadian rhythm.

One can accustom oneself to anything—yet none of these forms is pleasant.

Besides industrial shiftwork there exists a whole range of other types of "smaller" shifts, in relation to which the word "shift"[3] takes on a truly sociological ring: generally the working classes—who have no choice but to "shift themselves"[4]—do so on behalf of classes with which they rarely come into contact. One need only think of trash collectors, for example, who thunder through our city streets by night; or of the second wave of office workers who set to work after the first has gone home—or before it arrives. My desk and office carpet also are the realm of a working female trio—a Turkish woman and her daughter, and a German—whom I usually see rushing off whenever I turn up especially early to deal with a heavy workload. What do they think of me? What on earth do they think about in general? Nobody asks them.

Day and night appears to be a hierarchical arrangement. It is therefore interesting to note that hierarchies are flattened at night. Those with real authority go home. In general, those who work at night belong to the lower ranks. Consequently, a shift in responsibilities takes place at night too. By day, the doctor tells the nurse: "Monitor the patient's pulse, and call me if it becomes erratic." In the evening, before he leaves, the same doctor says: "If his pulse becomes erratic, deal with it. Here is the key to the medicine cabinet." Things that demand expertise by day are entrusted at night to any old girl Friday. Murray Melbin studied such shifts in interpersonal behavior, and identified similar cases in public life, on the street, in

3 [The author plays here on two meanings of the German word "Schicht," namely "shift" and "social class."]

4 [A British term meaning both "to change position, direction, place, or form" and "to provide for oneself, get along."]

restaurants, and the private stairwell. Solitary night owls should distrust one another, it is commonly assumed. Yet Melbin can prove they tend to trust one another a great deal in fact. People help each other more readily at night than by day.

We also colonize the night increasingly in our pursuit of life's pleasures. Pleasure is virtually synonymous with evening entertainment. Daytime is postponed, for whoever lives it up at night spends all morning in bed. In colonizing the night we renounce the daylight hours. Our endeavors to put a brake on this process are remarkably paradoxical: we switch annually to daylight saving time for example, then scrap it in winter in order that its effect can be felt the following summer. Instinctively, we experience summertime as an artifice, as an imposition on our lives: Italians call it "il tempo legale" (legal time), and Italian newspapers announce in autumn "la fine dei tempo legale" (the end of legal time), hence the return to natural time!

Work and play together dictate that services in the city continue to operate at night, or ought to: the goal is a city open 24/7, a city where anything and everything is possible, anytime. No metropolis, however large, has ever attained this goal. Closing down the Paris subway between 3 a.m. and 5 a.m. is a much-debated topic; some see it as a technical necessity, others merely as old hat. The lower the density of public transport, the greater the importance of the private car. A seriously detrimental side effect is the growing number of accidents caused by drunk driving.

How far should nighttime services go? Transportation, polyclinics, emergency rooms, and firehouses—all these seem indispensable yet of course they are not universally available, only in the cities. In the countryside we must first wake up the doctor, or ferret out volunteer firefighters from their beds or the bar; and after-work public transport does not even exist. My students can only work at night, at least they claim that is the case; yet their library is closed at night.

The library at Harvard is open around the clock—so no one there can claim a good idea came to naught for lack of ideal working conditions. And, on that point, here is a telling detail: a white man sits at the circulation desk by day, and a black man by night. Subtle hierarchies exist, even in the realm of knowledge.

But, with the exception of Harvard's library, the modern city is still a long way from 24/7 operations. In city districts, an unofficial timetable regulates the closing hours of places of entertainment. The lights burn brightest in the inner city, although business is restricted to limited areas there too, and by the early hours of the morning, only a few dedicated streets can offer an open bar or two. Anne Cauquelin[5] studied this nocturnal time-space pattern in Paris, and identified distinct changes in the cityscape: certain streets acquire and then lose a specific meaning at different times of day and night. Night-owls of a particular kind, people addicted to particular drugs, or members of singular circles, transvestites, for example, meet at certain hours of the night in certain streets that, one hour earlier or later, seem nothing special to the innocent passer-by.

And how do things stand with the night of thieves, crime, disputes, and lawlessness? This is a question one is unlikely ever to fathom entirely. By night, the police and criminals do battle; they chase through the streets, tires screeching. Who started this? Who first came up with the idea of staging this war at night? Presumably the custom dates from times when the eye of the law closed at night. But nowadays, the eye of the law sees all, especially at night, or so it seems. Or is Melbin's observation correct, that policemen normally sleep in their patrol cars? Nighttime police patrols have only a minimal success rate. Motorized police very rarely catch a criminal red-handed, and the police on foot almost never. The police force knows

5 [Anne Cauquelin, *La ville la nuit*, Presses Universitaires de France, Paris 1977]

this: it actually deploys police officers merely to increase nocturnal pedestrians' sense of safety. The motorized patrols do not exactly heighten this sense of safety. Aid for a pedestrian can come only from a pedestrian; and his forlornness amid the nighttime stream of traffic is precisely what heightens his personal sense of fear while, at the collective level, it drives slum deterioration. Any friendly advice, that he should use a car himself, or at least order a cab, accelerates the inexorable advance of the nighttime criminal city.

But streetlights now, they assure us safety! This is an old question: Whom do public streetlights really benefit—the criminal, or the person seeking safety? In former times people locked their house and yard at night. They ventured onto the open road only in exceptional cases, armed at best, and accompanied by torchbearers. To whom did public space belong at night, back then? Some researchers, Gleichmann[6] and Schivelbusch[7] for example, maintain that street lighting was the authorities' hobbyhorse, and disadvantageous to all common folk. But what constitutes "the common folk?" Did not large sections of the population also benefit from the fact that even men and women who could not afford an armed escort were henceforth able to walk the streets alone? While Schivelbusch claims that the cry "à la lanterne" meant a ruler was to be hanged from the very symbol of public order he personally had instigated, other sources dispute this. Aristocrats and the clergy are portrayed in cartoons of the day as being intent on extinguishing street lamps,

6 [Peter Reinhart Gleichmann, "Nacht und Zivilisation," in: Martin Baethge, Wolfgang Essbach (eds.), *Soziologie – Entdeckung des Alltäglichen, Festschrift für Hans Paul Bahrdt*, Campus Verlag, Frankfurt Main and New York 1984]

7 [Wolfgang Schivelbusch, *Die Entzauberung des Feuerscheins. Zur Entwicklungsgeschichte der künstlichen Beleuchtung*, Hanser, Munich 1983. A second, paperback edition was published under the title *Lichtblicke,* Ullstein, Frankfurt Main and Berlin 1986.]

and thus on refuting the Enlightenment. The question as to who actually benefits from nocturnal lighting evidently requires further study.

The question as to what we illuminate and why appears also to have been neglected. Increasingly, it seems that those responsible for lighting have no other goal than to make everything as bright as possible. Our street lamps illuminate not only streets but also house façades, which are ugly enough by day as it is. Moreover, such brightly lit façades do nothing to improve visibility for road users. Many cities now illuminate all or some of their historic buildings. This can look lovely on condition that the building is lit also from within. Without interior lighting, the façade looks like a ruin. All this lighting would be far more striking if other nearby buildings were left in the dark. Street lamps ought therefore illuminate only the traffic zone. All vehicles are equipped with their own lights; therefore, there is no need for streetlights on highways. Nevertheless Belgium, for example, lights its entire cross-country highway network, and thereby demonstrates that lighting today goes far beyond that which is technically necessary, and penetrates metaphysical or possibly, even theological space: man is endeavoring to turn night into day. This whole lighting caboodle does not, let me repeat, assure us safety: neither actual safety from traffic accidents, nor a sense of security. It is similar to a long-forgotten comedy from the 1930s, in which a married couple arriving home late at night observes, "It is so disagreeably bright up front, and so disagreeably dark to the rear."

To light the streets of Paris at night—and in a very odd way, moreover, namely by placing a streetlight at the beginning, the middle, and the end of a road, regardless of its length—was undoubtedly a design decision taken by the king. The change, whether welcomed with joy or rejected with suspicion, was in any case evident to all, and nocturnal behavior was adjusted accordingly. Equally effective are those resolutions and decisions we named earlier, which initially appear to have no visible impact: schedules, opening times, closing times, tariffs, regulations, laws, as well as—the absence and abrogation of laws. These constitute the framework that shapes our living conditions at least as radically as any visible and tangible elements such as walls and gates do. To illustrate that such resolutions are akin to designs, inasmuch as they put their stamp on our lives, we call this phenomenon "invisible design." One product of this invisible design is the night, man-made night: a temporal environment that is opened and closed in accordance with man-made rules. The theater closes at 11 p.m., the last streetcar leaves at midnight, and so we still have time for a beer. One instance determined the streetcar schedule, another the theater program, and a third the restaurants' closing hours. The overall result is the form our night takes. The end of the night is fixed also, and strangely staggered. The subway begins to run at 5 a.m., the streetcars at 6, and the workers at 7; bureaucrats begin work at 7.30, but open to the public only at 9. To call someone before 9 a.m. is considered rude, because everyone assumes everyone else belongs to the elite and thus can sleep late, be late for work, and lead a great nightlife.

Fake: The Real Thing (1987)

Real jewelry is not the issue here; it does not interest us at all. It is ephemeral, trivial, and fake—yes, fake; but first things first. Its high value, whatever that may be, makes real jewelry extremely short-lived. Only a few choice gems ever survive a generation. The Knights of the Holy Spirit presented Louis XV with a golden cross, studded with diamonds. Diamonds were just what the king was after. He had them removed from the cross and set into the hilt of his sword. When Napoleon came to power, he found this sword among the crown jewels. He liked the diamonds but not the style of the sword. A goldsmith worked a new sword, and set the old diamonds into its hilt. After the Battle of Trafalgar, this sword was given to the Duke of Wellington. To the delight of his wife, Wellington also had the diamonds reworked, this time as a necklace. Maurice Rheims, who recounts this tale, notes that the necklace is unlikely ever to be found. Presumably, Wellington's daughters and granddaughters are wearing the diamonds in their rings, earrings, brooches, and clips.

"But that is surely an exception!" cry those whose eyes pop out on stalks when ogling the Queen of England's crown jewels in the Tower of London. Let us assume, firstly, that everything on display there is genuine. The stones are not very old. Most of them date from the nineteenth century and have changed hands often. Crowns seem at any event more durable than merely ornamental pieces of jewelry, and for an obvious reason: crowns stand for something, namely for Empire, whereas merely ornamental pieces have no meaning beyond themselves. They are tautological. We have stated enough of a case now to be able to say something about fake jewelry. Fake jewelry—the glittering rhinestones made of paste and named for the *cailloux du Rhin* manufactured in Strasbourg—is of interest precisely because it stands for something, because it means something, because it stands for "the real thing." The real thing exists in its own right and has no further meaning. That is why fake jewelry is the real thing, whereas the real thing...

But that is impossible, a senseless, vicious circle. If fake jewelry imitates the real thing, but the real thing has no real meaning, then the fake stuff too will become boring in time. And that is why we must come to the very point that prompted our interest in fake jewelry in the first place: fake jewelry is genuine when it does not strive at all to be the real thing but simply transcends it. Real fake jewelry does not imitate real, actually existent jewelry but rather, real jewelry that does not exist—and could not exist, in fact, because no such precious gems exist, at least not unless they are fake. So, if the genuine jewelry represented by fakes does not exist then the fake stuff really is the real thing. Fake jewelry is a utopia. It considers what the jewelry really worth copying might be like, if ever it were to come into existence. This utopia has a banal name: glamor. Glamor is basically wishful thinking about how things could and should be. The history of teen fashion, as it is called, is closely interwoven with this preoccupation with role models and ideals, and likewise with the deconstruction of traditional meanings: hence the importance of glamor. Young Londoners who raided their grandfathers' wardrobes in the 1950s, donned stockbrokers' suits, and took to the streets, did not want to resurrect nineteenth-century capitalism. They were not interested in counterfeit as such but in investing the look with new symbolism. In the same way, squatters in the Westend district of Frankfurt Main were interested, not in living in bankers' villas as bankers do, but in appropriating the pillars, cherubs, and atlantes on the villas' façades for their own idea of utopia; for to debunk Establishment splendor as glamor gives rise to a new freedom, to the phony fake, and to the real thing.

And now we have used the word "real" again, which we were actually trying to avoid. The last century wore itself out on the problem of authenticity with its senseless paradoxes. In all walks of life, the spirit of bourgeois manufacturers united in praise of the real thing—which was perhaps, a just punishment for a class that made its living from the production of fake goods or *ersatz*.

For what characterizes the middle class as of 1848 is the fact that it no longer lives amid things it produces. It produces cotton but wears silk, manufactures rubber but wears leather. Nationalism in particular was attached to the notion of the real thing: monuments of stone, granite, sandstone, and marble trace the path of the Second Empire, and even in the Third Reich, eagles and swastikas had to be carved in real stone. Finally, plaster and paint was chipped off house façades in the name of heritage preservation, and the real thing was discovered beneath them: real stones, real buildings. Then paint was stripped from real timber doors too. — What else did we expect to find beneath it? This cult of the real thing was countered solely by its denunciator, the cult of glamor; and the claim that appearances are deceptive was countered by this discovery: appearance is the only thing that is not deceptive.

Papa Goethe thought all these thoughts long ago, with a mischievous smile on his face. Not that he was on the side of teen fashion, for he sided rather with the Establishment, with the nobility that still wore its jewelry with grace, and bore the real thing with humor, and dignity with charm. In Goethe's cryptic revolutionary drama *The Natural Daughter*, the duke plans to give his illegitimate daughter a jewelry case on the day he adopts her. The princess's joy is dampened when his housekeeper sourly demurs:

> "Yet not the appearance but the genuine worth
> Can satisfy the cravings of thy heart!"[1]

1 ["The Natural Daughter," Act II, Scene V in: *Goethe's Works,* Vol. 2, Philadelphia, G. Barrie 1885.]

In its ascetic pedantry, the emerging middle class distinguishes between the "appearance" even of the genuine article, and "true substance." Yet the fledgling princess has a ready quip, a truly charming Goethean couplet:

> "What is appearance having naught of substance?
> And what would substance be without appearance?"[2]

For the nineteenth century it was then clear: appearance lacking in substance is fake, fake material or fake jewelry. But what then is the substance that does appear? To demand such substance of real material would amount indeed to barbaric materialism. That is why we put our trust in the youngest generation's answer: the substance that appears is glamor.

While real jewelry was a sign of waste for the nobility, it was a sign of asceticism for the commoner. The nobility bought and made gifts of jewelry without a moment's hesitation whereas the commoner made investments. When he withdrew surplus value from the market and invested it at no interest, he did so for the sake of caution: by renouncing the interest, today's profit, he assured the stability of his assets. The middle-class daughters' jewelry case was the family piggy bank, quasi. Was such investment profitable? Moderately. Jewelry is valuable at times when everyone has money; when everyone is in need, no one gets rid of his jewelry. Thus in 1946, gold chains and diamond rings turned into nothing more than a few sacks of rapidly wolfed down potatoes. And long-term value is in any case nothing to write home about. The advertising campaign the diamond syndicate launched two years ago was symptomatic of the fact that there are too many diamonds, and too few

2 [Ibid.]

people to wear them. The price of these gems has fallen therefore, just like the gold price.

This brings us back to the question of value. Nothing illustrates commodity fetishism (to use Marx's term) so well as industry's search for diamonds and gold, nature's providential products. Something that should be discovered serendipitously, with a stroke of luck—the gold nugget, the rough diamond—is organized and rationalized here, and mined in huge concentration camps; an industry just like any other, although more macabre. The value of the product mirrors social relations, however. And nowadays more than ever, a fall in prices perhaps somehow reflects the fact that such methods of exploitation no longer rank among the finest, even in the exploiters' own books. The end of white South Africa is a part of the end of the era of good taste.

But let us return to that of interest to us: false jewelry and glamor. Appearances alone are not deceptive, we said, and this idea must be considered more closely. Appearances are not deceptive—and how could they be, given that they serve the very matter of discernment? Anatomists tell us it is difficult to distinguish a lion's skeleton from that of a tiger. Yet any child can tell the difference between a lion and a tiger. Obviously, the difference lies in their appearance or, to be more precise, it is their appearance that makes the difference. Two species of duck are closely related yet differ greatly from one another in appearance, more markedly so in the case of males in the mating season. This distinctive plumage occurs however, only in those regions inhabited by both species of duck. On remote islands where only one of the two species is found, the drakes look quite unimpressive, also in the mating season.

The emergence of—fake?—jewelry in teen fashion in recent decades seems significant to me. Broadly speaking, this trend developed thus: in 1968 the new era of modesty began, one symbolized by the hippie who did his best to resemble a poor Indian struggling to find enough to eat and to provide for his family. Clothing, hairstyle, and jewelry expressed the following position: a poor, but also unassuming, self-sufficient, and therefore happy people has values other than material gain and career advancement. This position implied the use of worthless materials to create modest but aesthetically pleasing jewelry. Sunflower seeds and similar worthless elements, it was discovered, can be strung together to make decorative necklaces.

The divergence of various tribes in the realm of teen fashion revealed a need for more nuanced differentiation. Even those who had remained loyal to the Indian gusto no longer portrayed "real" starving Indians, but Indians of the silver screen, Indians with glamor. Sunflower seeds disappeared in favor of gigantic jewels supposedly reminiscent of the treasures of the Indian rajahs. Roadside stores and stalls sprang up, where one could buy colorful glass beads and threads, the building blocks of this gem agenda. Naturally, such building blocks could be used to make more than only "Indian" things. The same kind of glamor might refer to European and American fin de siècle bohemians, to movie stars of the 1930s, or to social classes transformed by glamor. If one considers overall trends in the youth culture of that period, it becomes evident that the conspicuous display of personal symbols and signs turned into a style war: the mutual seizure, appropriation and reinterpretation of signs, pieces of jewelry, medals, uniforms, and hairstyles.

Phase three: the style war is over now; the "tribes" co-exist and no longer step on each other's toes. The signs people use are no longer intended for their opponents but for their friends, for only those in the know are able to read the deeper meaning of a stylistic gesture. That is why current fashion remains difficult for outsiders to understand. Seemingly contradictory features are combined for no apparent reason: a sailor's cap and a blond perm, an old-fashioned Teddy Boy look and a well-waxed rocker's quiff, or Punk and Indian emblems. The message is intended only for close friends. To see an outsider shake his head in wonder is considered a successful coup: "Hooray, I've got him stumped." Yet contradictions are very rich in meaning, and the more incomprehensible they are to outsiders, the more insiders find them highly informative: fur on silk, long hair combined with a mustache, jewels on a sweater—for initiates, these signs are like a horoscope of the person in question: "Although you are generally thrifty to the point of avarice, you can be generous when it really matters."—Well, what is he now, stingy or generous? Outsiders find this contradictory, but the person in question finds himself aptly described: It's true, I am sometimes petty; but money doesn't mean a thing to me when it comes to the crunch! The lace collar peeks out from beneath the Norwegian sweater and there is a flash of Rivière beneath the anorak. I am that kind of guy.

Real jewelry has nothing at all to do with any of this. Its message is linear and tautological: one piece of jewelry differs from another in one respect only, which is measured in carats. The intangible and seemingly supernatural dimension of jewelry, which has so fascinated mankind for centuries, is now banal. While, historically, gold and precious stones stood for a supernatural material—for that perhaps, of which Paradise is built, for platonic, immaterial solids, so to speak, to which were attributed an ideal value derived from celestial spheres—such real jewelry has long since been outshone by fakes. And this is the case because it is possible today, not merely to produce fake jewelry that is both indistinguishable from, and of equal value to real jewelry but also, above and beyond that, to produce "fake" jewelry that has no genuine counterpart, and therefore symbolizes much more than real jewelry ever can. Such fake jewelry does not stand for a Platonic world of ideas but for an imaginary world—yet one that, were it to exist, would belong to our worldly realm of the here and now.

Recycled Regionalism (1984)

The full title of the topic that has been assigned to me is "The New Heimat Style or an Architectonic Response to 'Hi-Tech Modernity' and the 'Global Village?'" This is a very complicated, complex issue and in order to make it workable and easier to handle, also for my own *gyri cerebri*, I have taken the liberty of breaking it down into five subsections through which this topic runs namely as the common thread.

The title speaks of an architectonic response and this prompts my first question. Who was asking? If someone gives a response then someone must have asked a question. My second question would be about the bit in inverted commas, "hi-tech modernity," which is evidently in the past. And my next question here is: Who killed it? If it stands here as a past monument then there springs to mind the catchphrase Habermas coined and which has since never ceased to haunt us: "Modernity, the unfinished project." Is that something we can get our heads around?

The third concerns the other bit in inverted commas, the "global village." This, I believe, is an invention of Marshall McLuhan's. I don't wish to ask a question in this case, but only to say that it is no longer topical. I'll return to it later, namely owing to an invention of my own, the law of the Tower of Babel. That leaves the question of the new Heimat style and I have fashioned it as follows: Is postmodernism the new Heimat style or not? This will be a hard nut to crack. And there is still the fifth theme belonging to our task. It is a verification not a question, namely: Papa's federalism is dead, and: there is the new regionalism.

The first question I asked unfortunately cannot be answered. If we say there is an architectonic response then there was evidently a question there, or a need: Please provide us with something new. My question here would be: Which came first, the shift in the cognitive requirement, the shift in style, or the shift in fashion? Have the architects brought a new message and is there a slowly growing understanding of that message, or did a new receptivity take shape, and the fresh architecture only then emerge in response? Where do styles or fashions actually begin? In the perceptive capacities of those they are aimed at, or in the productions of those who formulate messages of an artistic nature? That's a question that cannot be answered. If one needs to be the Dear Lord Himself in order to answer questions then one should stop asking them. If we could answer this question then we could create styles and say: next year this will be in fashion and then out of fashion; and this will follow; and we would know whether or not we'll be wearing ties again in ten years' time.

The second point concerns hi-tech modernity and its allegedly premature demise, or the question: Is it correct to speak of modernity as an unfinished project, and what would its completion mean? One could then ask a taunting question: Is modernity complete once our apartments have become as expensive as a hospital room is today? Is that the path of classic modernity? Or might modernity be perpetuated as the very opposite of its most recent trends, as "functionalism by other means," as a German architect recently put it. We all know that modernity morphed into academicism in the 1960s. I don't mean that negatively. An academicism is a style that follows rules. The rules of the modernist style are known to all, and to speculators in particular. I say so with the utmost respect for the actual achievements of the 1920s and 1960s. But it is evident, too, that every academicism—which is to say, every style that becomes a rule—brings forth counterreactions, just as Palladianism brought forth the picturesque, just as the French garden brought forth the English one, just as nineteenth-century Classicism engendered Historicism, just as the academic art of gardening calls forth the natural garden, modernism too, inasmuch as it is an academic concern and its aspiration to perfection can no longer be fulfilled, cedes to other movements—in the sense of a technocratic, total world order that alone the good dictator whom Le Corbusier secretly yearned for would ever be able to realize.

Now comes the question concerning the global village, and for this I have my new law, which is actually an ancient one, the law of the Tower of Babel. Sophisticated hegemonic structures tend towards abstract forms of expression. They think in terms of abstract models and they give expression to this in abstract styles. Modernism is one such abstract style. It is stripped of sensory imagery and depicts model thoughts. This is a process we can observe also in ancient history. Priestly cults, which are the equivalent of our technocratic systems of rule, were iconoclasts: declared enemies of the image. The Pharisees were iconoclastic because they thought in more abstract terms than the Sadducees, an old-fashioned aristocracy that counted Philistines among its kin and still kept the Golden Calves to which the ban on images directly applied. Or the iconoclastic movement in Byzantium when the Orthodox Catholicism of Byzantium attained a degree of abstraction such that it had to be enforced from above: it is at this moment, logically enough, that images are banned. Common folk think in images, however. They think in models, think with their senses. And this is namely the law of the Tower of Babel. Whenever the priestly caste enforces its iconoclasm, the cultural pyramid falls apart into its local and class-determined dialects. When Babel reached the point where its overall cultural discourse was focused on the tower, it collapsed into subcultures. And the iconoclasm of international modernism likewise came to an end; and we must take a closer look at that end.

Now comes the difficult question: Is the Heimat style a postmodernism, is postmodernism a Heimat style, and are the two in any way connected? I use postmodernism here as a neutral term.

It is used critically today, which means that all postmodernists say that they personally are not postmodernists whereas all the others are. Well, I am not using it in the negative sense. After all, we need a term for the changes now taking place in architecture. I mean one of the principles of postmodernism is that it regards each and every case as something special. That is the exact opposite of modernism, which treats the most diverse cases as if they were the same. Now we have the countermovement that says: every case is special—and this leads potentially to regionalism. We will see whether it really does. This rediscovery of regionalism in modernism is not altogether new. There is a significant movement in America—"Leave Chicago and discover the south-west: California"—and in Swiss architecture—"Forget Zurich and Basel. We love Ticino." So actually the movement has been around for a while. It is imperative to not mistake this revival for the Heimat style, because Heimat style is everything but the special case, and in fact is spreading sameness all over the Alps, setting up log chalets in regions where people build with stone, and Graubunden-style houses in regions where people build with wood. The Heimat style makes things uniform, in its German edition particularly thanks to the [since 1961 annual] competition "Our Village: Growing Lovelier By the Day." From Flensburg to Lörrach, all the villages that fall for this trend end up looking alike, since there are rules governing what makes a village more beautiful. There is a checklist: plant begonias around the fountain, etc. All the villages that take part become identical, regardless of whether they were once a place where agricultural labor took place in front of a house with a garden to its rear or one where work was done in the yard behind the house with a garden out front. Everything is measured by the same yardstick, and the same geraniums, begonias, and dwarf shrubs from the garden nursery make their appearance on what used to be working farms.

This Heimat style is certainly not what is meant—it is the very opposite of the special case. I posit that, inasmuch as modernism morphs into academicism, postmodernism breaks the rules of modernism by pursuing a new anti-academicism. Now, many will protest and say that is not the case at all; on the contrary, a new academicism is underway, for postmodernism recycles the academic architectural formulas over which modernist architecture only recently prevailed. On the one hand I had posited the rule: Every solution is a new one; postmodernism is anti-academicism. But now we must look at a second rule: These new solutions from the so-called postmodernist architects use comprehensible architectural formulas and anything comprehensible is old hat. In order to make oneself understood, or even to be able to convey anti-academicism, one must dip into the repertoire of existing forms. And that is the paradox of these new architectural styles, and this paradox is the mark of quality of good postmodernist architecture as opposed to mere epigonism. This is the crux of the matter: that the statements, which is to say the things borrowed from the existing stock of architectural formulas, are not bogus in the sense of deceptions but, rather, inasmuch as they express a dual message—I am like this; and like that—are patent fakes. And this is why they will never reference the old Heimat as it once was, will never build at this place or that as people built two hundred years ago—for to do so would be Heimat style pure or complementary heritage preservation. Instead, they build in a way such that fakes are so patently fakes that the issue of historical architectural forms must now be discussed in construction itself. The new regionalism evinces innovativeness by showing the old style in such a way that something authentic and new emerges from the dual negation, from the bogus counterfeit.

Now my last observation, the relationship of federalism to regionalism or, to use my catchphrase: Papa's federalism is dead. Who killed it? I must say a word or two here about how we Swiss and the German Federal Republic compare with other countries, with

France and Italy, for example. Federalism in our case is something traditional and conservative. In Germany too, there are people who say Baden-Wuerttemberg is a mistake, and an independent Baden, an independent Wuerttemberg must be reinstated. Those are conservative, traditionally minded people. In the new national states, France and Italy—France emerged from the French Revolution, Italy from the Risorgimento of 1871—traditional federalism is so dead that the new regionalism really is new—and also promoted on the whole by the left wing. Initiatives for regional autonomy in Italy or France come from the left wing while our homegrown federalism comes from totally traditionally minded circles in the depths of Glarus. We must be aware of this distinction. Regionalism in France or Italy is not bound up with dead and buried issues such as the reinstatement of the Kingdom of Angouleme or the Duchy of Parma and Piacenza. All of that is so dead and buried that regionalism is those countries is something progressive whereas in our case it's still looking very conservative.

Who is killing our old federalism? I would like to name its nemesis: Kaiseraugst.[1] Here, conservative technocrats are riding rough shod over an entire region. These men in the Council of States, these old federalists, are now riding rough shod over a region in the name of Swiss progress. And, for sure, this spells the death of their federalism. And what it means for us is that everything regarding federalism in the future will be new and of left-wing persuasion.

We are in the post-Babylonian condition. The great technocratic utopia, in its endeavor to create an abstract, national "language," has

1 [This town in eastern Switzerland gained notoriety as the proposed site of a nuclear power station. Thanks to concerted, long-term opposition, most spectacularly an eleven-week occupation of the site in 1975, the project was finally abandoned in 1988.]

destroyed regionalism along with everything else sensorily perceptible. That landed us in a situation of Babylonian collapse, of Babylonian (linguistic) confusion; and it is giving rise inter alia to the new regionalism, which is much more complex than the old one. For a complication now comes into play, one that I sum up with the words: "We are no longer one big family." Culture can no longer be arranged pyramid-like, as a family is, as in: Papa knows what is right and, although the children are still getting up to nonsense now, one day they will think just like him. Instead, culture has collapsed—and one cannot even say it has collapsed along class lines or along generational lines, for the daughter is perhaps still playing an old, quill-powered spinet while Papa collects jazz records. So: the fronts cannot be sociologically defined at a first glance. Rather, culture has collapsed into subcultures and the subcultures have become cultures.

What does that tell us now about the new architecture? It tells us that the new regionalism is not the same as the old regional styles. There was Baroque, which came from Rome, and then there were such delights as Mexican Baroque, which is a provincial style of architecture; for missionaries had brought along engravings from Rome and worked with local artisans and so something emerged that, while not as accomplished as the Roman Baroque, was oriented to it nonetheless, was a provincial variation on it, with folkloric touches. But precisely this regionalism is the one we will find no more. For certain it is dead, for the information is there: every architect now has the complete information. And provided he is at this global level he uses regional elements for works that are not provincial but that have a global level and are oriented to the global language of architecture. It is quite complex, but I have striven here to make the connection clear. Now once again I cite that very long title: "Regionalismus—The New Heimat Style or an Architectonic Response to 'Hi-Tech Modernity' and the 'Global Village?'" I believe that with our five questions we were able to answer that.

How Does Trash End Up In Museums? (1989)

In his book on urban culture Lewis Mumford explains the origin of the museum: "Through the material fact of preservation, time challenges time, time clashes with time: habits and values carry over beyond the living group, streaking with different strata of time the character of any single generation. Layer upon layer, past times preserve themselves in the city until life itself is finally threatened with suffocation: then, in sheer defense, modern man invents the museum."[1]—Thus, contrary to all our expectations, the purpose of the institution museum is actually to save room. To preserve exemplary artifacts relieves us of the task of preserving all the artifacts in existence. But which are the exemplary artifacts that we should preserve?

The city has yet another preservation problem, one from which we can learn perhaps: the problem of the dead. For public administrations, the dead are a huge calamity, since ever more land in towns and villages must be set aside for cemeteries. Here too, in sheer defense, man has found a solution albeit an absurd one: the dead are allowed to rest in peace for twenty-five years.

Nonetheless, there are still such phenomena as the Camposanto in Pisa. In this beautiful square there are graves from medieval times still, and while we are endeavoring to make out the inscriptions on them we notice a woman beside us, laying down flowers—evidently for a relative who was buried here some years ago. The Camposanto in Pisa gives the city the sense of: Here we all lie. Since the year 1100,

1 [Lewis Mumford, *The Culture of Cities*, Harcourt Brace Jovanovich Inc., New York/London 1938, p. 4]

"all" Pisans are buried thus on a square that is far smaller than the cemeteries in those cities of ours which dig up graves after twenty-five years.

And then there is the phenomenon of the Jewish cemetery: the Jewish grave lasts forever. If one extrapolates this fact one cannot but conclude that the earth will one day be a Jewish cemetery. And yet that is not the case at all: carefully laid out in their squares, Jewish cemeteries remain the same size for decades, for centuries. They too convey the sense of: Here we all lie—and their management of oblivion is insofar astute, in any case more astute than our twenty-five-year restriction.

Michael Thompson discovered this oblivion management quasi as a by-product of his trash theory.[2] "What was your grandfather called?" It's not difficult for me to answer that. "What was your great-grandfather called?" After a moment's reflection I come up with his name too. But when it comes to my great-great-grandfather I hesitate and then remain stumped. "And where does your family come from?" — Once again I can name an ancestor: a "first one," who doubtless had a father and a grandfather of his own yet whom one can no longer name. However, we name our common ancestors with no hesitation: Adam and Eve. Naming their children costs more effort while their grandchildren are known but—in our case—forgotten. "We all" is therefore an ingenious product of preservation and oblivion: society. Just as the rabbi in his cemetery square allows the graves of those with no more living descendants to sink into the earth yet wisely leaves standing the headstone of old Schmuel from 1550—"from whom we are all descended"—along with a string of headstones of deceased Schmuels and Meyrs from the seventeenth

2 [Michael Thompson: *Rubbish Theory. The Creation and Destruction of Value*, Oxford University Press, Oxford 1979]

and eighteenth centuries, so too in our memory (or our oblivion) an image of our origins, our family, our society takes shape. And the museum, if it is to save room, ought likewise to be structured according to this principle of forgetting and remembering.

Meaning

The museum draws on artifacts to tell the history of a society. Artifacts that are no longer (allowed to be) used convey to us information about their "meaning." For instance, there is the sleeve of a cloak that once belonged to Friedrich Barbarossa. And the glass from which Lenin drank his tea was once transferred with great pomp from Zurich to Moscow. The meaning of relics is then not so remote: there are many thorns, but only a few of them are the thorns of Christ.

An artifact and its meaning are not by nature irrevocably entwined; rather, it is we who read significance into things. This is why we bestow significance primarily on personal belongings, such as the binoculars I always used as a boy to watch golden eagles. Doubtless there are stronger binoculars to be had nowadays, but I still carry these around with me. In trash theory terms they are already trash. My companions advise me time after time to try out a modern pair. My own perhaps already look "immortal" to very young people but they still can't wait for the moment they'll be able to fish them out of my trash can. Not that they will then rush off with them to follow the chamois' tracks. Instead, they will place them on their smoker's table with conspicuous nonchalance. They too will invest them with personal significance, as in: the binoculars we once fished out of the trash.

If the artifact were to end up in a museum, however, its various layers of meaning would need to overlap or at least to be closely interlinked. My golden eagles are then not enough. Kepler's binoculars would be better or, for the modern era, the ones Neil Armstrong used. They leave room for one's imagination and thus give rise to a story. A series of binoculars might even amount to a history of astronomy / astrology.

Does the exhibit, the artifact on display, have the same significance for all who view it? — This brings us to the question of the pedagogic museum. In the nineteenth century, members of the educated classes were free to decide on the meaning of a thing: artifacts were to go on show and what each viewer might think of them was left to his imagination. The eternally praiseworthy Baedeker accommodated this paradox with an ingenious invention, the * asterisk. The * signifies: In Rome, you must see the *Palazzo alle Terme Museum. There, you can rush past hundreds of artifacts but should on no condition fail to stop in front of the *Ludovisi Throne, because … Yes, the * says little more than that. The Ludovisi Throne has significance, but it is the significance that you yourself read into it. Nevertheless we are all agreed that the Ludovisi Throne is more significant than the heads with or without noses that surround it in the Palazzo alle Terme—and, by comparison, what wealth, what impoverishment the explanation brings!

Contrary to our expectations, the more modern artifact requires the most explanation of all. "Prism glass from 1911. With the invention of prism glass, the Zeiss Company in Jena has …"—At least my paltry binoculars would have to be presented this way in a museum. For if no such social import were implied they wouldn't make the grade, not even as a curiosity. But let us note: the explanation serves not so much to explain as to alienate. An explanation of the artifact is the very reason the latter may enter the museum and be admired there. The unspoken prerequisite of the artifact's display is its obsolescence: the now useless manufactured product is alien to us and accordingly requires an explanation.

In this respect the ethnographic museum is the museum par excellence. Artifacts therein appear foreign to us because they are foreign to us, because they come from foreign countries. Today, well-meaning ethnologists are trying to establish museums in the third world. The agents of a culture are presented with that culture just as it is presented in the ethnographic museum. That is doubtless nonsense in trash theory terms. According to Michael Thompson, such products would not qualify even as trash, to say nothing of immortal. How then are they supposed to acquire significance?

The duty to impart meaning

That historical museums are by no means harmless was evident from recent debates about a German Museum in Berlin. Resigned to pessimism, people there are setting about the task while thinking with envy of the national euphoria evoked, for example, by the very name of Nuremberg's "Germanisches National Museum." In a more cautious land than Germany this debate was exhaustively explored in the late nineteenth century, namely upon the founding of the Schweizerisches Landesmuseum (National Museum of Switzerland) in Zurich. In the latter instance, the paradox of attributing national historical significance to an object that is older than the said nation itself respectively that stems from an area that was, in the artifact's lifetime, not yet part of the said nation's present territory was quickly recognized. One significant artifact in the Schweizerisches Landesmuseum is the Seedorf shield: and while it is true that the village of Seedorf lies on Swiss territory now, the person who once bore this shield had nothing whatsoever to do with Switzerland, and represents a tradition moreover that Switzerland was trying at the time to do away with. What does the Seedorf shield tell visitors to the Schweizerisches Landesmuseum?

Also in Switzerland, nationalism held sway back then and gave rise to the Schweizerische Landesmuseum. And a similar situation is unfolding now in the young African nations—for it is hoped that the institution museum will make the young nations historical fact. A cause for irritation, here, is that the permanent artifacts, in particular the permanent buildings, stem from the colonial rulers, while indigenous products not only have an everyday character but are also ephemeral in the extreme.

Thus the sum of the collective significance of certain artifacts is supposed to result in a national history. Without doubt, this is dangerous material. This context can give rise to a logic that is at best an artificial logic, at worst a bogus logic. History appears as a "non-coincidental" sequence: it is the stringing together of artifacts that gives rise *ex post facto* to an interpretation. History then arises out of the confused activities of mankind and becomes a logical narrative, a redemptive narrative, whereby the status quo is supposed to be redemptive. This logic is the logic of the German weekly news magazine *Der Spiegel*, which bestows "non-coincidental" significance on current events. It is no coincidence that Barschel ten years ago already... No coincidence that Kohl as an undergraduate... No coincidence that the Russians, for their part...—and the contemporary bogus logic manufactured by *Der Spiegel* is the same as that underpinning any history created by the stringing together of certain artifacts.

Artifacts tend all too easily to generate such logic. One good example is the pile-dwelling folk. It was once the pride and glory of Swiss national history and not a schoolroom in the land was without its images of the pile-dwelling folks' everyday lives: the mother seated on timber boards in front of her hut, gazing out over the lake to see if the man is returning from his fishing trip; the men dragging the slaughtered bear from the ship in happy anticipation of their welcome in the village of pile dwellings. The pile-dwelling people were as beautiful as they were logical and when German scholars asserted in their publications of the 1930s that the pile-dwelling folk had never existed, it led even to diplomatic imbroglios with the Confœderatio Helvetica. The Swiss clearly sensed that someone was cooking up the cultural sack and pillaging of their country. It is no coincidence that a Hitler came to power at that time…

How does the past become historical?

And nonetheless: contemporary life must not only age and hence become trash, but must also become history. It must become a part of that which we so pathetically describe as the "historical legacy." It is a matter both of our most recent history and, in material terms, our latest products.

What happens to it in terms of Michael Thompson's trash theory? A part of the artifacts remains trash, another part is immortalized. The trash is incinerated, the immortalized artifacts exhibited. And one day, those parts of the trash which were able to evade incineration will be pronounced fit for exhibition while those of our artifacts which we placed in museums will land—no, no, not in the trash; don't worry—but in the storage depot.

Another tale: in the 1950s, in the framework of a pathetic urban renewal project, the Treppenstraße[3] was created in Kassel and a fountain designed by an artist—in the 1950s style, of course—was installed on one of its terraces. In 1981, when Kassel was being spruced up in preparation for the Federal Garden Show, the director

3 [The Treppenstrasse completed in 1953 was Germany's first ever officially planned pedestrian zone.]

of the event noticed the fountain and declared: "That is no longer up to scratch."

A landscape architect was commissioned to pull the fountain into shape and make it worthy of the year 1981—and so he did. But then something unexpected happened. The artist, the creator of the fountain, was still alive, saw this (in his eyes) pretty mess one day—and went to court. The city was sentenced to have the fountain restored to its original condition at its own expense.

The moral of the story is: even the 1950s have to become historical if we are ever to grasp the fact that they are not our terrible past but our history. Just as we burn our trash, so too do we alter works of our recent past, because we actually think that they are ours, of our era, but are somehow no longer up to scratch. In reality they are perfectly up to scratch, so to speak, but they do not belong to us. They have alienated themselves from us, must be regarded by us as foreign. And not only Mumford's creation of space, but this too, is the true role of the museum: to bring us face to face with objects that are alien and yet, for that very reason, full of significance.

Color Is A Sign (1994)

I would like to demonstrate here, why a color theory such as artists and artisans tried to establish at the start of this century is not possible. There are no such rules, but merely reflections on why every rule ever discovered is not timeless, and on how the gradual supersession of the meanings of colors was able to take place over time. In addition, to begin with, a reminder: in the 1940s I studied national economics but some of my friends studied architecture, and I therefore came in touch with their work at the Swiss Federal Institute of Technology (ETH) in Zurich. In keeping with the example set by schools of applied art, color theory was on the curriculum there, and a pass in it was mandatory. The cleverer students tended to cut this class. But shortly before the exam they'd regret having done so and buy a copy of lecture notes to quickly cram. Among these notes were two rules. The first one always attributed a meaning to a rectangular block of color:

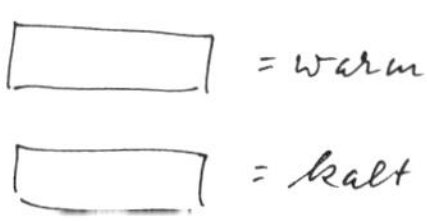

So, in this case, color is equated with a meaning. The second series of rules concerned good taste. It went like this: X matches Y

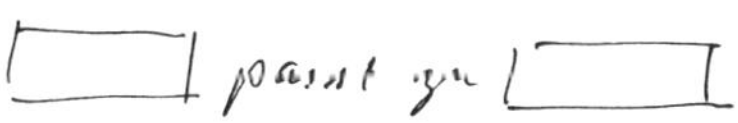

Colors were supposed to match. This played a major role in the culture of that era. It was possible that mother might say to father at breakfast: That tie doesn't go with this shirt. The rules disseminated by the ETH Zurich were topical therefore, yet they were lacking in content. Making a cheap copy of lecture notes made it impossible to fill in the blocks foreseen for color. The rules remained silent.

Farewell to color harmony.

The two series of rules, those on meaning and those on taste, came adrift in the following decades. I can remember the moment precisely, when the formula "X matches Y" suddenly lost all meaning. It was during a trip to London in 1964. We had some time left and were wandering down Carnaby Street, which was famous then for its novel young fashion. And what did this novelty consist in? — In its mix and match of colors that, in the eyes of the older generation, clashed: orange and crimson, blue-green and blue, and violet with everything it didn't "go with." And as for me, the harmonic color codes stored in my brain fell apart within fifteen minutes, as I found myself drawn solely to these novel combinations.

The language of color

Then around 1970 the first set of rules collapsed too. "Il n'y a pas de lexique"—"There is no lexicon," announced Roland Barthes on his visit to the ETH Zurich. We therefore could not put colors and meanings together in the lexical sense, by adding an equal sign. The relationship of meaning to an object, said the new science of semiotics, is fundamentally arbitrary, as in Umberto Eco's "struttura assente,"[1] the structure which we must presume exists but will never find. To make a meaning understandable always requires a proposition.

This dual collapse of color theory, regarding meaning on the one hand and color harmony on the other, brought us back to point zero, where Goethe began. There are two sides to Goethe's color theory: firstly, his lack of appreciation of Newton's physics, which back then already seemed rather odd; and, secondly, his introduction of the eye as the counterpart to the colored object. With the latter Goethe put an end to the objective, purely physical perception of color and pioneered the introduction of the eye, which is to say, the subjectivity of the viewer.

But when we take this as our starting point today, we have to dissect Goethe's "eye" in two: into the eye in the stricter sense, with its retina and all that conveys to us, and that which we now call perception, which is to say, all the things that unfold in the cortex in the back of our brain and which are, on the whole, a black box for us.

Newton and Goethe—reconciled

We therefore reconcile Newton and Goethe, namely on the one hand by admitting that Newton's color scale, the spectrum, really does exist. But we take Goethe seriously inasmuch as we ascertain that our eye perceives merely three slender excerpts from this spectrum yet is able to combine them in an extraordinarily rich manner. We see only three narrow bands of frequencies or wave groups yet

1 [Umberto Eco, *La struttura assente* (The Absent Structure), Bompiani, Milan 1968]

from these we can create box upon box of colored pencils, chalk pastels, oil paint blends, and color catalogs. It is in this rich mix based on only three sensitivities to color that the insecurity which finds expression in the link between perception and language originates.

The child learns colors with difficulty, and late. Translations into other languages do not function directly: for our *blau* the Italians have two words, *azzurro* and *blu*, for our *rot* the English have *red* and *pink*. Many anthropologists report that the indigenous tribes they have studied cover several of our colors, *blau* and *braun* for instance, with one word. Our generation has a further difficulty too: color photos, video projections, and TV are based on a mechanism that perceives and mixes only three color in a similar way to the eye. The outcome is a considerable impoverishment of our projected and printed visual realm. Anyone who has ever tried to photograph the rich blue spectrum of the alpine gentian—of spring gentian, stemless gentian, gentianella germanica, and whatever they are all called—ends up with nothing but a collection in Kodak blue or Fuji blue.

Color and image

So let's move on to the second part of Goethe's eye, perception. We emphasize here its black box character, since the latest findings regarding the workings of the cortex are neither available nor necessary for our deliberations. Our thesis is this: our perception is on the lookout not for a color but for an image. Or, to put it in the poetic terms of Deleuze and Guattari, perception always searches for a face or a landscape. A monochrome surface tells us little while the slightest sign instantly conveys to us strong data. A horizontal line suffices—already we see a landscape with sea and sky. Dot, dot, line and the face is done—a mere hint of two eyes and a mouth make a face of a blank surface.

When endeavoring to understand the meaning of color in our perception, analog to language, we must begin by considering what the monochrome surface means. In a language-like system, the monochrome surface must be something like the word "la parole." So what does "blue" mean? We think of the Madonna's blue gown in Siennese Madonna paintings as well as of the workman's blue overalls. Between these lies an invention: the blue of the Siennese painter consisted of finely ground lapis lazuli and it was therefore far more expensive to paint an area blue than to gild it. Everyone knew that no one but the Madonna deserved a blue gown. The proportion of blue in a painting was laid down in an artist's contract. The invention of aniline colors changed all that. Blue was all of a sudden the cheapest color. This is why the overalls that factories supplied free of charge to their workers were dyed blue. And so we see that the meaning of a single color can change over time.

Nevertheless we intend, as in language, to not overestimate the meaning inherent to any single word. A word per se does not prompt understanding. If I say "chocolate" everyone understands what is meant, but no one understands what I want. Should someone fetch chocolate now? Or have I just eaten my full of chocolate and would prefer not to see any more of it all week? To convey clear information I need a proposition: Please bring me … Or please take that away … So, which is the proposition pertaining to color?

The color spectrum and color card trends

I presume Goethe meant coloring. The original aim of Goethe's color theory was to produce coloring of use to painters. Anyone who reads his color theory and applies it is, so Goethe thought, a good painter. Does any famous good painter known to us stick with coloring? I know of none.

The so-called fashionable colors are the equivalent of Goethe's colorings. Twice a year, so rumor has it, mysterious gentlemen meet up in expensive hotels and show one another their color cards. Exactly two years later the general public receives the news: spring pastel colors will be back in fashion again this spring, fiery colors in summer, and a brownish sfumato in the fall. A new announcement is made each and every summer: and so it has always been. None of the young followers of fashion pay it any attention. All the young people nowadays wear anti-fashion, just as they used to on Carnaby Street. They thus follow a code that is not dissimilar to language but makes quite other, much richer statements than the color spectrums with the aid of which fashion designers suggest to the Queen of England which dress she should wear when opening a hospital or a preschool. Color spectrums are therefore not the proposition that makes any individual color understandable. But what then is the proposition with which the individual color is formulated as "word?"

To return now to my point: perception searches for the image. To once again quote Deleuze and Guattari, it is on the lookout for a face and a landscape. This search invests the object with meaning. Color invests the image with meaning and within the image the color itself is given meaning; it becomes symbolic.

Physical color and symbolic color

Traditionally, in painting, a distinction is made between physical color and symbolic color. Little Red Riding Hood's red-painted hood is physical color. The pink glow on the horizon in a landscape would be symbolic color. The distinction is highly questionable. None other than those artists who set out in the nineteenth century to paint reality for themselves for once—which is to say, they set out to use physical color—created the modern symbolic realm of color.

The reality of an image, the light, of course cannot be reproduced. Let us then imagine a nineteenth-century plein air painter seated now no longer in his studio but on the banks of the Seine, where he hopes to capture on canvas the reality of the sun sparkling on the water and the contrast of the dark shadows cast by the trees along the promenade. Had the man been equipped with a modern light meter such as photographers now use he would have ascertained the following: if, in the shade of the horse chestnut tree on the river bank, we have a luminous intensity of one, say, then the sparkling sun on the Seine has a luminous intensity of one thousand. Our eye can grasp that difference, but painting cannot. If we monitor the plein air painter's canvas with our light meter, we find that the shade under the horse chestnut is still one, whereas the patch of light on the Seine is ten at the most. In order now to emphasize how immensely bright this patch of light is, and how it stands out against the blue current of the Seine, our artist has added some color, has lent it perhaps a violet hue. So violet means: the brightest light. But violet is darker than white. The color is not used for its physical properties, therefore, but symbolically; the naturalist painters create a symbolic language of color. The symbolists and the expressionists who follow on their heels benefit from this. When Ludwig Kirchner came to Davos and saw the brilliant sunshine on the virgin snow he couldn't get enough of squeezing tubes of violet paint. I grew up in Davos and I can say in all certainty that the snow is white, not violet; but the brilliance of such white cannot be portrayed by white in a painting.

Color meanings in flux

There is no conclusion to my remarks here, except perhaps this: that the meaning of color is always in flux. Where does the change come from? How is meaning renewed? Meaning is always new meaning;

already existing, already known meaning is banal: it means nothing. A meaning that it is worth my while to take on board must therefore be a new one—and from where does this renewal stem? Let's follow Deleuze and Guattari once again. Meaning is renewed through the cultures and languages of minorities and the oppressed, immigrants, youth. Three examples should illustrate this principle in more depth.

Fashion

The first example derives from fashion. The older ones among us recall the rise to fame of blue jeans—propelled by the American West, the underground, the history of the poor, cinema, and in particular by James Dean. Students and people on vacation wore these blue trousers, which differed very little from workers' overalls, for a number of years. But then along came something new. I still recall the precise moment on the Kurfürstendamm: I was window shopping, rather bored, when I suddenly saw the stonewashed trousers with the faded knees. I realized then: there you have it. The eye had discovered the image in the color. The blue of blue-jeans is no longer a uniform all-over color, the non-opinionated surface but, rather, a proposition, an image stating that this pair of trousers has already been worn, it has already lived, it has a history; and in complete contrast to the gentleman's trousers with their neatly pressed crease, one knows in this case where the knee is.

Tableware

From the seventeenth century on, the European aristocracy liked to eat from white porcelain. However, the only white porcelain to be had came from China. Hoards of gold flowed into the Middle Kingdom simply in order that some porcelain could be shipped to Europe. Of course there were imitations too. A white zinc glaze had been discovered in Faenza and applied there to traditional earthenware. Delft refined white earthenware to perfection. Then, finally, Böttger in Meissen rediscovered porcelain. Soon the secret was out at several locations: in Sceaux, Berlin, Sèvres, and Vienna. White porcelain was now de rigueur on the tables of the upper classes. And accordingly it bored them all to tears. Things went on like this for twenty or thirty years: the gold no longer flowed to China, and artists painted little flowers on white plates and platters. But then along came the ingenious potter Josiah Wedgwood of Etruria. He did not use porcelain but simple potter's clay. He changed very little, glazing the clay not white, but almost: in a "cream color." This was what everyone had been waiting for. The czarina of Russia urgently sent to South Staffordshire, so as to be able at last to exchange her white for ivory-colored tableware. So, here too, the renewal of the meaning stemmed from the tradition of "the poor."

Synthetic boards

Sottsass's renewal of artificial surfaces of course does not concern color, not color alone. Sottsass too had the image in mind, from the very start. But from where did he get the image? The 1960s had invented the boring synthetic boards, Pavatex or whatever they were called, and given them a monochrome finish. It was all hygienic, shiny, washable, perfect, and boring. And Sottsass dipped into the culture of the poor in whose apartments remains of that linoleum could be found which we had already, oh so carefully, carried to the trash heap. Sottsass adeptly simplified, altered, and adopted their patterns and renewed—the color, yes, but also the image: "poor" linoleum was used for fun, meaningful, rich furniture. The eye, perception, does not look for the block of color, it looks for form and creates meaning from that.

Good Form and Good Color (1994)

The American agronomist Luther Burbank discovered a means of grafting new characteristics onto traditional fruits and vegetables. By thus crossing and separating he created the so very useful grapefruit, for example, the sole drawback of which is that one needs special utensils to eat it. By comparison, the common garden strawberry is probably the best-designed fruit of all. It has the perfect size and form to be eaten in a bite or two and without need of any utensils at all, since one can grasp the fruit by the little stem attached to it. A cute rosette of dried leaves protects one's fingers from coming into contact with the fruit's sticky flesh. If one so wishes, the once bitten berry can be dunked into a portion of granulated sugar, so even the matter of sweetening it can be accomplished without a spoon. The strawberry is more practical than the cherry, which is a bit on the small side, plus one never quite knows how best to dispose of the stone in a seemly manner.

Importers and wholesalers alone have never found the strawberry satisfactory. It is too soft to be transported—and yet of course no one wants to wait to eat strawberries until those in our climes at long last ripen. During transport from the south, however, berries bruise one another and grow moldy. The freight, when it arrives, smells and tastes wonderful but cannot possibly be sold. That is why the growers were commissioned to create a firm variety of strawberry that travels well.

Now, thanks to the aforementioned Luther Burbank, diverse characteristics can be grafted onto both ornamental and crop plants. But to successfully graft a characteristic and assure its stable perpetuation takes the grower at least twelve generations. And he can only graft one new characteristic at a time and must additionally bear in mind that others may be lost in the process, and that to regain the characteristics lost may take another twelve generations …

But the growers set about their task nonetheless and, twelve generations later, firm strawberries were on hand. They were now green, however, and tasted of nothing. But the traders were in a hurry. On no account did they want to wait another twenty-four generations. And so the question arose: "What is more important: that strawberries are red or that they have a strawberry taste?" — Anyone who ate strawberries this spring knows how the question was answered. And to be honest: Would you ever buy green strawberries?

Bad Form (1994)

Good form is dead. Good form, so says the true doctrine carried to the grave in the 1960s, is beautiful because it is functional. Good form was once the symbol of a sanitized solution—sanitized of all the unimportant minor matters, such as healthy raw materials, dangerous production processes, packaging problems, energy consumption, the difficulties of repair, the creation of dependency, the cost of replacement parts, and disposal. The award juries of the 1950s deigned to concern themselves with such negligible details.

Good form is dead. Has its opposite, bad form, meanwhile taken its place? Bad form would accordingly be the non-functional solution, the makeshift solution that just about does the job until something better can be found, the lavish solution from which one can omit something or other—although it is the extras, such as the hook on a telephone or the running board on a car, that make a thing all the more adorable.

One design that evinces the two characteristics of bad form is the dinosaur: a non-functional creature inasmuch as it didn't last very long—its extinction is proof of that—yet one that has remained popular since its inception with young and old alike. So what was it about the dinosaur that spelled its certain demise? Students that worked on a more viable redesign of it made a lot of proposals, ranging from Mickey Mouse ears to radar antennae, yet they failed to move beyond its evidently non-functional basic form.

How ever did the dinosaur come about? An English geologist by the name of Gideon Mantell found the first fossilized remains of a dinosaur in 1834. At the time, to speak publicly of periods of the earth's history that pre-dated Adam, or of creatures unknown to Adam, was still something of a risky business. The idea that certain species had not survived the deluge was acceptable; that mankind was absent from entire chunks of pre-history was not. The geologist Mantell therefore exhibited his finds in his own home and put out ads, inviting the public to visit him and form their opinions about these bony remains. To Mantell's delight, the painter John Martin turned up at his home, accompanied by his young daughter. As you see, although dinosaurs did not yet really exist as such, they already belonged to the children's realm. The geologist mustered all his courage and addressed himself to the famous painter: I was hoping above all to be able to show these remains to you, Honorable Sir, and I would be absolutely delighted, if you were to paint the dinosaur. John Martin, specialist for apocalypses, images of hell, and the fire of Babylon, did not wait to be asked twice. He thereupon painted "The Country of the Iguanodon," a steel engraving of which adorned the cover of the geology book that Mantell published in 1838.

Fortunately, Turner, Martin's mentor, had already painted a picture of a dragon in 1828, and this served as a model. For much had to be invented anew in order to conjure the dinosaur we know and love today. It did not have a color; the green skin with dark spots that tends then to a violet hue before finally ceding on the belly to a light grayish yellow was borrowed from the dragon. None of which mattered of course in the case of the steel engraving. But the structure of the skin—the thick and wrinkled belly and the armored back—all had to be fashioned. No one thought for a minute of fur or feathers, although animals with these do occur in the first image, the one set on land. In 1840 there followed a second painting, John Martin's maritime epos, "The Great Sea Dragons As They Lived." This image decorated Thomas Hawkin's book *Ichthyosauri and Plesiosauri*. The sea dragons and the terrestrial dinosaurs are almost identically portrayed, by the way.

Nature is the epitome of functionality. It can do no wrong. Even before Darwin, nature for Kant represents purposiveness without purpose and is beautiful for that very reason, because it is purposive, i.e. functional in a disinterested sense, which was Kant's way of saying its functionality held no profit or benefit in store for whoever observes it. Darwin then lends momentum to this functionality, telling us that the forms of nature have been tried and tested in the battle for survival, and hence the forms we see around us are survivors, are the most functional forms. Was the so adorably clumsy-looking dinosaur ever functional? And why then did it die out?

A purpose for the dinosaur had first to be found. Around 1840 it was evidently still uncertain whether the dinosaur moved about on land or in water, although this factor would definitely have resulted in extremely different forms. Even after a terrestrial lifeform had been decided upon, major questions still had to be resolved regarding the dinosaur's movement. Paleontologists were divided on this issue: some among them claimed that the dinosaur's legs could support its weight and that the dinosaur takes strides, others that the dinosaur crawls around on its belly like a lizard, thereby using its unburdened legs as oars quasi, to propel it forwards. Up until the First World War taxidermists continued to supply schools and museums with striding or crawling dinosaurs, as requested. The customer was always right.

Today, the dinosaur not only stands on a firm footing per se but is well established also in the toy industry, entertainment, schoolbooks, and natural history museums. Various forms and species have been distinguished. None of them looks convincingly functional. The lion, the whale, the eagle, and the modest horse are quite other creatures, which we can follow on their respective paths with a sense of empathy and understanding. And yet: our sympathies remain with the dinosaur, with its ultimately vastly undersized head, its weak legs, gargantuan rump, and long tail, the function of which I find particularly mystifying. Is bad form good form?

A Walk in Second Nature (1992)

To learn how nature as seen in our mind's eye translates into the image that we call landscape is a perennial object of our research. A walker's mind and his constantly roaming eye together conjure a seemingly stable image. In a broader sense, the walk accomplishes an even greater miracle: a chain of insights punctuated by distances ultimately merges in a single impression. We go along a road, across a forest, a glade, see a stream, the valley narrows and, eventually, from a hilltop, a broad panorama opens up; and by the time we arrive home we have seen a landscape. We can now describe how the area around Kassel looks, or that west of Schlettstadt, or in Montecatini. How, namely? It looks typical, typical of the respective region.

Here one should perhaps digress, and speak of the geographers' landscape. This is not the same as that of the landscape lovers, walkers, tourists, and landscape painters, although some links exist between them. One such link is all that is "typical." Do you remember geography lessons in school? The white cliffs of Dover are typical of England's eastern coast; homecoming coal miners in flat caps are typical of the Ruhr District ... Don't laugh. This concept of the typical may have consequences, for example whenever geographers become planners.

But let us return to the walk and its history. Born in the English landscape garden, it found its feet in the Scottish highlands then later in the foothills of the Alps, until a new invention—the railroad—triggered its crisis. The railroad reduced the typical region to the destination. It transported tourists to those hotels where the photo in the brochure, and on the picture postcards on sale there, corresponded exactly to the section of landscape on display beyond the windows of at least the more expensive rooms. Throw open the curtains of a morning and one would see the Giessbach Falls, the Matterhorn, or the Sainte Victoire.

These destinations represent large regions, or the early days of nations even, in the "typical" way. A connection exists between German unification and the image of the island of Helgoland, between the modern Swiss Confederation and the hotel windows in Schwyz and Brunnen. Do we need a brief digression on the topic of why, in the past, we never grew bored of always seeing one and the same landscape? Of course we also played cards and plotted schemes, but the answer to the puzzle occurred to me during a stay on the Furka: the weather used to change the scenery on our behalf, for we had not yet established that one-sided relationship with the weather such as is shaped now by the eternally blue sky of our travel brochures.

A large number of the old hotels at tourist destinations in Switzerland and elsewhere too have now vanished: I can name Rigigipfel—demolished; Furka—demolished; Giessbach—closed down. The hotels at these destinations are in decline while tourist numbers continue to grow. Today's tourists stay at hotels between destinations—for the walk of old has gained a new lease of life, namely in the form of the round trip by car.

The round trip by car has a larger perimeter. While the walk explores one hill to the west of Schlettstadt, the trip by car covers the Vosges, the Provence, and Tuscany. Consequently, the landscape experience is abstracted to a far greater degree. By the end of his long weekend, the motorist knows "what Burgundy looks like." Nowhere in Burgundy looks how he imagines Burgundy to look. He is convinced that the people of Burgundy have completely destroyed their beautiful Burgundy. He alone managed to construct an image from the typical remains.

In the 1960s, when suddenly everyone owned a car and regularly set off on a tour in the vacation season, the bells tolled for the extended walk. Civil engineers declared that it was necessary to channel traffic in order to avoid traffic jams, and they built the highway, thereby creating the very traffic jams from which they hoped to protect us. Once the highway was built, the problem of destinations raised its head, just as it had with the railroad.

This time around, too, the destination has to be typical because it represents a region; but, as we mentioned earlier, it must be typical to a greater degree of abstraction. The Matterhorn may represent the Alps, and the island of Helgoland Germany—but only very few tourist locations are constituted thus. Since the image of the region, of Tuscany or Burgundy, exists only in tourists' imaginations and not in reality, the tourist location must endeavor to live up to this great degree of abstraction. Often this is achieved by adding a further round trip to the trip to the original destination: one goes to Meiringen only to depart from there on the "Three Passes Trip," or the "Five Glaciers Tour;" and to Samaden to take the "Three Countries Tour," which takes one over the Ofen Pass, the Stelvio, and the Splügen. Five glaciers amount to the abstract essence of the single glacier.

Nonetheless, the place one stays should also evince something of this universally typical flair. Of course there are the vernacular, regional types of architecture, alpine for instance, but they developed their characteristic style at a time when neither hotels, nor large parking lots, nor swimming pools existed. So how might these huge buildings be made to look typical of their region? No role models exist, so it is a case of faking things without an original. In modern tourism architecture, the fake is the real thing, because a real counterpart to the fake does not exist. It is possible, therefore, that everything today is typical of everywhere; the style generated is that of ubiquitous regionalism.

Once the tourist location has successfully solved the problem of typical, regional architecture it tends to free itself from any compulsion to provide the round trip or the "Three Passes Tour" both of which in fact deprive it of tourism revenue. Is it not possible to merge all that is typically regional in a single location?—This requires a staged setting. The solution is an institution that combines the joys of an indoor swimming pool with a theme park that gives expression to all that is typical of the region. And since we can now pursue design completely free of local constraints, the region is the world. In an alpine hut on a tropical beach we can enjoy Finnish health with Japanese philosophy. Without moving an inch, we experience the whole world in the form of a second nature.

"I am a chapel on the landscape." Past and present — Today, the chapel has to announce what it is. Drawing: Lucius Burckhardt

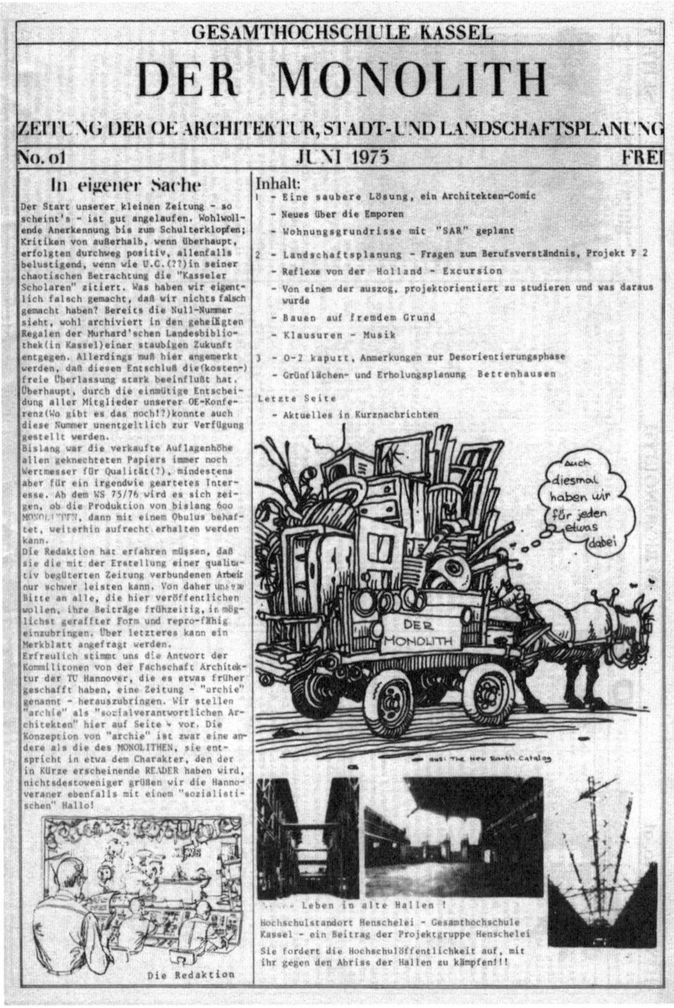

GESAMTHOCHSCHULE KASSEL

DER MONOLITH

ZEITUNG DER OE ARCHITEKTUR, STADT-UND LANDSCHAFTSPLANUNG

No. 01 JUNI 1975 FREI

In eigener Sache

Der Start unserer kleinen Zeitung - so scheint's - ist gut angelaufen. Wohlwollende Anerkennung bis zum Schulterklopfen; Kritiken von außerhalb, wenn überhaupt, erfolgten durchweg positiv, allenfalls belustigend, wenn wie U.C.(??)in seiner chaotischen Betrachtung die "Kasseler Scholaren" zitiert. Was haben wir eigentlich falsch gemacht, daß wir nichts falsch gemacht haben? Bereits die Null-Nummer sieht, wohl archiviert in den geheiligten Regalen der Murhard'schen Landesbibliothek(in Kassel)einer staubigen Zukunft entgegen. Allerdings muß hier angemerkt werden, daß diesen Entschluß die(kosten-)freie Überlassung stark beeinflußt hat. Überhaupt, durch die einmütige Entscheidung aller Mitglieder unserer OE-Konferenz(Wo gibt es das noch!?)konnte auch diese Nummer unentgeltlich zur Verfügung gestellt werden.

Bislang war die verkaufte Auflagenhöhe allen geknechteten Papiers immer noch Wertmesser für Qualität(?), mindestens aber für ein irgendwie geartetes Interesse. Ab dem WS 75/76 wird es sich zeigen, ob die Produktion von bislang 600 MONOLITHEN, dann mit einem Obulus behaftet, weiterhin aufrecht erhalten werden kann.

Die Redaktion hat erfahren müssen, daß sie die mit der Erstellung einer qualitativ begüterten Zeitung verbundenen Arbeit nur schwer leisten kann. Von daher unsere Bitte an alle, die hier veröffentlichen wollen, ihre Beiträge frühzeitig, in möglichst geraffter Form und repro-fähig einzubringen. Über letzteres kann ein Merkblatt angefragt werden.

Erfreulich stimmt uns die Antwort der Kommilitonen von der Fachschaft Architektur der TU Hannover, die es etwas früher geschafft haben, eine Zeitung - "archie" genannt - herauszubringen. Wir stellen "archie" als "sozialverantwortlichen Architekten" hier auf Seite 4 vor. Die Konzeption von "archie" ist zwar eine andere als die des MONOLITHEN, sie entspricht in etwa dem Charakter, den der in Kürze erscheinende READER haben wird, nichtsdestoweniger grüßen wir die Hannoveraner ebenfalls mit einem "sozialistischen" Hallo!

Die Redaktion

Inhalt:

1 - Eine saubere Lösung, ein Architekten-Comic
- Neues über die Emporen
- Wohnungsgrundrisse mit "SAR" geplant

2 - Landschaftsplanung - Fragen zum Berufsverständnis, Projekt F 2
- Reflexe von der Holland - Excursion
- Von einem der auszog, projektorientiert zu studieren und was daraus wurde
- Bauen auf fremdem Grund
- Klausuren - Musik

3 - O-2 kaputt, Anmerkungen zur Desorientierungsphase
- Grünflächen- und Erholungsplanung Bettenhausen

Letzte Seite
- Aktuelles in Kurznachrichten

... Leben in alte Hallen !

Hochschulstandort Henschelei - Gesamthochschule Kassel - ein Beitrag der Projektgruppe Henschelei

Sie fordert die Hochschulöffentlichkeit auf, mit ihr gegen den Abriss der Hallen zu kämpfen!!!

Der Monolith, Issue 1, June 1975, the student newspaper of the organizational unit 06 (faculty of architecture and urban and regional planning) at the University of Kassel. Annemarie Burckhardt was a member of the editorial board. Another homemade newspaper, *Canapé News*, accompanied Lucius Burckhardt's time on the professorial sofa at the Swiss Federal Institute of Technology (ETH Zurich). Its twenty-ninth and last edition, the so-called final report, was published at the end of the summer semester 1973.

Lucius Burckhardt plays Diogenes at the 18th Milan Triennale of 1992, as part of the German contribution organized by the "Rat für Formgebung" (design committee). Design: Andreas Brandolini/ Wolfgang Sattler. Photo: Annemarie Burckhardt

"Zwischen den Stühlen," a theatre play for three speakers written by Lucius Burckhardt to mark the occasion of the 75th anniversary of the German Werkbund and performed in October 1982 at the Münchner Kammerspielen festival (photo), in October 1983 on the 70th anniversary of the Schweizer Werkbund at the Kunstgewerbemuseum Zurich, in November 1993 at the launch of the design faculty at the Bauhaus University Weimar, and in February 1996 at the Deutsche Architekturzentrum Berlin. Photo: Monika Nikolić

A class is held outdoors in downtown Kassel in 1993 to demonstrate the re-appropriation of public space normally reserved for parked cars. The requisite fee was inserted beforehand into the parking meter.

A relief for the non-motorized public dependent on public transport: mobile bus stops in the form of balloons. The happening took place on Steinweg, Kassel, in 1993.

In 1976 a seminar on landscape was held on the edge of a forest in the village of Riede in Emstal.

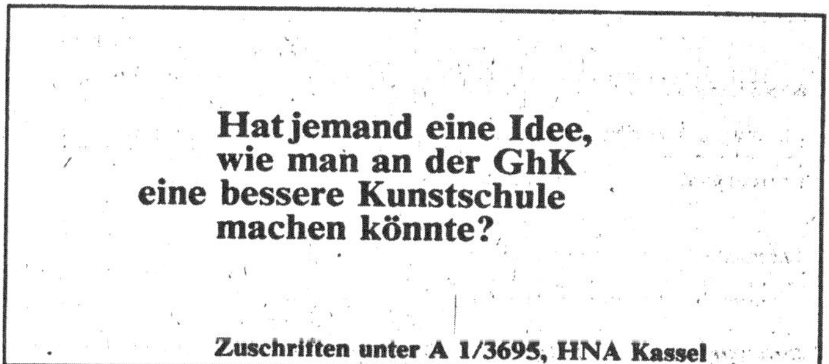

ANY IDEA HOW TO IMPROVE THE SCHOOL OF ART AT THE UNIVERSITY OF KASSEL?
Please send submissions to A 1/3695, HNA Kassel
Classified ad posted in Kassel's local daily newspaper, the *Hessische/Niedersächsische Allgemeine,* by Annemarie and Lucius Burckhardt and Martin Schmitz, October 27, 1984.

EDUCATION

University Planning and Urban Planning (1968)

Objectives and limits

The ultimate objective of the university system in its entirety, as the vanguard of research and education, is to provide insight: hitherto hidden or puzzling relations are to be raised into the light of understanding and knowledge and made transparent for anyone seeking to comprehend the scholar's thoughts. Thus the university is a part, indeed the most effective part of the secular democratization process—democratization meaning, in this regard, to counter the arbitrariness of the individual with the mindful consensus of the community.

The noblest task of a society is to set apart objective analytical instances that are capable of passing judgment on the said society. The university is one such instance: a place of reflection on society itself. It is a place where things can be said that have not yet permeated the consciousness and consensus of society. To call for a "critical university" is hence a pleonasm, since a university that has lost its critical capacities no longer deserves the name. If, today, the call for a "critical university" perhaps hides a bias then this itself reflects a further bias, one that knows how to hide behind a pretense of objectivity.

This duty, to bring transparency to hitherto unfathomable areas, goes hand in hand with a task that distinguishes the university from all other institutions of education. While schooling serves the reproduction of existing knowledge and hence the perpetuation of tradition and culture as well as the transfer to the next generation of all that has been achieved to date, the university serves innovation and reform. It not only preserves the knowledge gained and customs established thus far but also engenders new culture. And it is this, which makes the university far more a shifting entity than any school: it reforms itself and in so doing it changes society. Any discussion about the university and its remit is therefore necessarily a discussion about society itself. A society that does not wish to reform its universities does not wish to change itself and thus hastens its own decline.

In social terms, the university has a paradoxical task: it creates equality and creates inequality. Inasmuch as it imparts objective and universally comprehensible knowledge it addresses itself to all, and all are invited to pursue an education within its precincts. Yes, the university has a vested interest in all citizens having an equal opportunity to apply to it, for only so is it assured the cream of the crop. Yet with this cream of the crop it creates inequality. It gives the best positions in society to those who have stood the test of a university. To create such inequality is a great privilege and woe to he who thereby shows a bias!

While the university is an organ of society that towers over society and assumes judicial functions it is nonetheless subject to the social order from which it ensues. The university serves economic objectives too, and operates in an economic framework. In an appropriate manner and without becoming too much of a financial burden on society it is meant to educate the upcoming generation such that this can fill the top positions. It is a task of society to decide which resources should be made available to this end.

In this last respect the university is its own best advocate: for in disseminating knowledge it also sows awareness of the necessity of knowledge. Sociological surveys have shown that those who approve of state funding for research and education have personally benefitted from an education. Knowledge is the key to insight into the usefulness of knowledge. Here, the university once again slips from its service role into a leadership role: it must spread knowledge of knowledge. It has a right to promote itself.

Two concepts

The university system can be oriented to two different concepts. One can develop a university in a way such that it meets the population's current need for education, imparting education thus as a service; or one can develop it in a way such that those professional openings in the production apparatus which require a university education can be filled.

We call the first of these concepts the humanist one. It is premised on the notion that education is beneficial in and of itself, and that each and every means of fostering education is in the interests of society. If a young man wishes to learn Sanskrit or to know which minerals make up Greenland then that is a very good thing and deserves support. University imagined thus is a self-service store, in a sense, one that is all the better the broader its product range.

The system thus described is also often called the "German" or the "Humboldt" system. It is rooted in the idea that any kind of occupation at the vanguard of specialist knowledge creates access to general knowledge, which is the most worthwhile of all. The student cannot go wrong, for the rocks of Greenland or Sanskrit vocabulary will open his eyes to philosophy. Here, study is synonymous with research and research guarantees the originality of study. Each generation progresses questioningly through a field of knowledge, and thus remains eternally young and fresh. This argument is best represented by two figures, who while once the university's darlings have meanwhile become somewhat problematic: the eternal student and the guest professor. The eternal student confirms the belief that in-depth knowledge brings satisfaction and leads to a general education; the guest professor has to prove that the beliefs held by the established chairs are subject to the demands of the curriculum and therefore must be regarded as relative. The guest professor creates his academic position namely by casting doubt on his teachers' teachings.

The humanist concept finds itself up against the university's orientation to the professional structure of the country. Students are to be given instruction in those professions currently required by the public administration and the economy, as well as in those able to assure continuity in teaching and the advancement of research.

Such a rigorous concept sounds philistine and yet it is justified by the findings of modern classical economics, in particular by the growth theory. It was only in recent years that the connection between a country's economic development and the structure of its teaching and research came to light. The countries that make the most progress are those with an educational system that supplies the requisite number of graduates in the relevant disciplines. This system need not and indeed must not be rigorous: a certain surplus of teaching personnel serves to uphold the general culture of a society as well as the imperatives of so-called "edutainment:" the pursuit of learning as leisure. Yet these too form a cadre that is willing to toe the line of the production apparatus.

But if development and education are linked in this way, can any country afford to ignore the connection and continue with an education system that is "left to chance?"

Education and specialization

The traditionally educated person knows "everything." He has acquired a means of communication that facilitates conversation with other educated minds and indeed makes it a pleasure: a reference to a point in Plato, to a verse in *Faust*, to the Battle of Cannae, and his interlocutor understands and smiles. The educated minds were taught the traditional round of subjects in their schools, and they gained a certificate attesting their maturity, which in Switzerland is called the *Matura*. With this certificate they gained access to specialized knowledge, became engineers, doctors, attorneys, and thereby learned a great deal; yet they always considered their true knowledge to lie in their shared "education."

A common basis for understanding of this sort should not be underestimated. It considerably eases exchange among those who partake in it. The danger arises only when this education is mistaken for the real round of knowledge; when people say that it covers "everything"—except for specialized knowledge. Then this education becomes a value system that prevents insight into the altered circumstances of modern life. The educated person withdraws into the ivory tower of a kind of knowledge that no longer relates to real conditions; and because his colleagues give him constant reassurance, he doesn't even notice.

From the modern perspective, there is nothing at all round or complete about that knowledge imparted in schools and which we then call education. It is, rather, a really heterogeneous mix, a coincidental package that the history of the western hemisphere has cobbled together over the years. Whatever sympathy we may feel for this historical process, we are now no longer willing to see why the myths of classical antiquity have a greater educational value than those of India or China, say, or why Latin grammar trains the mind better than the abstract principles of linguistics do. Whatever we know of the Ancient Greeks is education. Whatever we learn about Ancient Mexicans is specialized knowledge. Why?

One could link this rejection of the classical education with the idea that models of modern pragmatic professions need to be created and taught at universities. Every university profession would give rise to a certain curriculum that would lead the student to his goal in the most appropriate way, namely to a professional position in his field. These curricula could also take into account the "new" professions, including those that people have hitherto arrived at as lateral entrants and, all too often, owing to a failure of some sort: the journalist, film director, or politician, perhaps. Don't they too need education and training? Could not a knowledgeable newspaper reporter be fabricated from language, politics and history, maybe geography too, and a course in military strategy?

He could indeed; and this is how it is done in other countries. But the fact that the classical education is no longer the sole means of communication shared by members of different professions should not lead us to believe that there is now no knowledge able to forge such connections. We need the sense of connection implicit in shared knowledge both for teamwork among scholars in different disciplines—an increasingly important type of work—and as a foundation for the development of the individual scholar, who should on no account lose his personality in the rapidly changing world of academia. With an all too narrowly specialized education one runs the risk of being ill prepared to adapt to future situations.

The goal of modern professional training at university level must therefore be to provide "operative knowledge" that, without resting on so-called "eternal truths," will equip the graduate for life. But just what is "operative knowledge?"

What should be taught?

Like the grammar school education, the university with its five faculties is a historically informed package, the origins of which lie somewhere in the liberal arts of medieval times. The last major shift was the highly consequential separation of the philosophical-historical and the philosophical-natural scientific faculties. This rupture—between schools of philosophy rooted in language and history and the various natural sciences—was the founding moment of late-nineteenth and early-twentieth-century pragmatism. It was analog to that separation of the fine arts and the arts of engineering, which, as we know, left urban planning betwixt and between. The rupture in the old philosophical faculty blinded us until recently to the fact that technical knowledge is not neutral but part and parcel of a society's development. From this we learn that every separation, every cut, has repercussions; and indeed many fields of knowledge—which we now regard as interdisciplinary—were left behind owing to this organization of the faculties. Sociology, information theory, semantics, linguistics, social psychology, and more besides come to mind. The classification of knowledge is accordingly by no means unbiased.

Should new and different content than before be taught at universities today? The fine arts would be one possible example: theater or music, where hitherto solely philology and musicology were taught. From a modern standpoint, one that regards art too as a means of information, to thus expand the university promises great excitement. On the other hand there is the risk that the university may become "a Jack of all trades" and circles form there which fail to make inroads into the commonalities of knowledge.

It is accordingly more important not to expand the curriculum but to make its modules freely combinable. The university should promote hitherto neglected interdisciplinary fields. These encompass also a field wholly ignored to date yet that ought truly be a university's prime concern: the science of the sciences, systems research, educational research, and educational economy, all of which offer counsel on educational policy.

In the immediate aftermath of the Second World War, the matter of restructuring the structure of degree courses was widely discussed. Thought was given to a general education that would give students a solid overview of all the knowledge taught at university; and thought was given likewise to preliminary courses, which would familiarize students with methodological issues before letting them loose on thematic content. The general education soon fell out of favor for it was recognized that it derived from an old and misguided concept of education—and failed even to remain wholly true to that. It fostered superficiality as well as the assumption that the faculties' knowledge falls into the "general" and "specialized" categories.

The matter of a foundation course evoked a sense of rank or hierarchy, especially in England. One may well imagine that students who are stuffed full of logistics, linguistics, ethics, and psychology during the first part of their degree course (whereby ethics can be taken to mean permanent self-criticism) are able to tackle the knowledge they later encounter on a wholly different footing. This does beg the question, however, as to whether one is right to teach such difficult sciences at the start of a degree course, or might be better advised to teach them continually throughout it. But there is no doubt that people educated this way are better equipped for certain positions than those who complete conventional courses. In this sense, every experiment does some good and no one ever went to the wrong school. Even such a modest experiment as that of the "Hochschule für Gestaltung Ulm" [Ulm School of Design] has shown that students raised to have an unusual frame of mind later do well in unusual positions. The drawback with all these "fantasy universities" is merely that exchange with other universities—coordinated exchanges—cannot be guaranteed. This puts at risk another means students have of broadening their horizons, namely that customary in past decades, of switching university several times during a degree course.

One aspect to which the university must definitely pay some attention is the further education of those alumni whose activities take them beyond the university precincts. Today, university education can no longer be limited to preparing people to embark on a career at the age of twenty-five then pursue that sole profession for the next forty or fifty years. The knowledge required in the higher professions changes so fast nowadays that no one can manage without further education.

This now falls into two categories, post-graduate education and life-long learning, and it is no accident that each still has only an English name. While the former follows directly on either the first degree course or several years' internship and is intended to equip the student for a specialized or interdisciplinary field (such as regional planning) not yet offered by the established faculties, life-long learning brings together the members of those professions obliged to keep up with scientific advances (doctors, for example) at regular intervals of five to ten years so they may study the latest findings. Both categories have the not negligible side effect of furthering the university's own education and keeping it abreast of developments.

New types of university

Quite apart from its highly diverse range of subjects, universities today have to educate extremely different types of student. One could consider whether some of these students might be better served by other types of university—whereby the established universities would be less crowded and the efficacy of teaching optimized. The types of student in question are:

- the student who wants to rapidly embark on a career and needs a diploma. As a rule he is intelligent enough to skip lectures and not fall for those seductive whispers telling him that a student must think for himself and do his own research.
- the student who wants to go into the sciences, gain specialized knowledge and, in parallel, get to know the research field.
- the student who hopes to poke his nose into different scientific fields and likes to attend the lectures prescribed for his own discipline as well as those seemingly unrelated.
- the student who wants to work in public administration and is best served by a fixed and tight curriculum.

– the student who wants to go into applied research, technology, or economics, and requires the university to always offer him the latest in cutting-edge content.

If, for once, one accepts this summary categorization of student types then it becomes obvious that the university is supposed to attain heterogeneous and incompatible objectives. For the adepts of science, which is to say those up-and-coming students who will one day accede to university posts, a relatively intensive degree course oriented to a very few students is required. Those "technologically" oriented students, who should not be underestimated now that the failing economy needs a boost, require a very different kind of diversity, inter-faculty exchange, and experience of professional practice. After all, the curious person testing the water, so to speak, should be offered something that he can understand and take away with him, something on which he can hone the hierarchy of his own personal value system. It is he who brings university knowledge into everyday life in the form of culture. If ever this culture seems dead and dusty, the fault lies with the university, not with him.

Not only for specific subjects but above all for these specific types of student, one could call for specific universities, those specialized in producing the necessary public administration personnel, for example, such as teachers, state attorneys, and so forth. On the other hand one could envision a type of university that combines technical knowledge with practical experience of economics. Such graduates would serve the country's commercial development. Certainly, such notions are anathema to fans of the traditional university. But the present burden on universities must be lessened somehow and it is more honest to spell out how it really is than to make an unofficial distinction between "better" and "mediocre," "prolific" and "modest" universities, as used to be the case in the old Germany.

Problems of teaching

We said at the beginning of this paper that the system of education is there to offer equal opportunities to all and then to distribute the positions in life. Our system of education achieves this either by making students repeat a year of school or by giving them a fail at exams. This system is a great loss both for the schools that apply it and their students; it already assigns the secondary school the task of dispatching young students on a fast track to the manual, semi-skilled jobs they are allegedly made for.

How does our university go about it? It is very obvious here how thoughtlessly an old system was transposed to new circumstances. One can tell immediately from the lecture plan. An important representative of the discipline in question gives the prestigious induction lecture—a custom that dates from when the lecturer's wage consisted of semester fees. If the principal lecturer applies himself to the freshman lecture who could be surprised to find he no longer knows the graduates? The old university system is still doctored nonetheless. The student still studies until he feels that the university chairs won't let him flunk his exams. The exams back then consisted of an academic discussion between an older research scholar and a younger one of his acquaintance.

The fictitious notion that the student is a young research scholar is upheld also in the dissertation respectively in the obligation to submit one. However, to research properly means to get to the bottom of an issue, even when this takes time. But the modern university wants to put the limited number of places in its libraries, laboratories, and seminars at the disposition of the greatest possible number of students, and it has no time for laggards. The doctoral candidate must accordingly be clever enough to conduct research in fields in which respectable findings can be made in a very short time.

The rewards hence go to those who have the knack of playing the research scholar without necessarily being one.

Many faculties or departments have tried to avoid this problem by introducing interim and final exams of their own. These are meant to separate the wheat from the chaff, the "bread-and-butter student" from the "research student;" the first is satisfied with a diploma, the second is destined for the doctor's cap. But "bread" and "non-bread" is too cheap a dialectic. It would make more sense to examine the efficiency of the teaching methods applied today at universities, and likewise to examine a method by which success might be allotted, one that would not so intimidate the candidate, because it would not entail the risk of all the knowledge he had previously gained being invalidated by a "fail."

Problems of study

We read daily in the papers that to be a student is to play a very special role—and owing to these reports, most of which come from abroad, one is tempted to say that this too is a "Swiss special case." One's time as a student is a time of major decisions, rapid development, and yet still limited experience, which is also why it entails a certain propensity for short-circuited thought processes as well as illuminating role models that inspire emulation. The proper student is soon alienated from his original milieu, accomplishes a steep learning curve under extreme circumstances and then is released into another milieu than that in which he grew up. However, this fellow does not tally with the Swiss student. One only has to think of that large proportion of students who live with their parents during their time in college! In Zurich (university and polytechnics) it is 45 percent; and of those students who live in rented accommodation, 64 percent regularly go home to their parents on weekends, and a further

15 percent only now and then. The remainder, who stay away from home consistently at the least for one whole semester, probably consists to two-thirds of foreigners. The Swiss student is therefore never completely released from his family bonds or the circle of hometown friends and former schoolmates; he retains a bond with these circumstances and will in all probability return to them one day. The formative influence of student life is slight under such circumstances, probably slighter than that of life as an army recruit, say.

One can see this as advantageous or disadvantageous, depending on one's viewpoint: the political "common sense" of our students, to which these circumstances lead, can be glorified as particular maturity or dismissed as hopeless naivety. Either way, the ability to open up to fields of knowledge that can deconstruct or convert the traditional notions one grew up with is generally less marked among those students who remain in the family circle. Information that cannot pass the filter of traditional notions falls on deaf ears.

One must always bear this state of affairs in mind when there is talk is of founding new universities—as now in Aarau or Lucerne. For as long as such universities exist only to save local youngsters from making the journey to Basel or Zurich they contribute little to the modernization of Switzerland.

The formal system

The formal system, which is to say, the hierarchical and organizational expansion of the university, comes in for much analysis and criticism nowadays. The main focus of criticism is professorial tenure, i.e. the long-term appointment to a professorial chair. The full professor is at the pinnacle of his discipline. He is accordingly overtaxed with academic as well as administrative duties. Of course he has opportunities to organize his affairs, but prefers to lighten his load with the aid of assistants, secretaries, and other staff rather than of persons who might assume not only his duties but also his rights. In particular, he makes sure that no professional colleagues of a rank equal to his own ever come along, since they, owing to their fewer administrative duties, might accomplish more than he in the scientific arena. Often, this third party, whom the full professor fears is laughing up his sleeve at him, holds the position of extraordinary professor and is therefore in every respect worse off than the full professor and yet likely, thanks to his scientific work, to perhaps gain more renown than he.

The professorial realm depends on assistants and, in part, on guest lecturers, the latter increasingly in the spotlight nowadays, and rightly so, as "non-professorial teaching staff." Given the fact that scientific insights rapidly change, the youngest scientists are often the most productive, especially if they have recently garnered experience abroad. Criticism is voiced—and again, rightly so—regarding the fact that their advancement depends on a single individual who on no account wishes to have a rival on his heels or pushing ahead of him. Here we have a point for which the university is unlikely ever to find a cure, for it is the sole instance able to initiate reform in this regard but in so doing might reasonably expect to weaken its own position.

The one thing common to all reform proposals worth their salt is, therefore, that the department head must intervene in place of the professorial chairs, the department being now an instance of a size and scope somewhere between the chair to date and the faculty.

The effective system

Whenever a vital society is harnessed to an outdated organizational scheme, all kinds of semi-official and unofficial configurations come about, one example of which is the rapidly expanding system of institutes.

Institutes can be divided into the small and large ones, and one must also differentiate between those "incorporated in" or simply "at" a university. Small institutes serve to endow those professors who are elsewhere unable to acquire the matter-of-fact means to pursue fruitful work with these precisely, namely an office, a telephone, and a woman who ensures that he is not constantly interrupted in his work, plus a small library of books, and credit enough to be able to enlarge it. Small institutes thus comprise an emendation, as harmless as it is necessary, of the formal system. Large institutes, however, are professorial chairs blown up out of all proportion, the long arm of omnipotent professors intent on setting up an unofficial realm in addition to their official one. Of course, large institutes—given the present circumstances—are also necessary; effective research is conducted at them. However, the imminent university reform will have to ensure that institutes too are under the management of the departments and that their non-professorial teaching staff is not denied the rights it has been granted at last at universities.

The institutes "at" universities, for their part, are often institutions bordering on the commercial. The university's name is used to land research contracts, but ones that are carried out at a price and independently of the university. This is by no means reprehensible. Such institutes provide scholars with opportunities to pursue and enliven practice-oriented lines of research and insofar mitigate the often precarious, financial situation of certain scientists. The assistants of the institutes "incorporated in" the universities are more au fait with economic reality and therefore often find worthwhile positions.

Growth and reform

As a result of the rise in student numbers, the different demands now made of education, and the expansion of science itself, university education is undergoing change. It can do so in three ways: as it is today, by proliferating and splintering; by carrying out reform; or by founding new universities. Ultimately, it can also resign itself, limit the availability of student places, or restrict its most distinguished task, which is to welcome foreign guests.

The reform to date of proliferation and splintering as aspects of growth, in particular of their organizational and structural consequences, will be discussed in the next article, which will follow next month. When it comes to reform, the first question to ask is: Who can carry it through? We find ourselves now in an unfortunate situation, since the instance in society that should be one step ahead of events and therefore in a position to reform society has become stuck in a rut and is no longer able even to help itself. University reform can be carried out neither by the university's own instances nor solely by the cantonal administrations on which the universities rely for funding. University reform is an operation concerning one of the most important instances in society, in the entire country, and its implementation therefore requires the full participation of the general public and its political organs. University reform must become a political issue for all Switzerland. To those fearful of putting so subtle a matter in the public eye, we say: This is the sole and final arena in which a youth grown restless and an intelligentsia that feels itself slighted can publicly argue and publicly reconcile itself with all the other forces in society. And a discussion of this sort will serve not only the university but also the entire country.

It is easier to found a new organism than to reform an existing one. This truth is the innermost core of the aspiration to found new universities. In Germany, it took the founding of the University of Konstanz to lend momentum to reorganization of the study of medicine. If founding new universities has an effect on the system overall, it is truly worthwhile. If it doesn't, it is not.

Educational policy

University policy is a part of educational policy. Educational policy—well, there is actually no such thing in Switzerland, officially, since education falls under the sovereign remit of the cantonal administrations. Yet educational policy of course exists nevertheless, and even to forgo it would amount to a policy of sorts, just as letting a ship go adrift is a decision of the captain and has a certain outcome.

Now, one need not imagine that educational policy consists in confidently drawing up curricula and distributing credit in keeping with an overall research program. The university is also a part of an economic system and a social system. Research and its application, in and for the economy, armaments, and other areas, along with the repercussions of its application for research, comprise a "superstructure" that acquires a momentum of its own and dictates the laws of trade. We cannot look at research and teaching in a vacuum, detached from politics and the economy.

Under these aspects knowledge per se looks different from the classical education: knowledge is not an even field to be extended at its margins so as to keep out the unknown, whereby everyone is intent on keeping the field round and free of gaps. More accurately, one might say that knowledge is a fleece full of holes and pockets, misshapen by wear and tear in places, and neglected at others. Knowledge is not to be broadened by endeavoring to fill in the gaps, but is dictated, rather, by what happens in the "superstructure." Research can be triggered by politics, by the economy, or by research itself. In any case, research requires money and must obtain it from the state or the wider economy. Anyone who gives credit to this end is not disinterested, is not wholly without ulterior motives, but rather a man endeavoring to understand something of a matter, and to steer the course of research according to his own lights. The research scholar, for his part, is no less innocent of the machinations of politics or big business, nor has he chosen his area of research by accident, nor his potential sponsor by accident.

There thus exists neither research for its own sake nor purely disinterested patronage solely in the interests of science. The task of the university cannot be to produce or reproduce such purity, if indeed it ever existed. It can only emend events by raising awareness of the actual state of affairs, by assuring transparency and publicity, and by making a public matter of educational policy forged behind closed doors. To do so, however, the university must first get to know itself.

When students today demand a "critical university," it cannot be taken to mean either a "biased university" or a "pure university," the latter independent of all circumstance. We can regard the demand for a critical university as meaningful only if what is meant by this is a university that consciously formulates educational policy and uses it to political ends. For education, inasmuch as it upholds and regenerates the culture and the traditions of a society, is the true object of all political activity.

Infrastructural prerequisites

The university does not prosper in a vacuum; rather, it needs fertile soil—which in our case is the city. In the United States and in England there are universities that are independent and distinct from the city and have constituted their own fertile soil. To do so requires either a long-standing tradition, or a very large university, or a large sum of money per head of lecturer or student. In our case, on our small scale, the university needs a city to be able to grow. Does this mean only Switzerland's larger cities can provide all the university needs? Are they alone a viable environment for a lecturer from elsewhere, for example? Certainly, one can lecture in biochemistry without going to the theater or attending concerts, and one can visit art exhibitions on Sundays, if one takes the car. Certainly, students can live in student halls instead of with professorial widows, and they can eat in the canteen, make beat music of their own in the common room, and go for a walk in the countryside instead of to the cinema. One can do all that and more, if one has to.

What one cannot do, however, is to lecture and pursue scientific research at a place where there is no consensus with the local population—one is better off in that case on a campus. The university town must have a richly developed society, not the noble society of old, the counterpart to the elitist, exclusionary university, but a society that wants to know what is happening in the field of knowledge, that participates, inquires, joins in the work, and joins in the celebrations.

This society will also govern its city in a way such that a university finds within it the infrastructural prerequisites of its existence. For the planning of universities is bound up with urban planning—and that will be the subject of the second article in this series.

Ulm Anno 5. On the Curriculum of the Ulm School of Design (1960)

Germany 1955: lapsed development in the arts field since 1933 and the need to make up for lost time had necessitated a review of the situation of the early 1930s, and led to a veritable renaissance of Modernism. The sudden change in Germany, from historic bankruptcy to commercial proficiency, proved to be lasting and lucrative. Then the first few turned up their noses at this Wirtschaftswunder—they reeked of youth movement, and were on the lookout for a new fools' paradise. The choice of the Kuhberg (Cow Mountain) district of Ulm, rather than a location more apt to provide cultural and industrial contacts, points dangerously in this direction.

Thus neo-Modernism, commerce and the tramp of sandals paved the way to Europe's first school of design. That these forces were obliged to rid themselves of Max Bill, the first rector of the school and a man of a wholly other ilk, surprised no one. The ideology used to do so was typical: just as Teutonic irreality cedes to cynical pragmatism more easily than one imagines, the rallying cry now was the supremacy of science. We shall deal here neither with the superficial incidents surrounding the overthrow of Bill, nor with the subsequent interregnum that is expected to reach its end this fall. These stories, although at times of downright Castrian fidelity, are at a disadvantage vis-à-vis the ostensibly similar Bauhaus gossip insofar as they are not backed up by the accomplishments of the Bauhaus crowd. Therefore, those students in Ulm who are busy creating a mini-archive in Ulm from gossip retrieved from wastepaper baskets are wasting their time: Darmstadt will not buy it.

Given that 150 years of industry and 50 years of Modernism have proved that the form of an object never follows merely from the demands made thereon, and that the quest for a style that represents freedom from style is nothing but a likeable yet misguided aberrance of human illusion, it is difficult to understand the following: namely that, not in 1919, not in 1929, but in 1959, in the wake of the Bill crisis, an endeavor was made yet again to re-establish the positivism of functionality, and consequently to criticize as "formalist" every design that could not be explained solely in terms of its technical features. The outcome of such disregard for the style issue is that almost all the objects created by Ulm students for their final exam, unless they happen to be electric drills, evince considerable "formalism" and are strongly reminiscent of the aforementioned 1920s and 30s. Lecturers too, when it comes to criticism, are confronted with questions of form, which they resolve by resorting to design coherency's *je ne sais quoi*. An Italian visitor who pointed out this discrepancy was fobbed off, insofar as he was understood at all, with the retort that such attitudes are remnants of the Bill era. For it is not permissible to admit that the consummate form evinced solely by technical objects is a premise of freedom from style.

Paradoxically, the theory of technical expediency came to be complemented now by a second theory that addresses the social and sociological contingency of form. People discovered the social aspect of the development of form and fashion. And as people in Ulm live by their convictions, this had unexpected consequences. Sandals were suddenly out, and stalwart Swabian ladies became fashion conscious: they threw out the stocks of sack dresses already written off as market flops, sank up to their high-heels when scaling the clay of the Kuhberg then fluttered green-shadowed eyelids in a mute cry for help. They failed nevertheless to draw the correct conclusion from their masquerade, namely that form, whether it be a style or a fashion, always possesses a degree of freedom independent of purely technical factors. Ulm's stock of forms proved just as ephemeral as fashion: after all, the font Accidenz-Grotesk, shades of gray, orthogonality, and the technological look now comprise the luxury style of 1960. I have nothing against that. Yet one should not allow one's students to believe this alone will teach them absolute design for all time. Once this fad has run its course—as it surely will, for all of them do—then Ulm graduates will become slaves to mere "styling" with even less reserve than everyone else.

Guests are not always welcome in the cloistered backwater Ulm, for the less foreign matter arrives to ripple one's retreat the easier the world can be shaped in one's own image. Reyner Banham's visit took place around that time. This ingenious and humorous architecture critic defends the (here unduly simplified) hypothesis, that any products of our era which the artistically-schooled eye is likely to find lacking in taste—exaggerated automobile chassis, cinema advertising, pin-up girl magic—in fact constitute a kind of folk art: applied art for mass consumption, which Ulm would ignore at its peril given that it has nothing itself with which to counter that suddenly fashionable spoiler, the "consumability" of form.

Yet the "bündisches heart"[1]—which continued to beat even in a sack dress—could not believe our clever guest from Albion. People shied away from this experimenter's consistent realism: the idea namely, that an ultimate outcome of the study of the sociological contingency of form might be the capitalist entrepreneur who personally anticipates a market for the expressiveness of form, thereupon begins to plan the course of fashion himself, and to heat up or cool down conjuncture by recourse to design and in accordance with demand.

A compromise was sought therefore, a social market economy of design, so to speak; attempts were made to reconcile two opposing

1 [The reference to the "Bündische Jugend" (as the German Boy Scout movement was called after 1914) is presumably meant to imply loyalty and steadfastness.]

theories: the theory of absolute technical expediency, and that of the social contingency and economic freedom of form—nothing easier than that, in the land of Hegel. The resolution of opposites was posited in an imminent era, an era already embarked upon in Ulm, an era in which the fashionable marketing of form is united with advances in production, an era in which every new form is inspired by a new technical twist. The core of this belief was the doctrine of the imminent worldwide demise of the American automobile industry and the Fidel Castrian ascent of the legendary Fiat 600.

Manipulation of the present is a far more difficult task than any conquest of the dreamers' realm since time began—the future. Several Fiat 600s have been sold meanwhile in fact, even in the USA. Likewise other objects of design have gained ground, even those of Ulm provenance, the renowned Braun radio in particular. Dazzled by their vision of the future, people failed—despite all sociological zeal—to notice that this development concerned only a tiny percentage of the market: the only people buying belonged to the class that had long since devoted itself to the "fine arts," good taste, and the beet juice of contemporary lifestyle. In humanity's department store, Ulm has leased a stand in the Modernism department to serve a small and wholly unchanging clientele of not-all-too-angry young men and village schoolmarms. These are vaunted as the face of the future while people keep quiet about the other 97 percent of the population, whose natural need for varied ornamental and showpiece forms keeps the wheels of the economy turning.

Instead of succumbing to such gloom, people prefer to preoccupy themselves with a new theory, the theory of "human engineering." Every object requires a user. A stove is of little use without a cook. The actual cooking machinery might be said therefore to consist of cook-plus-stove. Cooking is easy with this combo. Anyone who builds such man-machine systems must recognize that humans are unalterable and machines are able to adapt; until now, misguided opinion held that man would surely learn in time how to handle the machine. And we put everything else—color theory, drawing theory, and perception—at the service of this learning curve. How much more easily we learn to pull a plug from a socket when the plug is ring-shaped; for the ring shape graphically invites us to insert a finger and to pull. Yet besides the metaphysical accomplishments of "human engineering" there are physiological ones, for instance, how we must cramp our fingers in order to grip a fork! Calloused, crippled hands are the result. So the grip research group is put into action. It studies the gripping operation, the act of lifting the edibles, the path followed to the facial food slot—and what is the result but a Modernist form of cutlery. And the latest fad is a typewriter keyboard with sufficient space for the long fingernails of the machine's better half. (Needless to mention that real "human engineering" in the USA is presently researching the adaptability of surgeons.)

But now, misfortune is fast approaching. The number of lecturers had declined rapidly in the meantime, and to such an extent that operations at the school were under threat. When the school administration embarked on self-sufficiency, retaining its recent graduates as teaching staff, the students went on the defensive. Their threat to sue the school without further ado, for non-fulfillment of the curriculum, proved highly effective; and it also shows how far things had gone by this point.

But it was not our intention to go into detail. Suffice to say, the rector's supporters shrank in number so drastically that his re-election was a matter of doubt, and he resigned so as to be on the safe side. This paved the way for a new solution. At the start of the school year (in October 1960), a new rectorship took office: the author Gerd Kalow, who became chairman, the Ulm native and nestor Friedel Vordemberge-Gildewart, and the mathematician Horst Rittel. The fresh start will prove difficult, perhaps more difficult even than founding the school was, for much initial enthusiasm and goodwill has evaporated. It will succeed only if the future remains in the foreground, not as a bizarre ideology but as a task of education. Two things are top priority: firstly, to clearly define and limit the spectrum of professional training offered in each of the four disciplines at Ulm and then to appoint a convincing staff.

Ulm justifies its existence solely by claiming to offer professional training courses that do not exist elsewhere. In those cases where it must compete with existing state institutions—"visual communication" (graphic design) is one such example—it is not up to standard. On the other hand and despite all idiosyncrasy it must not be allowed to produce a type of professional for which the production process has no use. The architecture faculty threatens to do precisely that. In our world with its division of labor, quite other professional training is required for the design of prefabricated construction elements than for the planning of settlements and urban districts, and their construction from prefabricated elements. It makes little sense to teach these two specialized areas to one and the same student. Anyone wishing to pursue the first profession would require a solid foundation in construction, which for various reasons is not available in Ulm; anyone wishing to pursue the second would need to be taught the modern methods of rationalization, construction site planning and logistics, installation, and much more besides. For prefabricated construction will succeed not on account of its ideological benefits but only if it proves economically viable.

At least in the other two disciplines, the "product formers" have no problem when it comes to finding employment. Demand for designers is high, and Ulm is still Europe's leading school of design. Almost all the work produced by students for their final exam is commissioned by industry, and graduates are assured thus a springboard. Nevertheless a new border must be drawn here, in particular to delimit that which virtually makes Ulm purely an inventors' school. When going through the students' final projects, it is striking to find that almost every one of them is distinguished first and foremost by a technical innovation, which is of course what students most enjoy, and it is gratifying also, so long as it proves fit for production. Yet when a technical twist overshadows design in practically every object, it does little to advance the cause of design per se. If, as in Ulm, we reproach entrepreneurs for allowing their "construction staff" also to pursue design, we cannot simultaneously train designers who wish only to construct things.

And, finally, the information department: if I am correctly informed, Bill's initial intention in setting up this department was to train critics for the industrial manufacturing sector. Later, a more general course aimed at copywriters came into being, whether for print advertising, PR, radio, TV, film, or whatever. In practice, these branches require both a broad general education and rigorous specialization. The upcoming generation assumes its role and possibly even becomes a "doctor of" by training on the job with the support of specialized technicians—photographers, typesetters, sound engineers, and so forth. In Ulm one can provide neither an adequate general education nor the skills and capacities required of a technician, and one must therefore ask oneself yet again, whether the profession created here actually fits into the existing division of labor. Whereby the issue of training for a run-of-the-mill copywriter is completely open-ended. That such a common profession can still be pursued today by a circuitous route and often owing to failure in another discipline is a waste of energy. Now that a lecturer in "information" has been appointed rector in Ulm, this course will presumably be restructured. Did not Gerd Kalow once call for a "poets' school"?

By the time this article goes to print, we may perhaps know more about the appointments the new rectorship will be obliged to make. Under the present circumstances, it will not be easy for anyone to make a binding and long-term commitment to Ulm. The overly exploitative methods pursued previously by Ulm are now making themselves felt. Word is out about the instability of conditions there, and about the fact that the Geschwister Scholl Foundation, the school's financial backer and hence also its adversary with regard to contractual appointments, does not maintain the requisite distance from school affairs. The situation on Ulm's Kuhberg accordingly forces everyone to sever important links with professional practice, with universities, and with a richly endowed library. We must hope nevertheless that the talent and idealism needed to take up such a teaching position will be found, along with the fighting spirit required for self-assertiveness. That is what talented students are waiting for.

Should Ulm manage to extricate itself from its sectarianism and intolerance, it will become a thoroughly indispensable institution: firstly, as a school, because an industrial product poses challenges of an interdisciplinary nature. It must be simultaneously functional, appealing, and marketable. The designer must receive an education that lies somewhere between technical training, the art academy, and a trade school. Where will he find that but in Ulm? And, secondly, as a place of reflection—for research into the powerful dynamics to which taste and hence also the desire to consume are subject is still in its early days. It must fuse sociological, economic, psychological, political, and technological findings. Ulm is the only institution that on the one hand addresses concrete design tasks and thus maintains contact with professional practice, and on the other fosters a keen awareness of the theory underpinning all such operations.

The Exhibition Medium (1965)

The nineteenth century endowed us with another major means of communication in addition to the press: the exhibition; the world exhibition, primarily, but also the regional variety, and trade fairs. Despite the subsequent invention of TV and radio, two further means to influence the masses, the exhibition seems not at all outdated. No other form of mass media but the exhibition draws the visitor into its own ambience and influences him for hours or even days on end, through all his senses and with a myriad of impressions. That this medium is used so rarely and with so little specific intent is due probably to its great expense, which generally cannot be borne even by states and has to be raised instead by the collective endeavor of heterogeneous interest groups.

The exhibition makes no secret of its origins in the nineteenth century, the era of exultant industrial progress and free world trade. Stylistically, behind its totally up-to-date façade, it still bears traces of its earliest days. The exhibition park is the "jardin anglais-chinois," an artificial, artful natural garden of the late revolutionary period, with temples and ruins as staffage. Exhibition venues themselves are extrapolations of such garden structures as glasshouses, orangeries, pleasure palaces, and follies.

The object of interest par excellence, however, was the exhibition content, which prompted in visitors both astonishment and an appreciation of progress: patriotic pride in the domestic industry's manufactured goods, cosmopolitan delight in the commercial wares and rarities from distant shores. A hint of the atmosphere of those world and regional exhibitions of old greets us to this day perhaps, when we visit the older zoological gardens.

At these early exhibitions the object itself was the issue: the fact that it existed, that it could be manufactured, was the sole source of interest. No one asked: For whom? To what end? At what price? It was the World Exhibition that made rubber famous. Everyone marveled at the little unbreakable elastic boxes made from the resin of a tree. The architect Semper of course lost no time in proposing how they might be ornamented. No one guessed that they were not luxury goods at all, but the premise of a revolution in transport and lifestyle. Yet luxury goods were, initially, the crux of this nascent era of invention: the well-to-do gentleman treated himself to a motorcar, a gramaphone, or a ride in an airplane. The great majority of the population did not come into contact with such products; or, if at all, then only on the assembly line. Agriculture and small and medium manufacturing were not yet mechanized, or only rarely, and barely.

With the two wars the situation changed. The military demanded new vehicles and means of communication and industrial capacity was expanded in order to produce them en masse. Inventive minds were no longer applied only to objects themselves but also to their rational manufacture. Exploitation of the new advances enabled an ever broader public to be supplied with industrial goods ever more cheaply. Mechanization continued a-pace now, in all sectors of the economy: the small and medium enterprises in particular were compelled to rationalize in order to retain a competitive edge. So everyone now comes into contact with mechanization, regardless of his social standing. In parallel, a perfected global traffic system assures the availability of all conceivable raw goods.

The object as such accordingly now loses in interest. The invention alone no longer suffices to make an exhibition. With the advent of automation, machines have grown more alike: gray-painted boxes with content that is hard to understand. They can do more and yet they are much less imposing than the steam engines exhibited in London at the World Exhibition of 1851. One of the most popular exhibits at the Swiss Exhibition of 1939 was an electrical charge one meter in length. Doubtless one could exhibit a charge twice the length—but would this expensive demonstration bring home to the public the issues then at stake, namely efficient sources of energy, the methodical exploitation of local energy sources coupled with the simultaneous protection of the landscape's natural equilibrium, and the systematic development of new energy sources? It is this, which shifts the focus, from the object itself to consideration of the principle, from the machine itself to how it is used in the workplace; from the product to productivity, to its use, its influence on lifestyle; from the new vehicle to traffic problems, from the mowing machine to the rationalization of agriculture, from medicine to hygiene.

This shift to abstraction was the basis of changes in the art of the exhibition and exhibition technology. How should one portray abstract themes? How does one display in an exhibition, things it would be better to read in a book? Is the exhibition still an apt medium? Is the exhibition as a source of information still up-to-date? Anyone wishing to launch himself into the inevitably expensive adventure of a major exhibition is confronted with all of these questions.

Not only problems and hence potential exhibition themes are increasingly abstract but also the style of the means of representation. The non-figurative nature of the things to be portrayed perfectly suited modern graphic designers. After the Second World War the applied arts broadly returned to those stylistic means created by the De Stijl movement and the Bauhaus in the 1920s. People worked preferably with script, symbols, and vacant spaces; the object itself was taboo, revealing itself now only in the distorting mirror of a form of photography intent on creating the most rigorously stylized effects with contrasts and light. The exhibition itself, the way it was hung, served only to emphasize how far removed it was from the figurative. And exhibits were mounted not on the exhibition venue itself but on special, emphatically flexible scaffolding, which heightened awareness throughout of the permanence of the building and the ephemerality of the exhibition. As elegant and aesthetically gratifying this type of exhibition may have been for the connoisseur, it ill-served its true purpose, which is to impart information. The viewer was confronted with a dual difficulty: he had not only to understand an abstract theme but also to decrypt an encoded means of communication. It is therefore no wonder that the public did not warm to this type of perfect and yet incomprehensible exhibition, and that visitor numbers left much to be desired.

There was only one way the turnaround could go: back to reality. Not to the reality of the themes but at least to that of the means of the exhibition. The first step to be taken concerned the exhibition architecture: the only very recently so meticulously emphasized separation of the exhibition venue and the exhibition structure was revoked in favor of a single entity that we describe as "environmental." In the style of similar experiments in the visual arts, André Bloc's *sculptures habitacles*, for example, the visitor was to be completely surrounded by and immersed in the means of representation. A formally rich and in technical terms more flexible architecture introduced this movement.

With regard to exhibition content, this return to reality took the form of the "environmental" exhibition in three different ways, as far as we can see: firstly there is the attempt to integrate artworks in a way such as to charge spaces with atmosphere and turn them into channels of communication. One such space at the Italia '61 [trade fair] was the Venetian Pavilion, which offered nothing but a beautifully conceived architectonic ambiance, which, thanks to its cascade-like chandeliers of Murano glass, walls of colorful glass mosaic, and sparkling water in an ornamental pond, was meant to be vaguely redolent of the lagoon city itself. Admittedly, more explicit allusions and portrayals are conceivable in artistic translation too yet the information in the case of this exhibition technique always reaches its limits at the point where modern art, also that of the more figurative variety, ceases to be "representative;" we can no longer really stand the work of art as an objective message. The artist therefore strives to use objects symbolically, as they were used for example in the "General Section" of the Swiss Exhibition of 1964: a sober railroad station clock in one atmospheric space stands for emigration; a surreal, strangely ticking machine is a symbol of parliamentary democracy; a glimmering lightweight frame of anodized metal is a vision of industrial cities of the future.

The second possibility for a return to reality lies in the use of modern reproduction techniques, both film and audio. The disadvantage of this, in terms of exhibition technology, is that the visitor must be lured into—and locked inside—a dark information cell. However, once he has landed in this trap he can use his eyes and ears to garner information. Two variations present themselves, here too.

One of them aims for the total illusion of reality, which most closely approximates Walt Disney's Circarama. This option soon comes up against a new limit: the total illusion is as banal as reality itself. The future looks more promising for the more rigorously styled solutions: visual compositions on several screens, with diverse plots, standing projections, music, and explanation. The possibilities revealed here are not yet exhausted—far from it.

The third type of representation is difficult to describe, but with a stroke of luck it proves the most successful. It is the attempt to alienate the actual presence of the object itself in a way such that reality becomes transparent and interesting. We can draw on an example from the Swiss Exhibition of 1964, namely the office equipment concert composed by Rolf Liebermann and based on an idea of the architect R. Gutmann, of Zurich. Over one hundred pieces of office equipment and other sources of sound in modern life, such as the alarm clocks, railroad station bells, telephones, and signals that accompany our everyday lives, are all of a sudden harmonized in a rhythmic concert that we will never forget and indeed will hear again persistently, every time we step into an office. For this kind of alienation no recipe exists—a brainwave alone does the trick; but certainly, the greatest potential for the art of the exhibition lies here, and will do also in the future.

Yet not even all this can solve the problem of how to communicate abstract issues. These usually consist not in a single fact but in a sequence or network of thoughts that must be understand in terms of thought "processes" or "passages." To do so requires sequences of spaces, sequences of different moods. A spatial sequence of this sort was shown for example at the Milan Triennale of 1964: the Italian section, in its endeavor to depict the problem of leisure, developed the dubious pleasure of a weekend at the seaside. A first space, pleasantly lit and acoustically enveloped, symbolized the lost and yearned-for harmony of the natural way of life. There followed a dark corridor of terror, with traffic lights, car taillights, and a dissonant concert of car horns: the return journey, there and back. Then came a space that demonstrated the unbroken majesty of the ocean and an encounter therewith. A wildly gesticulating figure points to the ocean, which is represented by an evenly revolving drum. But behind the backdrop to this drum, through which the visitor strides, unfolds the other side of the story: having fled the world of consumerism, the short-changed man of leisure comes upon a new world of consumerism, temptation, and pillage, upon the whole assortment of so superfluous yet seemingly indispensable equipment, from the diving mask to the private yacht.

The thought process is comprehensible in its sequence and also impressively portrayed. But what space, what staging it takes to impart this simple deliberation! And, moreover, the thought is one-dimensional: it must be followed step-by-step in the right direction. A viewer gone astray won't understand it. Objections, parallel considerations, variations are ruled out. There arises hence the new demand for multidimensional sequence, firstly, in order that the viewer might go around at will, but also in order to combine several thought processes. The fashion pavilion at the Italia '61 in Turin attempted this. In the large hall the exhibition content was laid out in the form of a checkerboard. The themes theater, sport, fashion, interior design, tourism, etc., were laid out in the longitudinal axis, in a temporal sequence. If the visitor strode through the hall lengthways, he oriented himself to a branch of social existence, to tourism, for example, and its development from 1860 to 1960. If the visitor strode through the hall on its latitudinal axis, he garnered a cross-section of all the aspects of social existence in a particular decade, for example that of the fin de siècle. The industrial pavilion at the Swiss Exhibition of 1964 goes a step further, because its form derives from a spiral. Its outer contour was meant to show the workplace in manufacturing, the inner contours the impact of industry on civilization, specifically for the worker, the consumer, and, further in, for the part of the country in which the respective industry is located, while the very core of the spiral is devoted to portraying the problems and limits of industrialization, nationwide. In the curves of the spiral the visitor sees one and the same problem occurring in all industries whereas, if he cuts across the curves' radius, he learns about all the problems of a single industry. The exhibitors failed to fill in all the sections of this ambitious program; yet they nonetheless made clear that the workplace is now the locus of industrial progress, and there was a warning in the inner contours that rash investment has secondary consequences. At least it served to demonstrate the exhibition's potential as a vehicle of conceptual development.

All this has consequences in turn for exhibition architecture. For as long as we can recall, exhibition architecture has stood between the poles of a large exhibition hall with flexible fittings and a temporary pavilion structure adapted to the exhibits in question. As we have shown, modern exhibition design's "environmental" and spectacular concept really calls for individual buildings that are adapted to their content or even fuse with it in a single work of art. On the other hand anyone who has a large hall and finds himself thus instantly relieved of sticky issues, such as putting a roof over his head, protection from the elements, and the whole matter of statics, is freer than anyone else simply to get on with his work. For the same reasons one might opt for a large hall with the maximum possible open-plan space within it, such as Pier Luigi Nervi built in Turin in 1961.

At the Swiss Exhibition of 1964 in Lausanne an in-between solution was tested, so to speak. The exhibition directors called it the *multicellulaire* approach. The buildings were temporary and were dissembled in October 1964. Nevertheless, unlike at earlier exhibitions they were not adapted in every case to the content exhibited within them: the agricultural exhibition is neither a farmhouse nor a little village; the interior of a local household is not shown in a sample house; there is no "Atomium" and no "talking" architecture. Rather, the buildings had a logic and an aesthetic all of their own; they were flexible and *multicellulaire* simply because this made them more adaptable to the exhibition content than a large, permanent hall can ever be. And the last word about this experiment has not yet been spoken, although at least two objections have been raised: for one, that if the ephemeral, flexible building type is to be stable then it should be no less sturdy than the permanent building type, and that the modular "building block" systems used in the former case are not always quite as freely adaptable as people like to think. And the other objection is that architecture, even of the provisional sort, is much more cumbersome than the usual exhibit, so much so that its full and complete integration is ultimately impossible. Given our present level of technology we must set about creating a building two years before we tackle its interior design—and who on earth has a totally conclusive exhibition concept ready to go at that early stage?

One final objection picks up an idea mentioned at the outset, above: there is a limit to the amount of information a person is able to absorb. The visitor can deal only with small doses of new impressions; the fatigue that exhibitions cause us is brain fatigue, not leg fatigue, even though we feel it in our legs. So the visitor yearns for the crutches that all things familiar comprise, the familiar things that help him go on, and that also put across to him unfamiliar, unknown things. And the greater the proportion of unknown things, the harder time he has of it. This too must be considered if architectural exteriors wish to display innovative and free forms that challenge a person's cognitive abilities. Neither the best idea nor the most impressive effect relieves us of our obligation to follow those pedagogic and information technology rules which alone make the exhibition an effective means of communication.

documenta urbana—What Could That Mean? (1982)

The idea of complementing the documenta in Kassel by holding another art fair there, the documenta urbana, stemmed from Arnold Bode, but his notion of the form it might take changed repeatedly over time. It was, however, driven always by the same major concern, namely that the documenta, which is meanwhile an institution in Kassel, will not survive unless it puts down strong roots in the city and among the local population. His ideas were initially oriented to that which used to be known in Germany as "Kunst am Bau"[1] then later came to encompass artistic happenings or installations in neighborhoods and on public squares, in the city's large landscaped parks, or at the Hercules monument on the Octagon. Bode personally came to believe that a documenta urbana might contribute to improving the quality of life in Kassel, either by offering artists' residencies in studio houses or pursuing exemplary construction projects that throw a spanner in the works of routine urban planning and construction.

This was the springboard for all that is demonstrated today under the single title "documenta urbana:" that routines must be interrupted, eyes re-opened, and the spectrum of ideas enriched. Almost forty years have passed since Kassel was destroyed and blame for the current state of the city can therefore no longer be put solely at the Allied bombers' door. And if the problems we face today were

1 [The "art in architecture" program, often a city ordinance, obliges major federal development projects to donate a percentage of their overall budget to the production and installation of public art.]

created in part by planning and reconstruction then we will not solve them by holding onto the tools of conventional urban planning and conventional development.

But if planning is unable to help us solve the problems that planning has sown then we should not delude ourselves that art might come to our aid, or at least not directly. Given the power of the construction industry "Kunst am Bau" is an obsolete concept: members of the public pass by art in public space with as much indifference as if it were a bare concrete wall. The hasty tags or terse prose of a graffiti artist have more impact. So, would spontaneous action prove helpful? Although we would prefer to spare ourselves the embarrassment of hearing local residents spout their opinions on art under professional instruction, let us make room for the subversion in spontaneity, for the public in public affairs.

At documenta 7, two incomparable actions are to be carried out under the name "documenta urbana." Incomparable for the simple reason that one of them was official from the very start, received funding, was destined for the public eye, and will indeed be carried out in public. It can be viewed at a designated conservation area in Kassel, the Dönche, on a scale of 1:1, in concrete, wood, and glass; and it is already partly inhabited. The other action "documenta urbana—sichtbar machen" (documenta urbana—making visible) was the outcome of a seminar at the University of Kassel: participation was voluntary and free of charge, and a public performance, if it takes place at all, will be short-lived. It is available for viewing solely in the form of design proposals, plans, and a printed catalog. The relationship of the two "documentae urbanae" is thus that of the paper tiger to the concrete cat.

Yet all their differences notwithstanding these two expressions of the idea "documenta urbana" do represent two opportunities, two extreme opportunities for intervention, be this in the form of an exhibition, setting an example, mobilizing public opinion, or prompting discussion. The “Dönche documenta urbana” stands in the tradition of those permanent sites created for exhibition purposes, which is to say in the tradition of the Garden City Hellerau, the Werkbund housing estates in Stuttgart, Vienna, Basel, Breslau, and Prague, and the IBA Berlin architecture competitions as exemplified most strikingly by the Hansa district and the Friedrichsstadt. Kassel’s perpetuation of this tradition consists in the densification of its suburban zones and hence is a measure to prevent its city margins being parceled out solely with single-family residential neighborhoods in mind. With this doubtless topical choice of issue—one that is to be dealt with extensively in a special catalog (*Die Stadt* of August 1982, a magazine of the “Neue Heimat” consortium)—Kassel is contributing only indirectly to solving the problems of the inner city. More specifically, it is cleaving still to the ruling valid to date, namely that when it comes to housing developers, designated building land belonging to the city is non-designated building land whereas non-designated building land is designated building land.

This is why the “documenta urbana” seminar convened ad hoc at the University of Kassel considered it necessary to carry out an action that would serve to shift the balance at least a little in favor of the inner city. The Deutsche Werkbund was the first to publish the idea, in its journal *Werk und Zeit,* Nr. 2, 1980. The outcome of the action was published in the catalog (Issue 2 of *Schriften der documenta urbana*)

The broader framework of this action is quite modest: a selection was made of fifteen points in the inner city that represent problem zones inasmuch as they are problematic in terms of urban planning, traffic and transport, urban development, and the economy. The fifteen problematic zones were documented in a catalog that was then dispatched to artists, architects, planners, and educational institutions. We requested all recipients of the catalog to submit contributions—ideas on each of these fifteen points—but did not launch a competition, since we hoped that the sheer number of contributions would broaden perspectives on these fifteen points. And so, although neither an award nor implementation was foreseen, we received over one hundred contributions, all of which we published in the said second issue in this series. So this action, above and beyond the actual conceptual content it prompted, is proof of how much is possible even without recourse to financial resources or organizational (administrative) instances, as well as of people's willingness to participate voluntarily in actions of this sort. The themes of the "documenta urbana—making visible" action were premised on the following three ideas.

- The task of a "documenta urbana" is to improve the environment not only in residential areas but also in places of work, consumption, administrative business, transport, and downtown leisure, and on the routes leading to all of these. To focus design capacities solely on the issue of housing would leave the inner city high and dry.
- One cannot improve the everyday life of the urban dweller if it remains invisible. We remain blind to the shortcomings of the inner cities because they have become part and parcel of our everyday lives and therefore seem to us to be immutable. What we need to create, first of all, is a "sense of everyday life" that will once again raise awareness of the monstrosities of our routine and put them up for debate.
- The designs aspired to in this first endeavor cannot be "solutions;" for it is precisely such "solutions" that have put the inner city in the state it is now in. We were surprised and pleased to note, when examining the contributions submitted, that not a single one of them was a technically feasible "neat solution" comprising a one-track approach to the problem while simultaneously bringing other, worse problems in its wake. Thus all the participants grasped that the technician's "effective" interventions do not lead to the

goal. All of the designs submitted were proposals that, if they could be realized at all then only for a short while, as monuments quasi, in order to make a point.

A word must therefore be said here, about the possible use of the contributions or rather about what we can learn from them. The contributions should help break the circle that has always led our cities directly from the diagnosis to the solution and thereby always created new problems. The vicious circle is to be broken, the circle that says: "There is a shortage of parking spaces, so we must build some more. The parking spaces subsequently block the access roads, which must therefore be widened. Then the widened access roads foster an increase in the number of vehicles, and so we have to build more parking spaces … and so on." But what is the alternative to this type of technical solution based on the equation: diagnosis = solution? Perhaps this: to plan minimal interventions that, when undertaken not individually but in strategic combination, improve living conditions in the urban environment.

To Expect Quick Results from the Planned Reform Is to Underestimate the Braking Forces (1972)

The present turmoil at German universities is a part of worldwide protests by young people, the greatest intellectual event since 1945. But it is also a consequence of the specific circumstances of German universities, just as student protests in other countries were sparked by the prevailing shortcomings there.

The start of the protest movement at universities is often portrayed as if barely a thing had changed from 1950 to 1967 and then, like a bolt out of the blue, students and assistants felt all of a sudden dissatisfied with their lot. Yet although the structure of the universities has remained the same, a great deal has changed in recent years, first and foremost the ratio of students and assistants to professors: and that this change was not underpinned by a reform of the university hierarchy is nothing less than fundamental negligence on the part of the authorities. Thus the tenured professor found himself promoted to a position in which he was often out of his depth, in terms of organization as well as of his professional or even personal abilities. His bias, of a sort kindly tolerated in the paternal professor of old, now prompts resistance to the unanswerable powers that be holding sway over institutions and research funding.

And there is another matter too. Since the Second World War, young and middle-aged European intellectuals have been left-wing—except for those in German-speaking countries. It was only a matter of time as to when the retrorocket of the German intelligentsia would run out of metaphysical steam. It did so at the end of the Cold War and German youth henceforth drifted on in zero gravity—one need only read Habermas's study of students' political abstinence and ignorance in 1961.

The momentous revolt of international youth had an explosive impact on this state of affairs. Yet, spectacular riots aside, it must be noted also that the timing was right for young people in the German-speaking countries to join forces at last with their international peers ... Sooner or later they had to learn the codes and content through which young people elsewhere on the globe were communicating with one another.

Concerning the end of the protests and whether lectures or structural improvements might bring it about, my response is as follows: the student protests, a part of worldwide youth's growing sociopolitical awareness, will cause upheaval for quite some time to come. That students should be given new course content, also of the Marxist variety, is self-evident in my opinion. But such course content will not spell the end of the protests.

More decisive than course content are teaching methods, selection criteria, exam regulations, and so forth, which is to say, the university's internal structures. Yet to expect quick results from the "planned reform" is to underestimate the braking forces. In our experience, progressive university regulations do not permeate the university and it is also as clear as day that even young forces very quickly make use of the old jog trot once appointed to a professorial chair. Also in our experience, progressive impulses run aground on old rules and the legislators' traditional mind-sets. A slow process of transformation is underway yet, if it is not to come to a premature halt, the student protests will, and indeed must, propel it along.

From Design Academicism to the Treatment of Wicked Problems (1973)

However great the changes imposed by pioneers of modern architecture may have been, and however great the impact of the achievements of the 1920s and 30s on the whole of contemporary architecture, professional teaching practice has remained unchanged. The relationship of professor and student has remained the traditional relationship of master and apprentice, and the students' tasks continue, as always, to be those of abstracting from actual implementation: a case of designs for the desk drawer, as folk of the last century used to say. Conventional design training continues to set the task it has always set, namely that of creating a specific building on a real or imagined terrain. In the course of the "Lehrcanapé,"[1] we called such tasks the "Youth Center on Paradeplatz." In the case of such designs it is assumed the terrain is available, that the purpose of the building is correct, and that both the client and prospective owners unanimously welcome the proposed building program. Land prices, traffic congestion, urgency, and profit yield are all problem areas that remain outside the scope of such design proposals. The student is educated in an atmosphere of abstraction, at a remove from the real world, which means he is in for a bumpy landing later, on the hard facts of reality.

1 [Lehrcanapé: the "professorial sofa," as opposed to the usual professorial chair, was the name given to a temporary professorship at the ETH Zurich, held jointly by the architect Rolf Gutmann and the sociologist Lucius Burckhardt, from 1969 to 1973. Cf. also Silvan Blumenthal, *Das Lehrcanapé: Lucius Burckhardt und das Architektenbild an der ETH Zürich 1970–1973*, Basel 2010]

Any student of the conventional design method learns to take a "trial and error" approach. He endeavors, in one way or another, to put down on paper the task entrusted to him, and after a while he fails, or assistants point out the non-feasibility of his approach, whereupon he tries out a new one. What distinguishes the master from the student is the former's so-called experience. Only rarely does the master embark on paths that do not lead to a goal. The student also takes note of this experience, and instinctively weighs up which paths are relatively sure to lead to goals without demanding too great an effort.

The design method born of experience born of intuition conceals from the designer even essential features of the decision-making process. One scribbles a few lines on paper and dozens of questions are already resolved: site development, the number of stories, perhaps therefore the building materials, and even many things inside the building, which reveal themselves only later to be design constraints. The design proposal fails because a disproportionate amount of time and skill is expended from this point onwards on relatively unimportant individual factors. Finally, the semester nears its end, the pace of design increases, and dozens of decisions are once again pushed through in secret. The conventional architect behaves the same, particularly when it comes to competitions. Major decisions are to be found in a certain sense in two pockets: hidden at the beginning in a paper napkin, along with the supposed brainwave one suddenly brought home; and, at the end, in the bustle of work that precedes project submission.

In the 1960s, the growing complexity of the planning and construction fields made a new approach to training indispensable, and led to a phase we call "enlightened academicism." This posits that a design be premised on a prior phase of analysis. Enlightened academicism believes that a methodical approach is assured by integrating the following in the decision-making process, in an order expressed in German by the acronym ZASPAK: goal identification, analysis, synthesis, planning, implementation, and control. This approach overlooks two prerequisites of its successful application:

- Goals must be identifiable from the outset. However, in most practical exercises the real goals come to light only during the design process.
- Synthesis is required so as to incorporate the insights gained from analysis during the planning process. However, the planning methods taught presently at our universities do not demonstrate how such a large amount of data may be synthesized and incorporated in the planning process.

  Enlightened academicism led thus to the now familiar two-part task definition. Let's say, the semester theme is the theater in Hintertüpflingen. The analysis phase serves to determine what the city of Hintertüpflingen most urgently needs; then the design phase proposes development of a railroad yard in Hintertüpflingen in order to obtain a platform on which a theater can be built.

A Weltanschauung underpins the "enlightened academicism" method: the image of a harmonious world whose problems can be solved through technological intervention. This is the world of tame problems such as we learned to solve in school: the Greeks are philosophers, the Romans statesmen, the Germans belligerent, and the math teacher's sums correct. The laws that rule this world are supposedly eternal: whatever we learned in the past, we can apply to the future. Basically, if we had Laplace's cosmopolitan esprit we could predict the future completely. Yet we lack such a wealth of information, and so restrict ourselves to "essentials."

However, to restrict ourselves to essentials, and to those facts we currently find most relevant is precisely what has put an almost unbearable strain on the resilience and tolerance capacity of our real environment. The problems and limitations concealed by the prosperity euphoria of the 1960s are now erupting on our horizon at an alarming speed.

In light of the above, we consider the premises in which conventional and "enlightened-conventional" academic work is rooted to be fatal. While schools demand that a solution be found for a clearly defined problem, real life demands that the architect map out the scope of problematic issues himself. What he must learn therefore, is to deal with unsolvable, "wicked" problems. It is a mistake to imagine that one's experience and intuition are the best guides in this uncertain field. Methods do exist, in any case, also for dealing with wicked problems. The study of such methods seems to us all the more urgent, given that both the architect's influence, and its impact on policy-making bodies obliged to take decisions on lofty goals, are intensifying exponentially. This is the reason we named our approach, not "project training"—for conservative academics too could lay claim to that term—but rather, "problem-oriented training."

Problem-oriented training and methodical design

The "Canapé" defined problem-oriented training as a form of teaching focused on one or several issues of such complexity as to be representative of real professional issues, as well as on solutions that ideally evince an integrated, interdisciplinary approach.

This approach to training—and moreover, this goal of training—served quasi as a lens through which to consider all other associated goals and measures, be these endeavors to carry out methodological design, or to handle problems within a team comprised of teachers and students. This appraisal of professional design training led away from the popular creative design topics such as a house on a slope, or a weekend lakeside retreat, to more comprehensive issues of sociopolitical relevance, which could not be solved by construction alone. These were, for example, the problems of education and training for students and professionals.

Certainly, one result of this approach was that students at the time received no training in "classical" design techniques. They were confronted rather, with problems whose solution demanded much broader understanding than is required when implementing a structural solution to a spatial program. They were obliged to acquire a problem-solving frame of mind, for this put them in a position to solve problems that could be defined more precisely solely through a step-by-step approach. This capacity to solve undefined problems, which is to say, the capacity to collate, to process, and to apply relevant information in order to solve a problem, we called the "problem-solving frame of mind." Certainly, students were initially overwhelmed by this kind of "design," because it was very difficult for them to correctly categorize the wealth of information and to evaluate individual data with proper regard for the problem at hand. This is evident from the data collated during the far-ranging analysis phases, which was much too extensive, dealt with unspecified issues, and thus later simply impeded a project's progress. Yet one can still assume that the frame of mind fostered here enabled students to deal with an issue and to arrive at a result, without knowledge of the habitual solution strategies.

The "Canapé" considered that its task was to heighten students' appreciation of the fact that social problems cannot be solved simply by a design proposal, or by fully implementing a construction project, as well as of the fact that planning, if it is ever to produce comprehensive solutions to identifiable problems, must encourage the formulation of alternative goals. For this reason we tried to proceed methodically, that is, to use systematic reduction to generate the alternative solutions likely to attain previously formulated goals.

To this end, and in addition to the regular semester schedule, a methodology seminar was launched in order to teach students the rudiments of design methodology The seminar was divided into two parts:

- The study of various design and evaluation techniques
- Application of these techniques to selected test cases

It must first be clarified what is actually meant by planning. We premised our approach on A. Faludi's definition: planning entails the application of systematic methods to the task of formulating social goals and their translation into concrete action programs. This definition provided a springboard for the presentation and discussion of different types of design. This was followed by an assessment of evaluation techniques, their effectiveness, and their validity. The subjectivity of evaluation systems was the central problem. On which factors does the result of an evaluation depend; how can it be manipulated; and how much value should be attributed to it when deciding in favor of, or against an alternative? Given that most problems in the field of planning are heuristic search tasks—hence wicked problems whose solution depends crucially on the personal value system of the person addressing them—the evaluation discussion was broad in scope.

The first phase revealed that three key insights seem to have been important for students:

1. Since we are dealing in the planning field with wicked problems, it is important to make the problem-solving process transparent, which is to say, easily comprehensible. Various techniques and methods can be used to meet this demand for transparency; all of them involve the systematic production of diversity, as well as the systematic reduction of this diversity through the evaluation procedure.
2. The goal of all planning is to eliminate disruptions. To eliminate such disruptions requires a very specific frame of mind, a

problem-solving frame of mind. It is a process that begins with identification of the disruptive factor and ends with an actual state of affairs, namely the "Ist-Zustand" (status quo), which is the fulfillment of the "Soll-Zustand" (target state). This process is ongoing, because the demands made on the built environment are constantly changing, and the limited adaptability of the built environment constantly gives rise to disruptions. Anything built for a specific purpose (a school, a hospital, etc.), is generally already outdated the day it opens.

3. Planning inevitably has a crucial political dimension. Every evaluation gives expression to a system of values held by an individual or a group. To create an objective evaluation system is impossible. For this reason, evaluation systems should not be prescriptive—in the sense of laying down universal laws—but should be used only to support an argument.

The second phase—application of techniques to various test cases—was unfortunately not the success we had hoped for, as students found this approach rather dry and only reluctantly took part in these exercises. It was planned to conduct a series of smaller test cases, so as to be able to apply all that had been learned within the lecture framework. Some seminar participants did work on the first two test-case exercises, albeit quite half-heartedly. These were:

- Exercise 1—To evaluate three different three-room apartments
- Exercise 2—To design an apartment building for a specific context, in line with the AIDA[2] method

Unfortunately, the results of their work are available in fragmented form only, and therefore cannot be documented.

2 [The AIDA Reaction Model created by E. K. Strong in 1925 posits that the sales process has four phases — Attention, Interest, Desire and Action.]

On the Difficulty of Teaching Modesty (1979)

If we were looking to name the trend that shapes our work at the faculty of architecture and urban and regional planning, and likewise the work of some lecturers and students in the neighboring faculty of industrial design, then "poor design" would do. As in the case of certain representatives of Arte povera, Modernism's whimsical heirs, this poor design does not consist in reducing everything to simple forms and straight lines but in the use of cheap and widely available everyday forms and materials. It goes without saying that poor design of this sort, especially that of students of regional planning, can be integrated in ecological programs. Agricultural and leisure landscapes alike should be sustainable, which is to say, every cycle occurring on them should be perennial, and neither irreparably deplete substances nor cause them to seep into the groundwater.

A second reason for "poor design" is the large scale at which we sometimes work. It is probably an abuse of the term landscape to speak of "urban landscape" with regard to how green zones might be viably integrated in a neighborhood. In North Hessen however, the region where our university is situated, the primary problem is not overpopulation but the shrinking population, not overuse but wastelands. The pressing matter here, therefore, is to prevent the deterioration of large-scale landscapes, and to maintain them as attractive locations for tourism, leisure, and future uses.

Nor do we deny, ultimately, that our poor planning is in the final instance also an artistic position, however ambiguous and paradoxical thoughts on this last point may be: as paradoxical as the non-utilitarian kitchen garden of Rousseau's Héloise.[5]

The difficulty, in pedagogic terms, is the constant frustration of the student who is not supposed to express himself. How quick it is to conjure the superficial charms of the common garden styles. And how much more effort it takes to proceed in such a way that nothing is yet done, and the users, or nature itself, can still do their part.

Instead of drawing up snazzy designs, therefore, students and indeed we ourselves must concern ourselves with three bothersome sciences: firstly with the science that has an answer in store for the question: "What grows all on its own?"—namely plant sociology. And then there's the question of what people get up to in everyday life, and what their places of work are, whereby we take father's garden at home, the housewife's whereabouts, and children's games to be everyday work and places of work. The science in this case is a sort of rubbed-up-the-wrong-way sociology.

And, finally, there are the sciences of agricultural exploitation: not the official agricultural science, which is geared to maximum yields, nor the nascent alternative means of production, which we approve of whereas farmers do not, but rather, knowledge of the everyday husbandry practices of the modern farmer, who faces certain economic constraints yet also acts in keeping with certain ideas, traditions, and recommendations made by certain third parties, which is to say, a science that lies somewhere between agricultural sociology and agricultural technology.

But if the goal is a design, a plan, however poor, then the image to the rear—the backdrop, so to speak, that landscape is—must be analyzed and discussed. Otherwise we'll wind up like the conventional landscape designers and planners, quite a number of whom are underway in these parts and entrusted with great tasks, since they

3 [Jean-Jacques Rousseau: *Julie ou La Nouvelle Héloise—Lettres de Deux Amants*, Vol. 4, 11th letter]

are permitted to produce landscapes. Opencast mining for brown coal (lignite) is common in the North Hessen region and all that remains once deposits are depleted is lunar landscapes. The task at hand, therefore, is to transform these depleted areas back into landscape and to organize opencast mining wherever it newly occurs in a way such that the future landscape there develops more positively. It now appears that these new artificial landscapes are oriented to images of the *locus amoenus*, the "charming place," such as established agriculture or agroforestry provide. So, with subsidies from the mining and forestry sectors, it is possible now to create at the former opencast mines precisely those landscapes now deteriorating elsewhere on account of the economic constraints under which agriculture must operate.

In our endeavor to define what landscape is we organized two seminars, two years apart. Both seminars were devoted first and foremost to making a scientific record of a landscape, which is to say, we examined plant sociology, usage histories, climatology, and soil science. In these respects the two seminars were identical. But in addition, each group set up a working group on "landscape aesthetics," each to tackle a different issue.

Our first seminar took place in Riede, a village that has, like any average German village, a local landowner with a castle who practices agriculture on a larger scale as well as some farmers who do so on a medium scale and some villagers who commute to jobs elsewhere and till their fields and gardens, if at all, merely for supplementary income.

The "aesthetics" working group established in this village an "aesthetically optimal" walk that led whoever undertook it to the *locus amoenus.* From this charming place—the lime tree at the spot one leaves the village behind, the entrance to the woods, the rise with a panoramic view, the melancholy of the barren place, the satisfaction exuded by the fertile and well-tended place—from all such spots we

Lucius Burckhardt and Paul-Armand Gette make preparations for "The Completely Straight Walk," a seminar held on Mount Hoher Meissner in 1978. Photo: Annemarie Burckhardt

distill our ideal images. We invest all such spots with poetry and painting, and we try to derive the walker's satisfaction from the difference between the anticipated ideal and the actual look of the spots, as found. As for theory, we draw on the teachings of topoi in poetry, such as Ernst Robert Curtius once laid down for medieval times; and as our resident expert we had taken along Bazon Brock, whose book "Ästhetik als Vermittlung"[4] the students read.

On the second excursion, which took us to Mount Hoher Meissner, we were accompanied by the French artist Paul-Armand Gette. The Meissner posed a much more complex aesthetic problem than Riede village, in particular owing to the fact that it prompts much greater expectations in the visitor and fulfills them much less. Geo-

4 [Bazon Brock, *Ästhetik als Vermittlung. Arbeitsbiographie eines Generalisten* (Aesthetics as Education), Cologne 1977.]

graphically, it offers a forested basalt peak and an extensive plateau. The very name Meissner fosters two emotional expectations in the German visitor: Meissner is the setting of popular fairy tales, specifically of the pond of "Frau Holle," Old Mother Frost; and it was on the Meissner that the "Jugendbewegung"[5] assembled in 1913, an at the time still politically unaligned protest wave that was later to splinter into right-wing and left-wing extremist factions. The "High" in the name "High Meissner" stems from the Jugendbewegung. Lastly, the Meissner, which is a designated natural landmark and also enjoys the protection of some enthusiastic civic initiatives, is faced with three interventions.

A great deal of brown coal was mined hereabouts for decades and although that's now past history there are rich deposits to be mined still on the Meissner peak. Secondly, NATO has installed towers on the Meissner, which are visible from afar; and for the third and last intervention, the Meissner has tourism itself to thank: access to its peak, which at times has to welcome a great number of visitors, is now assured by extensive road networks, parking lots, well-marked hiking paths, inns, and, astonishingly, adventure playgrounds. Efforts made by the forest administration to replant the area in order to hide the scars left by opencast mining can likewise be described as an intervention.

This time, with Paul-Armand Gette as our guide and inspired by the students' ideas, we did not go in search of the "charming place" but were prescribed locations instead. We followed the geological section on which the soil science group had worked and treated each of its drill holes as a potential *locus amoenus*. A second phase of the study consisted in making two different sections of the same bit of landscape: the artist's section, the line of which snakes its way across

5 [German Youth Movement]

hills and thickets, each time tracing a tolerably charming image; and the surveyor's section, a straight one, which first followed the central axis between two forest margins and was then continued geometrically. Accidental positions on these two sections came about owing to the appearance and disappearance of mountain ranges and thickets. As we were dealing here with an area aesthetically under the supervision of the forestry department, we also attempted to depict its future composition: we included in our drawings the trees as they would look after a period of normal growth and saw that the forest department's replanting program will drown out the natural composition of alder and willow shrubs. — At the students' suggestion, the landscapes thus gained should be compiled as an "anti-brochure" for the Meissner: in analogy to the local tourism board's publication, which aims to boost tourism, the anti-brochure would contain images of the landscape that, while genuine, would be less likely to evoke the charming place than to mysteriously frighten off visitors ...

This brochure has not yet been produced however. But the thought given to the project sufficed to show that Mount Meissner's truly charming landscapes, those that actually provide what they promise, are the places where the, in the eyes of the nature conservationists so regrettable, opencast mining interventions took place and the forestry department has not yet succeeded in "healing" these "scars" in the landscape. Couldn't we just, here—yes, at this pit where the most coal was mined, which is full of groundwater now, and its steep sides already covered with fantastical trash dump flora—couldn't we just sketch in a perhaps over-ambitious yet to a large extent already established ideal typos, such as the view across Lake Averner onto Baiae Bay, as discovered by Vergil and Horaz and immortalized in art by many a Romantic painter? In short, wouldn't it be for the best, in the tradition of poor design, to do nothing more here at all? But who on earth would dare?

The Minimal Intervention (1982)

To this day, the press keeps on repeating its same tired mantra: reconstruction of the Sicilian towns destroyed by the earthquake of 1968 will be a long time coming; the mafia has long since pocketed the money donated to this end. Anyone visiting the Belice gets another picture altogether. A new highway, traffic on which is admittedly still very light, now assures access to the entire region. The earthquake-damaged towns have acquired new neighborhoods fresh from the plotting tables of academic urban planning departments. Some of them are already inhabited: the town of Gibellina, for example, which is modeled on an English new town. Other projects, such as the new districts of Calatafimi, another instance of academic urban planning, have not yet progressed beyond the road building stage; likewise the highway intersection at Partanna, with which the road builders have demonstrated to a town of only a few thousand inhabitants how the intersection of a metropolitan road network and a highway should look.

The earthquake-damaged valley of Belice was therefore the perfect place to hold a seminar on "the minimal intervention," the declared goal of which was to examine a chunk of the latest developments in planning theory. This seminar was the third in a series of panel discussions organized by the earthquake-damaged town of Gibellina on the topic of parks. The discussions of parks are a means for Gibellina to raise awareness of the problems still to be solved there—given that the open spaces in this "English" new town are much larger than is appropriate for a small Sicilian town's scorching hot days of summer—and simultaneously, to make a contribution to the interregional cultural programs launched in cooperation with the University of Palermo.

So, we were in search of a theory of minimal intervention and the approaches pursued at various levels were intended to bring it about. Some lectures were derived from the critical planning field and drew attention to centralist interventions' irrevocable impact on locally determined situations. Other lectures remained at the landscape design level, in keeping with the seminar's objective, and inquired into what may have caused the current decline in the art of gardening, an art reduced to the simultaneous use of contrasting motifs drawn from the stock box of academic routine, and the message of which, of whatever sort, hence is lost. Finally, the speakers addressed how history can both be destroyed and rendered visible, and the importance of this theme for a recently reconstructed new town located 18 km from the razed town.

Common to all these approaches was the awareness that man lives in environments that are partly visible and partly invisible. This is why physical interventions in the exterior world bring incalculable shifts in consciousness in their wake, which may in turn prompt a need for new, planned types of destruction, such as demolition.

From the viewpoint of established planning, the theory of minimal intervention is an aberrant digression into spontaneity: the guild remains stuck in its old routine. Nor is any help to be expected from official art circles, which are currently retreating into the "true realm of artistic activity"... Nevertheless, the debate about this byword, minimal intervention, is now at the very vanguard of modern planning and design. To negatively define one's own stance as the opposite of that of one's opponent is always the easiest option. The theory of minimal intervention is a critique of the aesthetic of academic planning's "neat solution." The planners' guild works with the one-off intervention, which provides the perfect solution. Such solutions are supposed to serve moreover as exemplary, universally applicable models. The planners' educational establishments teach solutions per se, but not how to devise solutions. In psychological terms, the aesthetic of the neat solution corresponds to the puerile notion that reality can be fundamentally grasped with the aid of simplified models, and that the solutions arrived at through models can be seamlessly transposed to the real world. The fact that our comprehension always rests on a reduced likeness of reality and that we are therefore basically incapable of estimating all the consequences of the consequences of our interventions is simply suppressed. The puerile pleasure of understanding and curing reality from a single perspective is all too tempting.

The second level, as we have said, is the search for a landscape reading of the minimal intervention and hence the critique of the very term landscape. The way in which we describe an environment in its entirety as "landscape" is an ideological trick. We divide the objects in our environment into typical and atypical: for instance, typical of the painterly landscape are the agriculture workers hard at work in the fields beneath a scorching sun. But we don't consider the real estate speculator's car parked up in front of a farmhouse to be a part of the landscape. So the term landscape lends us a practical pair of glasses that deludes us as to the real processes of landscape destruction currently underway, and allows us to believe in the feasibility of producing beautiful landscapes.

That demolition and reconstruction can result in alienating circumstances and inhabitants' loss of identity is no secret today, even among conservative planners. Items that served in people's earlier everyday lives to anchor a strong sense of self are lacking in the new environment. The latest architecture believes it can compensate this lack by referencing other styles. Yet it is impossible to foresee which associations these references will evoke in which persons, or whether building a sense of trust perhaps requires quite other webs of visible and social signs. Either way, the minimal intervention cannot consist merely in sticking some sign of a former existence on the façade of a new life; what is needed instead, is a more attentive approach to the everyday concerns and living conditions of those people in the hands of our planners.

The town of Pavia has adopted minimal intervention as policy, reports its director of municipal construction, Federico Oliva. The town has resolved to plan no longer for the year 2000 and the so-and-so many inhabitants who will have migrated there by then—and hence, on behalf of housing developers—but solely in the interests of the people living in Pavia now. In consequence, it regards all planning as a careful and gradual transition from whatever has been to whatever is yet to come. Nothing that was previously of importance is to be destroyed unnecessarily by this transformative process. If ever another intervention proves necessary, then the rule is to protect everything already in existence as far as humanly possible. When it comes to the landscape having to be altered by new access routes, say, or the economic restructuring of agriculture, then there is no better way to describe the type of approach foreseen than in the words of the town of Pavia itself, in its comments on the development plan:

"Why, for example, should one regard a surface area under planning as a tabula rasa and allow the caprice of purely formal investigation free rein there, when on this land there are not only farmhouses whose survival is stipulated in the development plan but also terraced fields, thickets, simple trodden paths, drainage canals, and the seeds of an urban or rural landscape of great value? Why aim to invent a settlement on a blank sheet of paper ex novo, only then, in order to breath life into the development, to artificially reintroduce terracing, plant thickets, lay out footpaths, or even fill a small lake with water, to destroy the existing rudiments of a landscape and create others that will be hard put to rival them. (…) Moreover, our experience of all such new developments that turn their back on what already exists—however valuable the single project may be—teaches us that they should be built in stages, and also that before they reach the aspired-to final stage (if ever they do), they stand around for years incomplete, cold, and lacking in expression, since alone their completion engenders their expression, their warmth, and their meaning."

At a much more abstract level, there are the thoughts of the English literary critic Stephen Bann. For him, the minimal intervention is bound up with the mythical reading of the landscape. Allusions are made to previously existing meaning, a poetic landscape is conjured without any need of the gardener's modern accomplishments—replanting mature trees now ranks among the routine tasks of the trade. The role model here is Chinese landscape painting, which familiarizes us with the landscape and fosters identification with it inasmuch as it seeks to overrule the antagonisms prevailing therein. Western artists preoccupied with land art are as ill placed as modern architecture with its endless references to offer experience of the minimal intervention. They are far too easily satisfied by the traditional techniques of western artistry, with perspective, geometry, and abstraction.

For the French landscape artist Bernard Lassus every intervention in the landscape initially derives from a misunderstanding of that which is already present. Anyone who replaces one view of the landscape with another must weigh up what we have to lose from such an intervention and what we have to gain. The astonished defense of the landscape architect—"... but there was nothing there before!"—is no longer tenable. Anyone who designs a landscape must weigh up whether the meaning he creates is of a sort that other people can understand, also those with other cultural backgrounds. In our pluralist society a design must be open for several interpretations: one and the same park must have a different meaning for children than for the adults accompanying them. In the zones of suburban landscape design, the landscape designer should not only harmonize but also create landscapes with critical meaning. To simply magic things out of sight with a wave of a green wand, as today's gardeners are supposed to do, makes our everyday environment illegible, impossible to read; for it makes otherwise distinct objects part of a continuum.

In the view of the German vegetation expert Karl Heinrich Hülbusch, intervening in gardens encourages weeds. As we are obliged to note in urban gardens today, relentless weeding with a trowel or hoe, to say nothing of toxic matter, is a consequence of the fact that a shift in our view of aesthetics has made unwelcome weeds of the city's spontaneous vegetation. This is because the modern art of cultivating flowers is oriented now to production. The flowerbed, a basic element of academic landscape design, imitates the vegetable patch; and the latter must be rid of weeds, admittedly, if one hopes to reap a harvest.

A plant therefore, so the minimal intervention theory, may not be declared a weed simply because landscape gardening has degenerated into the mere production of flowers.

Bazon Brock, finally, addressed the preservation of our historical environment inasmuch as he argued that rubble and ruins must remain signifiers of everyday life. To illustrate what ruins can do he spoke of a situation in Berlin, interpreting it in the light of history. The patch of land in question is flanked on one side by the Berlin Wall. Without information, the onlooker cannot guess that a similar wall stood at this same spot as early as the eighteenth century, a wall surrounding a barracks in which the Prussian emperors kept their press-ganged soldiers locked up until they had "sworn allegiance," as people used to say. Back then too, absconders were shot. The minimal intervention consists therefore in raising awareness of the continuity of circumstances that would otherwise mistakenly appear to us—or be misleadingly presented to us—as one-off aberrations in a logical line of development.

If the ruin is to a very notable degree a signifier—a conveyor of information—and thus enables us to process the present, the theory of minimal intervention must seek to build ruins. A thing incomplete or in ruins is the very opposite of those invariably know-it-all and inevitably catastrophic "neat solutions" which are destroying our world.

75 Years of Bauhaus—On the Tame Approach to the Wicked Problem (1994)

We are celebrating the seventy-fifth anniversary of the founding of the Bauhaus, that institution which endeavored from 1919 to 1933 to answer two questions: What is contemporary art? Can art be taught?

We must begin our study in the nineteenth century, the century in which the new middle classes rapidly became the mainspring of cultural renewal. The criterion by which this new bourgeoisie viewed fine art and the applied arts was "good taste." Until then knowledge of the arts had been the domain or even the prerogative of the nobility: alone he who had read the books of Vitruv, Serlio, and Vignola was able to pass judgment on art. But about architecture at least it was possible to speak objectively, as in: this truss shouldn't be on this column; that ornament is wrongly applied. But that is no longer possible, now taste is the criterion. One simply says: I like it. Someone else says: I don't like it at all.

The concept of taste has a dual function for the bourgeoisie. Anyone who can claim to have taste may also criticize the nobility. "They have no taste" also means however: anyone who does not share the lifestyle and education of the upper middle classes cannot join in expressing an opinion on questions of art and beauty.

The upper middle classes of the nineteenth century were also at the pinnacle of industrialization. This begs the question: Can industrial products be tasteful? This question first reared its head at the World Exhibition of 1851 in London, where all the industrialized nations exhibited new materials, such as vulcanite (hard rubber), and new products, and where it was noted that industrial production might take two directions: it could mass produce cheap goods and refine luxury goods.

In reaction to industrialization the latter half of the nineteenth century saw the rise of a new respect for, and appreciation of, handicrafts. This movement called into question not only industrial production methods but also, at the other pole end of production, the figure of the artist. In the early days of the industrial age, only those who painted or sculpted were regarded as artists—but not craftsman. By contrast, the Arts and Crafts movement revived the medieval ideal of the artistic craftsman or artisan. By these lights, an artist is anyone who personally designs artifacts then produces them himself. The artist matures by gaining a fundamental knowledge of his craft.

Historiography revolving around the Bauhaus normally traces a direct line from this revival of craftsmanship to the functionalism of the Bauhaus. Books with the title "From Morris to Gropius" or the like[1] tend to represent this view of history. We faithfully parrot all of that, too, even though we have already reflected in secret that there is something amiss about this equation of Morris, industry's sworn foe, and Gropius, who sought salvation in industrial form. While Morris printed his own texts on a manual press and scorned anyone who went to a printer, the functional designer's principle was to not produce his own design but entrust it instead to a factory.

The theory "From Morris to Gropius" notwithstanding, it is historically incorrect to assert that the supposedly handcrafted luxury products of the late nineteenth century were in reality handcrafted. Let's take furniture, for example: historians of modernism claim that cheap furniture is industrial, luxury furniture handcrafted. In the late nineteenth century however, the reverse was true: cheap furniture was manufactured by hand in small craft workshops and sweatshops,

1 [Cf. inter alia Nikolaus Pevsner: *Pioneers of Modern Design. From William Morris to Walter Gropius*, Faber & Faber, 1936]

whereas expensive cabinetmakers could afford to mechanize their production and hence optimize its quality and sophistication. One example is the rise of the fin de siècle Art Nouveau style, in particular its early French variety, the École de Nancy.

Furniture for the lower middle classes

In the Deutsche Werkstätten [German Workshops] founded in 1908 in the Hellerau district of Dresden a compromise was sought: *Typenmöbel*, meaning furniture consisting of standardized parts. It was designed by artists who had a background in manual crafts yet manufactured by craftsmen, in rationalized and partly mechanized serial production. The initial motivation was to produce affordable furniture not only for the upper but also for the lower middle classes; and given the durability of well-built furniture, it was reckoned it would be cheaper for workers to buy such furniture once in their lives than to have to replace a broken stool or a cupboard with ill-fitting doors every few years.

In the very premises in which the Bauhaus was founded in 1919, Henry van de Velde taught until the outbreak of the First World War. There, this major exponent of modern applied arts provoked a debate that would go down in design history as the "prototype conflict." In spring of 1914, shortly before the war, the Deutsche Werkbund assembled in Cologne, where the architect Hermann Muthesius gave a crucial speech in which he called upon artists to henceforth design prototypes for quality industrial manufacture. On hearing of this, Van de Velde rushed off to Cologne bearing a contrary manifesto. He called upon artists to personally realize their own designs or to at least supervise their manufacture; and, also, to make a fresh design for each new piece of furniture. Interestingly, Van de Velde's proposal won the approval of the assembled Werkbund members.

Then, in fall, the First World War broke out and with it came an immeasurable loss of human lives and material as well as a great leap forward in industrialized mass production. The factories set up to produce ammunition, uniforms, telescopes, and field telephones could also now assure the production of household appliances. In addition to such material progress the—for Germany—lost war also engendered a colossal psychological shift in expectations: people hoped to build a new world but did not yet know exactly how it should look. For some members of the avant-garde, the ideal was the industrialized city, for others, the dissolution of the city and a return to rural self-sufficiency. The Bauhaus began with very heterogeneous and vague objectives while Gropius himself wavered with regard to issues of style, politics, and industry. But visionaries, artists, and social reformers were unanimous on one point: students were to be trained in the crafts, as artisans.

Only he who never undertakes a thing he cannot do becomes a master. This principle culminated in the renowned preliminary course,[2] which sealed the reputation of the former Bauhaus. Students on the preliminary course were set abstract exercises for educational purposes. Make a cube from cardboard and paint each of its sides a different color! Cover a white surface evenly with black dots! As we see, each exercise is bereft of content; only whoever can hold his own on abstract terrain can proceed to the actual object. For if the black dots turn into a text then gray shadows appear in the graphics. The preliminary course launched in 1919 was the institution with which the Bauhaus put an end to the traditional art academy and its conceit. But today we no longer regard that as necessary.

2 ["Preliminary" is the preferred term in present-day Bauhaus publications, but cf. also the work of former Bauhaus teacher Johannes Itten: *Design and Form. The Basic Course at the Bauhaus*, New York: Van Nostrand Reinhold 1975.]

More importantly, we must ask ourselves: Is it right to set exercises that have been emptied of content? Why can we not set students the task, say, of designing a student newspaper for our faculty? But students are not capable of that, (people will say), since they have never done it before! But why should students not be permitted to make mistakes? Making mistakes is the best way to learn.

The history of the Bauhaus is well known, albeit usually in its more prettified form, such as historians of modernism prefer to showcase. Gropius found his style after some to-and-fro-ing, but it was the style of some ambassadors of the Dutch De Stijl movement then sojourning in Weimar. Their clear formal idiom, white cubes, clean contours, and lack of ornament became emblematic of the new architectural ideal propounded by Gropius. And architecture cleansed thus of its dross was to make room for the new society.

Of course not every teacher at the Bauhaus was inclined to follow Gropius's not always straightforward concepts. Above all his position on art remained unclear: if indeed the prototype designed with artistic aspiration but without any frills can be industrially produced en masse then our environment will soon be all that it should. But the question is: What will become then of art? Will not we all then live in art, and artistically? If everything is art then there is no further need of art—this is the one position. But precisely in architecture stripped of ornament there is a need for modern art—this is the other position.

The Bauhaus student Max Bill

I cannot make that leap from the Bauhaus of the 1920s to the founding of the faculty of design in Weimar [in 1993] without mentioning a hugely influential interim stage: I mean of course the Hochschule für Gestaltung [HfG, School of Design] in Ulm, which was founded by Max Bill, a former Bauhaus student, and existed from 1955 to 1968. It was deemed imperative, after the Second World War, to apply the ideas of the Bauhaus to the new historical situation. And this implied, in the eyes of Max Bill, that design must be turned into a science. The designer proceeds rationally, following a step-by-step approach we name ZASPAK, which is an acronym of the following German words: Z for objective (*Ziel*): name the objective; A for analysis (*Analyse*): analyze the problem; S (*Synthese*): synthesize one's analysis; P (*Plan*): formulate a plan; A (*Ausführung*): move towards implementation; and K (*Kontrolle*): monitor the result.

Let me give you an example. Name the objective. Our objective is to eat a soup. I analyze the situation thus: a warm liquid in portions of circa 20 gram each are to be transported from a vessel to mouth height and then, in a horizontal plane, into the mouth. The synthesis: a tool is required, one with a handle and a depression able to contain the relevant portion. We draw up a plan: to our astonishment the drafted prototype looks like a spoon. We stride on to the realization phase then, in conclusion, monitor the outcome: a drop of soup lands on our shirt. Somewhere we have made a mistake.

The following difficulties arise with this methodical procedure: it is impossible at the start of the exercise to exactly define the goal. — Analysis serves the collation of data that we later do not need; we are not proceeding rationally. — The plan and the implementation pin everything down. — In consequence, the monitoring phase happens too late.

In the later phase of the Ulm School of Design the mathematician Horst Rittel lectured on design methodology. His theoretical work on design methods strongly influenced pedagogic debate. Rittel classifies design tasks either as tame or wicked. Tame tasks are those for which a solution has already been found. We are often set such tasks in school, especially in math. Students have to divide a large number by a smaller one. Of course the sum works out: there is no remainder. Design tasks however are often intractable, which is to say, the optimal solution to them is not always possible. Every advantage in one respect brings drawbacks in another. Let's take the intersection. An accident happens sooner or later at every intersection. Of course it is possible to build the totally safe intersection by adding an underpass or an overpass. But the drawback of this is that one can no longer turn off the road. Well, we want a proper intersection with clearly marked lanes for turning off in either direction. One could solve the problem by judicial means, by decreeing that cars in future can cross intersections only at a snail's pace and with someone on foot leading their way while waving a flag. This would dramatically reduce the number of accidents—but it is impossible to enforce. The intersection problem is evidently a wicked one.

For me, the Ulm School of Design stands for the point at which the Bauhaus pedagogy reaches its limits on account of its methodology and moves into a new pedagogy, namely that of dealing with wicked problems. Typically, such exercises are always determined by their content. The non-drip soup spoon cannot be tested on a preliminary course, for without soup this is impossible. The students who graduate from the faculty of design in Weimar will later be faced with exercises of a wicked nature. Their clients, industry, journalists, political instances will all call on them only when there are difficult problems to solve but not, however, on account of easy ones.

Not A New Bauhaus! (1993)

Many will not understand. And yet it is actually very straightforward. Anyone who founds a new educational establishment must think about the students, their future qualification, and their professional prospects. And about nothing else. Neither about reviving the Bauhaus tradition, for instance, nor fostering debate between the two parts of Germany. Neither about liberating art, product design, and graphic design from the current craze for postmodernist frills, nor any of the other stuff bandied about these days.

Design by no means operates only between two poles, as in: the Bauhaus, here; arbitrariness, there. Not that the point is, now to condemn artistic positions that made perfect sense in their day. The Bauhaus, Gute Form [good form], and Neue Sachlichkeit [New Sobriety] are movements that should on no account disappear. And they couldn't, even if they tried. For they have meanwhile been "subsumed" in the cultural canon on which design still draws today and will draw likewise in the future. But we do need new concepts.

For those interpretations of contemporary life grown so dear to our hearts are starting to look mistaken. Let's take the economic crisis. Normative thinking tells us that whenever people have less money then more competitive products are required, i.e. industrially, serially, and mass produced goods. Nothing could be further from the truth! The crisis came about precisely because every last businessman was hoping to supply the whole world with his own particularly good-value, mass-produced wares—most preferably a car. But putting assembly lines back into operation, supplying Japanese cars to America, American ones to Germany, and German ones to Japan, will not suffice to overcome the crisis. After the present crisis—which is a structural crisis, not the usual sales crisis—manufacturing will be different than before.

One consequence of the crisis is that the liberal-conservative ideologists currently in power are urging the government to privatize state-owned infrastructures. But precisely these great public institutions—the railroads, mail service, healthcare, and schools—have traditionally been the biggest consumers of serially produced products. So the crisis is limiting the progress of serial production lines that are geared to functionality. The need for conventional "good form" design ware will decline. For it thrived actually on encounters between the businessman with faith in this production method and the major buyer of similar bent and working on behalf of the government, the mail service, or the railroads. However, since these days we go to a store ourselves, the telephone we buy is likely to be colorful and fun rather than black and square, and rarely do we find one of the same design as ours when visiting our friends' apartments. Is that a bad thing? Opportunistic? Should we keep quiet about this development in front of our students?

Another example is that the forecasters have unanimously agreed since 1960 that while the production of goods may be rationalized the service sector may not. It was subsequently prophesied that the proportion of the population working in industry would drop from 50 to 10 percent while a rising number of employees in public administration, provision industries, and distribution would one day amount to 80 percent of the working population. These beliefs have strongly influenced economic planning, regional and urban planning, and industries' forward planning. In the meantime, however, there is evidence to suggest that service industries too can be automated—through electronic data processing—and also that industry will disappear, not because it can be automated but because it will be outsourced to low-wage countries.

So, what will our younger and our older people do in the future? — The high-wage countries' hopes lie in the limited edition, the unique product, the artistically enhanced product, the intelligent product, the luxury product, in anything but the good old practical yet pedestrian form of the black table telephone.

Creative design hitherto rested on the conceptual isolation of the object. Purposeful form, it was said, ensues from precise definition of the task in hand. "The neat solution" is what people called it. But the designer facing tasks in the future will have to think about their context, their environmental impact, and their social implications in the very broadest sense. Objects are not innocent, are not abused by evil people; rather, there are "tools of conviviality" (Ivan Illich) and the opposite, namely asocial objects. For the designer, therefore, the border between the object and its environment will dissolve: he must not only deliver the perfectly constructed device but also consider its appropriateness as well as its consequences—or otherwise end up with something like that perfect automated ticket vending machine, alongside which a railroad official was obliged to stand, inquiring after the customer's destination then taking his small change, and using the machine on his behalf.

There are consequences to these observations. The objectives and methods of professional training will change. This is why we in Weimar are first and foremost pushing through project-based teaching. By this we mean teaching methods based on a specific set task, which impart to students the necessary know-how and ultimately lead to the requisite expertise. We thereby consciously negate the great traditions of the Bauhaus. Everyone is familiar with the concentric rings of the Bauhaus curriculum: firstly you must learn about the materials, then learn how to handle them and only then are you permitted to work with colors, before ultimately acceding to the design stage. And only when you can already do this, can you do that …

We take a different tack, one we call "project-based" teaching. Here, one can try out things one has not yet mastered and in the course of which one will make mistakes. But one will learn from those mistakes too, will learn that one still needs to acquire specific knowledge and skills. It is accordingly our opinion, that the study of theoretical matters best proceeds by drawing on examples. We think up "problematic" projects. This implies projects that have never yet been solved and for which perhaps there is no solution. Non-compatible solutions are making our world fall sick: the engineers' "neat solutions" are polluting the environment; the promised solution to the traffic problem is choking our streets; the modern kitchen is prompting residents to eat out. We imagine that designers and graphic designers will be "consultants" in the future, rather than problem-solvers. Brainstorming—together giving thought to contiguities, future changes, shifts in consumer behaviors, and the like—is more important than any "perfect" solution.

A University Must Foster a Sense of Belonging and Hone Resistance at One and the Same Time (1996)

Stephan Dillemuth: You speak of the "science of strollology." Is that a joyful science?
Lucius Burckhardt: The science of strollology is a theory I developed on the perception of landscape in order to counter the predominance of that "one image" familiar to us from geography books, as in: this is the heath and this is how it looks. Reconstructing the heath generally means reconstructing not the heath as walked on but the image of the heath that hangs in cheap hotels. I took the contrary view, namely that one perceives the landscape differently, as episodes. One takes a walk, leaves the town, reaches suburbs, villages, and forests, and in the end one tells of images that one has not actually seen but only reconstructed, strung together, from whatever one already knew, from things one had heard about the Eifel, say, or the Taunus region. It is a theory of perception for practical application.

I was thinking that you also take a stroll between the sciences?
One picks up on fragments and then collages them in one's mind's eye. This theory actually combats the "perfect image" and tries instead to outline perception as it really is. One has prior knowledge then garners additional diverse fragments and portrays it all afterwards as if it were a single entity.

You are occupied with urban and landscape planning?
My background is in urban planning. The [strollological] approach of course grew out of a critique which back then was still original but that everyone advances nowadays, namely that urban planning

means more than simply traffic planning and runs counter to the interests of local inhabitants.

Is your focus to study existing social and community structures before they are organized, regulated, and fixed by urban planning? That at least is what I gathered from your catchphrase "Design is invisible."
My intent was to broaden the concept of what design does, so to speak. Design designs actual social relationships, lifestyles, and procedures. And it must therefore take the degree of acceptance into account, the question as to whether this or that object disrupts or improves human interactions.

So, once carried over to the urban and landscape planning context, design is also about challenging sociopolitical issues?
Yes, thought must be given to the social and at times also historical aspects that even if no longer visible are still a part of people's mind-sets.

To what extent does thematic and aesthetic design determine challenging social issues?
The word "problem" is always used in combination with the word "solution." Yet the word "problem" is actually the word for an intractable task perpetuated by strategies. The urban traffic problem cannot be solved. All those who stand up and claim the traffic problem in Cologne or Würzburg can be solved are either conmen or trained engineers. The problem "traffic" leads to irresolvable complex relationships in which one can at best displace the pain. We can let the motorist suffer to the benefit of the pedestrian, or vice versa. We can say that running down a few schoolchildren is no big deal if it means motorists can race through here. Or we can say: [running down school-children] is so terribly bad that we can't ever again allow anyone to drive through town.—Thus we displace the pain but we don't

remedy it. This is known in mathematics as "the wicked problem," the problem that cannot be solved. And design too revolves around this precisely.

Is one then automatically in the dilemma of having to deal with a social issue that one believes can be solved only by political work or de-politicized aesthetic design?
We can influence politics only to a certain degree. To say we cannot solve a matter only because it cannot be solved politically is to shift the problem to a higher level. Nonetheless we must tackle the problem. In the pedagogic perspective the problem cannot be pushed into the public arena by saying the problem is global or political. On the other hand we must bear in mind that there are no neat solutions. — Our generation can do no more than manage the traffic problem, say, and pass it on to the next generation. And perhaps the next generation will have other views than we do on speeds and the like.

So we cannot find an ultimate solution, but merely tinker around with end moraines and then pass the problem on?
Yes, and we'd better get used to it. In the 1970s, people still believed there was a neat solution. But they solved one part of a problem and created new ones in the process. Environmental damage is the outcome of neat solutions. Water is cleansed so thoroughly of bacteria these days—but the equipment used to do so pollutes the groundwater. We turn the problem into a solution plus environmental pollution. In "solving" the problem we just move it elsewhere.

So the processes of being problem-oriented and solving problems are presumably decisive for your models for the Hochschule der bildenden Künste Saar, [HBKsaar, Saarland University of Art & Design] and the Bauhaus University in Weimar? Have your proposals been implemented there?

"Bauhaus University" is a contradiction in terms, just like "violin-piano" or "piano-trumpet." The institution I founded is a faculty of design. I didn't invent problem-oriented learning but we [in Weimar] do distance ourselves from the Bauhaus, which was geared to solving problems. People there thought, first solve the minor problems then tackle the big one later. We, for our part, think that realistic education and training today must gear students to tackling problems directly, and not only after they've tried to neatly form a perfect letter of the alphabet on paper. In Weimar the freshmen produce a student newspaper. They may produce it badly—but they produce it nonetheless! One can always come along and criticize a thing. But the fact is, they made a start, and a start is never perfect—no newspaper has the perfect layout, but one makes a start and then learns by doing.

Learning by doing …
…with all the problems that entails. Not: form a perfect letter of the alphabet on paper and I'll give you an A grade—but rather: Just do it!

How does the concept look in reality?
My problem turned out differently than originally foreseen [laughs]. — The government of Thüringen set me the task of founding a faculty of art and cultural studies, which was to be a kind of service faculty for the students of architecture. Giving prospective architects access to art and cultural theory, whatever that is, was meant to cure them of their East German pasts building prefab slab housing.

It was clear to me that this was no way to attract professors, for professors don't want to teach the architecture students next door, but students of their own. Which is why we established courses in art, design, and visual communication, and opened them up also to the architecture students.

So instead of creating a purely "autonomous" chair of art you put together this triple package?
Yes. I revised the structural planning and proposed the appointment of four chairs for each of the three study blocks. In addition there is a theory block. So we now have four artists, four designers, four specialists in visual communication, plus an art historian, an architecture historian, a sociologist, a lecturer in aesthetics, a drawing teacher, and a media theorist. That makes a total of eighteen chairs. That is how many I was able to fill. And at the core of the curriculum are projects, each supervised by two professors.

One leaves the school then embarks directly on real life in order to solve concrete topical problems?
One embarks on life and on theory directly on the spot, and arrives at very diverse solutions.

Is that research or teaching?
One puts students in a situation in which they must seek out information for themselves. They have to go to the library, or make inquiries and telephone calls, or conduct experiments on their own initiative. To do research is to go beyond what is already known.

And your structural planning for the entire process adds the didactic layer to all of this?
There's that old catchphrase: "Learn to learn."

Students' school career would be a slalom through several projects of different orientation? Then there is no accumulative structure to the degree course?
Study is structured and regulated in a way such as to ensure that students do not pursue specializations in too extreme a form. Grades must be acquired for course modules in three different subject areas.

It is possible to float around in three different subject areas: that doesn't count as a change of degree course, as long as the first and last projects are in the same subject area.

So it's conceivable that a set of twins work on the same projects, but that one of them ends up as an artist, the other as a designer?
With just one restriction, namely that they don't work together on the first and the last projects. The thesis must be written on the subject area they each opted for at the start.

Nevertheless it seems to me that, on this course, it's only a matter of perspective or emphasis whether what I do is called art or design, whether after one and the same education I call myself a graphic designer, a designer, or an artist.
The artist's career and the designer's career are not as unambiguously laid out as people think. That artists study then rent a studio and sell paintings is likely straight out of a fairy-tale. Nor is it a matter of course for designers to immediately find a job, start in a factory, or open a store of their own. Things are not quite that straightforward—which is precisely why a broad-ranging degree course makes sense.

What is the image of the artist, in your view?
The image of the artist [laughs]... I think it's important to prepare artists to earn their money with a broader range of occupations, preferably with work that is not totally alienating. Not doing the dishes all day and painting by night but rather some kind of work that at least enriches their art and keeps them more closely wrapped up in it.

But this broader range of skills shouldn't just be a means to bridge the gap before the artist starts selling her work. It's imperative also to call into question that which art itself and the conditions of its production and sale have meant until now.

I think the school fosters this ability inasmuch as it offers a certain breadth of subject areas—the absolute minimum being architecture, graphic / design, and art. (—Here, Annemarie Burckhardt adds that a lot of artists have no wish to study art theory, because they believe art just happens of its own accord and needs only to be "sensed."—) Yes, teaching artists is really an experience apart, because they have all been fed this old notion of the genius. They mostly come up with only one idea in response to the problem I set them but they defend it to the death. Whatever the artist's idea, he feels it is a good one; and the crazier the better. One can say the idea isn't really viable but that just proves his point: he is patently a genius.

Forum Stadtpark, a club run by artists for artists, has worked well until now, so why the need to found a faculty? The artists you have spoken of seem to do fine all on their own.
I believe that an essential task of the university is to air certain questions so as to create breathing room, in order that students can develop for a few years, undisturbed.

Why does one need teachers for that?
Because one can then ask oneself what it makes sense to have happen in those few years [laughs], to ascertain that certain things are taught. I think breathing room is important, but it's wrong for an art school to see itself as breathing room alone. And in my view, it is also old-fashioned, a re-run of that nineteenth-century image of the artist, like the time I said to a young student of mine: "Come by tomorrow morning at 9 and we can discuss the project." Whereupon she replied: "At 9 in the morning? But this is an art school!"

Would you structure a school differently than an institute?
What is an institute? A place where the teaching staff pursues research?

The academy perhaps comes about more through a loose form of interdisciplinary exchange while universities and their institutes tend instead to pursue a didactic program for the transmission of knowledge. To what extent should the students' existential, individual search for meaning à la "what is the world and who am I?" play a role in education, and to what extent the development of a collective persona?
Both forms of teaching have benefits and drawbacks. At the academy freedom is important and also the fact that one is pretty soon grown-up and starts things straight away. The risk with the academy, I find, is the master class. The academy professor takes students under his wing like the mother hen her chicks, and forbids them to go to other professors, or to attend other seminars or lectures at the school, since the academy professor can of course teach them all they need to know. He has an all-encompassing philosophy, one can ask him anything, he has an answer for everything. The proper student is always at his side, having developed an instinct for whether he is now in the canteen or the cafe; the student then runs along there too. Sure, that is a caricature of the academy. But in my experience that is also how it is. — The university by contrast has a scheduled curriculum, and one can go wherever one likes. From 8 to 9 there is this, from 9 to 10 there is that, and from 10 to 11 there is the other. One can pick out parts of the mosaic at will. The benefit of the academy is its degree of latitude; the drawback is its formation of classes. The benefit of the university is its broad-ranging curriculum; the drawback the risk of being spoon-fed as in school, or of cramming.

Have you attempted to create an in-between solution in Weimar?
The freely selected slalom is one option. — A university must foster a sense of belonging and hone resistance at one and the same time. To critique the teaching staff is vital. I also find the role of the assistants important. They must on no account be under the thumb of the professorial chair. After all, the role of the university assistant is

to say to students: "The old goat was dishing up some pretty odd ideas today, you know. Views have progressed since his day." — We need this tension to build up between professors and assistants, because students can learn from it.

Are you in favor of lifelong tenure for professors?
Not really. We've been mulling over whether we should advise the government of Thüringen to appoint professors for a six-year term. As far as this university is concerned I am all for it. But I am not sure whether people in Germany can take a six-year break from their profession and then re-enter it as easily as people in America do. Incapable professors can be dismissed there too, whereas in Germany they cannot. Excellent results have been attained in America with limited periods of tenure.

What do you think about a relatively self-run operation for inviting guests, so as to turn the hierarchy of lecturer and student into the relationship of guest and host? Admittedly the guests would have to leave again after one month or six months.
I do think that students should have an opportunity to say they have read this and that, find this interesting, and would like at some point to invite him or her. But if it were a case of students running the school and they alone being able to invite guests … Well, I'm not prepared to concede total latitude. When newly founding [the faculty in] Weimar and restructuring [that in] Saarbrücken I discovered that students are actually conservative. And that one doesn't get very far, if one listens to them. They have already studied a good while under the old goat and they don't want to see that experience invalidated. If we tell them we'll bring in better professors then they really put their foot down, because they feel then that their previous year was in vain. Students are conservative because any improvement loses them the credits they have gained.

We cannot let that stand as your final word on the subject.
Why ever not? That is my personal experience.

But it's very negative. The point surely is to tackle this very matter? The matter of developing a capacity for criticism, also for self-criticism, so that one can give up whatever one has learned to date in order to gradually move forward, move on?
Your question was whether the students themselves could manage a school completely independently, and now you yourself are saying that a didactic instance is required.

Ok. But I think that, whenever possible, one shouldn't give teaching staff permanent tenure. I am wondering rather whether things can be structured in a way such as to propel self-criticism and fruitful dynamics. For this would be didactic enough.
I don't believe in self-propelling models. Regulations or personnel input of the stable sort are still required.

... I don't know otherwise, how it might work without repeating the old reproductive mechanisms.
The best bet would be total freedom from repression of any sort, but that is a pipedream; the world is not like that. We used to say—it was a common idea in '68—"we live in semi-repressive structures." We cannot evade them and so the best we can do is to build not a free system but one that is "only" semi-repressive. But this is probably the most complex system of all, because it requires a complex combination of mainstream educational establishments, regulations, and breathing room. To build a repressive system is easy—no question about it. And to build a free one is easy too.

Really? And how does it look?
My free system is: diplomas are awarded on day one; everyone gets top grades; and you can all go home! You are chartered engineers, certified artists; you have your diploma from our school. We also offer three extra years of study, free of charge, so you can stay here and learn something; or you can go out there and claim you are already it.

Not bad at all.
And those who stayed on would undoubtedly be the most fun [laughs]—and the most interesting.

So why don't you do things that way?
Because we need semi-repressive systems in order to hone resistance. Now, that's enough!

As you will. Thank you very much for the interview.

Do Examinations Make for a Better Education? (1996)

When that better world we are all hoping for has finally come around one fine day, we will not do away with diplomas. Instead we will award them on the students' very first day in class. And with those who wish to remain nonetheless, we will embark on an exciting (and angst-free) period of study. But until that day comes ...

Jeremias Gotthelf already explained to us just how examinations should *not* be. The teacher asks the little schoolboy: "Do apes live in Af___?" and already pretty much sets the scene for how things will continue even at tertiary level. But to cram for this type of examination is a waste of time. At best it hones the short-term memory, but this at an age in life when the development of quite other skills is paramount, such as the capacity to combine data, to think systematically, and to pursue matters to a logical conclusion, to say nothing of creativity.

But can such capacities be examined at all? And are such examinations conducive to effective study? I believe so. However, I am not thinking of examinations that take place on the last day of semester, last only fifteen minutes per subject, and consist of little more than a string of rattled-off questions. I am thinking of regular oral examinations, which is to say, conversations that take place at regular intervals all throughout a study program and during which students are faced with a specialized question of the sort they are likely to encounter in professional practice, namely a problematic and complex one. In cooperation with the "examinee," one then develops strategies that, while not necessarily solving the problem in hand, at least come to grips with it. The point here is not to identify the best—which in any case typically means the best first available—

—"How would the world be without the Bauhaus?"
—"Horrible!"
Drawing: Lucius Burckhardt

solution, but rather to examine alternative approaches and thereby weigh up their benefits and drawbacks.

The obligation to keep a clear head in anticipation of such—graded—conversations fosters students' development and resilience. Teaching staff will admittedly see such oral examinations as time-consuming and inefficient. Cost efficiency cannot be measured however only in terms of paid time; study time too is of value.

Problem-oriented Project-based Teaching (1999)

Thrice in his life, the present author had an opportunity to contribute to the foundation of an educational establishment devoted to design and planning—first of all, following his appointment to a chair at the University of Kassel after the inauguration there of the faculty of urban and landscape planning, and the faculty of architecture. The second occasion followed his appointment to the advisory board convened to oversee the foundation of the Hochschule der bildenden Künste Saar (HbK Saar); and, thirdly, in 1992 he was commissioned by the government of Thüringen to found the faculty of art and design at the Hochschule für Architektur und Bauwesen (University of Architecture and Construction), which now goes under the name Bauhaus University Weimar.

Every step in educational policy unfolds against the backdrop of expectations of the future; after all, the younger generation must be equipped to deal with whatever time brings next. Two prophesies of the postwar period have meanwhile proved to be wrong, although everyone has not yet realized it. Firstly, the view that production overall would develop along Fordist lines, i.e. as mass production on the assembly line. Yet mass production has proved viable only for certain product types: motor cars, refrigerators, and televisions. This put a dent in Fourastié's prognosis that the number of manual activities in industry would progressively diminish. In fact, the industrial complex did not reduce the number of jobs available but opened up several sectors. One was the repair economy: many products are still so expensive that they are not put in the trash and replaced when found to be defect. Cars, for example, are repaired. Secondly, setting up production lines with automatic assembly machines on no account depends on mass production; for it is truer to say that, in Fordist terms, they are put together by hand. It can be noted that industry is increasingly outsourcing these experimental types of manufacture. The production of an automatic machine gives rise to problems: respecting wage contracts and delivery dates proves impossible, and conflicts with purchasers threaten. Into this gap move small experimental operations, which often form ad hoc, for a single order. Such operations can survive waiting times and absorb losses on their own. Major companies prefer to take on watertight contracts that assure them profit in the stipulated period. The small experimental firms that carry out such contracts cut costs and recruit young people who have already familiarized themselves with technical tinkering as a hobby. Such labor networks are flexible, on first-name terms, willing to give help and advice by phone, and also to disperse if an order falls flat. Today's educational establishments do not cater to the educational profile of these youngsters. Indeed we are shocked to see how little the state invests in the education and training of this young talent—in putting workshops and equipment at its disposal, for example. The money spent on unemployment benefit would be better invested here.

This brings us to the second false prophecy, namely that 80 percent of the population would work in tertiary occupations in the future. It was supposed that Fordism would lead to the automation of all industry and that labor requirements would continually decrease, as in agriculture. On the other hand it was held that sectors such as administration, insurance, and trade, the so-called "service industries," could not be rationalized. It was believed, therefore, that this tertiary sector would become a refuge of sorts, where those dismissed from the primary or secondary sectors would find work. Meanwhile, thanks to electronic data processing, automation of parts of the service sector has indeed proved viable. Therefore, if we want to continue to go to work in order to feed ourselves we must open our eyes to a further production sector. This new sector encompasses design, representation, reproduction, invention, and "tinkering." Educational establishments in the design field are supposed to prepare our young people for the future and must therefore address the needs of this sector and train people in the requisite skills: fantasy, decisiveness, imagination, spontaneity, and an aptitude for lifelong learning.

During planning for the faculty of art and design in Weimar, the advisory board convened to oversee its foundation was continually being reminded of the great role model that had operated from 1919 to 1925 on the very same premises: the Bauhaus. The preliminary course was held to be of particular importance. We consider this position to be historically incorrect. For what we can learn from the Bauhaus is not so much which teaching methods it applied, and how, but rather the fact that teaching methods, in any era, must reflect contemporary concerns. The Bauhaus stepped up after the First World War as an educational establishment for the arts, one that was intent on moving beyond its two historic predecessors: the *Kunstgewerbeschule* (school of applied arts) and the *Kunstakademie* (academy of the arts). It was of vital importance to the founders of the Bauhaus to overcome the academy's conceit: no student should take himself for the genius who strolls through Munich dressed in a velvet suit and bow-tie in order to demonstrate to the locals what an artist is. The Bauhaus accordingly took a leaf out of the working class's book: it called its students apprentices, its professors, masters, and its graduates, junior masters. But behind these agreeable titles lies an ideology that would be catastrophic, today, the preliminary course ideology.

The Bauhaus welcomed its freshmen but had a total distrust of all that they had previously learned: in the parental home they had learned bad taste, in school, particularly in the drawing class, they'd had their natural line bent out of shape and been taught the tricks of old academicism—and the preliminary course was designed to knock this out of them or at least to iron it out. "You know noth ing," the new arrivals were told. And: "You can't even draw a straight line!" And the rule hence was: "Do only that which you know how to do, because otherwise you will *Pfusch machen*—or "botch it," as craftsman are wont to say, when insisting that everyone do only the tasks they have already learned so that no mistakes are made or materials wasted. However, we recommend a very different sort of welcome for new students.

Their prior knowledge should be acknowledged and if one or the other student already has a skill then he or she should apply it. Moreover, *Pfusch* (a botch job) is allowed. Our advice is that new students should be set tasks that overstretch their previous capacities. The Bauhaus task—which is to arrange a few blocks of color or letters of the alphabet on a white sheet of paper—is immediately outplayed by our own: Design the cover of the student newspaper! For even someone who has never even heard of a layout can design one, and while the result is doubtless a botch job—a botch job can teach you a great deal. Thus, after eighty years, the three ground rules of the historic preliminary course—You know nothing and can do nothing; Your taste is depraved; Do only that which you have perfectly mastered—became obsolete.

Training at the conservative polytechnic is premised on reaching design decisions by following the sequence of steps we call ZASPAK:[1] name the objective; analyze the problem; synthesize one's analysis; formulate a plan; move towards implementation; and monitor the result. This sequence overlooks that its application is contingent on the following two points:

– objectives must be identifiable at the start. But in most practical matters, objectives come to light only during the design process.

1 Cf. also p. 285

- data collated during analysis must be synthesized in a way such as to feed into the planning. In practice, however, such data is classified and introduced into the design process in highly subjective ways. Furthermore, the clients, which is to say those who set the task, mostly mix up objectives and means. A road in the historic city center is to be widened. Is the objective here to accelerate traffic flow? Or is widening the road merely a means to demolish historical houses or put them on the market?

In a streetcar, early one morning, one boy asks another: What did you make of that sum we were set in math? And the other boy replies: A remainder of 5. And you? His answer: I had no remainder. And the other boy: Then your result is correct. That is how math textbooks are in school, and likewise the tasks one is set in traditional polytechnics. All the sums that don't tally, that fail to give an unambiguous result, are erased from the math textbook. The design tasks set at university do tally. During summer vacation the assistants have drawn up the relevant plans and demonstrated that there is room on the lot for the proposed building. Consequently, all the designs proposing that an ancillary building should flank the larger one are patently incorrect.

Teaching at the polytechnic is premised on the notion that the future male or female professional will be set problems that can be solved. However, the issues facing today's designers cannot be solved in the usual sense; they are wicked. The wicked problem is characterized by the fact that it requires decisions to be taken, but decisions that rest on the stated opinions or the votes of all the parties involved. Such issues are: How much may it cost? How much damage is it to be allowed to do? On whom shall we unload the design's disadvantageous aspects? To improve the traffic is to allow motorists to reach their destination faster but also entails a higher incidence of accidents involving pedestrians on crosswalks. How many accidents per annum might that be?

Our society has a very labile response to such issues. We tolerate that traffic causes a whole string of accidents because traffic, in our view, is vital. We therefore continue to design traffic systems that are more dangerous still than those that went before. In other instances the authorities react very strictly. For example, although it is highly unlikely that a human being will be infected by BSE (mad cow disease), the EU aspires to absolute security. But this security has its price, and the livestock dealers pay it. Evidently we agree on the fact that virtually total security in this sector justifies discrimination of the agricultural sector.

Horst Rittel, the design theoretician who coined the term "wicked problem," often used the following example: Where exactly in the city should an urban planner locate firehouses? Close to the city center, where the most valuable properties and the largest number of citizens would be protected? But this would be disadvantageous for the single-family residences scattered on the city margins. Can we, in order to benefit the city center, expose houses on the city margins to the risk that firefighters would be able to reach them only after a one-hour ride? Who decides—the specialist or the general public? Either way it is a wicked problem, because a house that burns for thirty minutes is done for. Only buildings that a firefighting team can reach within twenty minutes are safe.

Problems confront us thus "in problem form," which is to say, no expert solution to them is available. Moreover the expert solution cannot be separated from the moral solution. The idea that the expert finds a solution to the problem then puts it at the politician's disposal is untenable. In the case of wicked problems, ethical aspects are so wrapped up with technical aspects that it is virtually impossible to neatly separate the two. It is expected that the expert, in the course of his daily routine, neatly deals with and packages the ethical aspects of an issue and integrates them in his solution. The expert, for his part, expects that the client keeps abreast of technical data and involves himself in the technical aspects of an issue. It is therefore rare to see a decision being publicly debated as follows: According to our calculations, this exit from the underground garage causes three serious accidents per annum. — Then should we build it? — The business community expects us to.

What those in the profession of planner, architect, or designer need to learn, therefore, is how to deal with wicked problems. Our society is full of problems that cannot be solved. The traffic problem cannot be "solved," no more than the "school problem" can, or the problem of housing, of senior citizens, of youth, etcetera. In all these areas, experts have been standing up to offer a solution since time began. But the traffic problem has not yet been "solved" anywhere. We all know there are problems that will burden our society for many generations to come. We therefore must learn how to deal with problems because we cannot solve them; at best we might mitigate their effects for several decades.

Not only the major problems of a society are of this wicked sort. The designer is likewise confronted with many problems "in problem form." And in every case his solutions delight certain users while putting others at a disadvantage. Please design a ticket dispenser for the federal railroad so we can cut staff numbers! Who do we want to suffer the drawbacks—the far-sighted elderly, the travelers in need of information, or the railroad authorities themselves? Teaching people to deal with wicked problems is, in my opinion, the most pressing reform needed today in education in the fields of planning and design.

Modern pedagogy also casts doubt on an important requisite of the classic education: the examination. This actually ranks among the ceremonial rites of university life: my exam is coming up; I have to cram; I have no spare time. In the briefest time the entire pack of knowledge one has acquired over several years is crammed into one's short-term memory. Some students prove to be failures at exams while others don't. It is questionable whether the energy invested in the exam is put to optimal use.

At many universities, exams are still conducted with a great degree of informality. There is often a shortage of exam supervisors, be they students or staff. The professor seems to be infallible; in contested cases, his word counts. A person's entire fate depends here on personalities that may be under stress or (mis)guided by emotions.

There is a means to avoid the fears that examinations prompt, namely to recognize grades awarded for coursework. Students should go into an exam in the knowledge that the grades already acquired are in all likelihood enough to secure them a diploma. And even those who fall short in an exam should still be given a satisfactory grade. The grades awarded for seminar contributions and projects during the semester should account for at least 75 percent, if not 90 percent, of the final exam result.

This raises the question as to what needs to be in this pack of knowledge, and of its connection with project-based teaching. Must or ought an undergraduate know "everything" in his professional field of choice? Traditionally such knowledge was imparted throughout the four-year degree course by means of lectures: "Theory of Load-bearing Structures I," then "Theory of Load-bearing Structures II," and so on. It takes a very good memory to cope with this pack of knowledge. Project-oriented study would mean something like: Let's design a roof structure. Students would either be given the necessary knowledge for this task directly or required to go and find it for themselves in the library. Clearly, this type of learning leaves a much more memorable impression. It is possible, however, that a student by the end of the course has still not covered a certain aspect of his prospective profession. Perhaps a certain construction material never occurred in the planning scenarios he worked on and he accordingly knows nothing of its properties. It is expected that "a medical doctor" will always provide first aid.

Must not engineers and designers likewise be trained for every eventuality?

If so, then the number of technologies to be taught in the design field would be much too large. A designer should be educated in a manner such as to ensure that he can think his way into any problem ever put to him. If, for example, a glass blower takes him on as a designer, he doesn't need to first master the employer's technique. All too many types of craftsmanship are too caught up in their traditional forms and methods; so they really are in need of the expert from another field entirely, who asks questions such as: "Why is it done that way?"

To put project-oriented teaching into practice is also a problem—admittedly, an almost intractable one. Teaching would need to be organized such that the content of lectures would be of help in the design exercises. Problems, exercises, and lectures would therefore need to be minutely planned and coordinated in advance. The traditional study schedule—in the first year this, in the second year that, and so on—is child's play by comparison. To design an open-ended, problem-oriented style of teaching is therefore, for its part, an intractable problem, such as we have described above.

The Sermon Given in St. Jacob's Church, Weimar, June 30, 1994

I have chosen a motto for my sermon. It is from the Prophet Ezekiel, Chapter 36, Verse 26, and it says: "[...] I will take away the stony heart out of your flesh, and I will give you an heart of flesh."[1]

It must be said that prophets, contrary to popular belief, do not predict the future. They don't predict that I'll hit the jackpot next year or have an accident. What prophets do have to say to society is both timeless and timely. We'll return later to the verse's timeless significance. Interpreted by the light of traditional church doctrine, it means mercy replaces the law and the New Testament replaces the Old. We want to consider what a heart of flesh means for we who are alive today and working at universities of applied science. To answer that I'll need to briefly digress. One skill that man possesses yet animals probably lack is the ability to plan. An animal reacts; it responds in a certain way to a given stimulus. Man also registers a stimulus, a nuisance, or an impulse—yet he is able not only to react but also to plan a permanent countermeasure. This characteristic attains a professional dimension in the person of the engineer, and it is about him that we shall speak next. We'll also reflect on how his skills can be taught and learned.

Engineers come up with two types of blueprint: one type I call "the masterpiece," the other "the neat solution." The masterpiece ensues from an academic tradition, the neat solution from the polytechnics. The masterpiece is the work of a great master. He has

1 ["The Major Prophet Ezekiel 36 (KJV—King James Version)." Blue Letter Bible, 1996–2010.]

intuition, likewise an important human quality, namely that of summoning imaginative powers enough to be able to act and to plan, even in circumstances about which one is not adequately informed. The great master needs intuition when he is young, in order to forge great plans while carrying out the minor tasks entrusted to him. Gradually, in the course of his career, he gains that which he calls experience, and which we believe to be the first sign of his heart growing stony. Later in life, the master is given major tasks for which he delivers paltry solutions. Namely he draws on his experience and concludes that whatever was right for small tasks will do equally well for large ones. To extrapolate thus gives rise to the gigantic failures of planning we know only too well, to Chandigarh, Brasilia, the Salt Institute, and so forth. Therefore, when we ask here for a heart of flesh, we do so in order to avoid being paralyzed by past experience, to avoid feeling that we have nothing more to learn simply because we think, "I've done that, been there. This is how it's done;" and, above all, in order to avoid telling our students, "What you've begun there will never do. I tried that once, and it didn't work out."

Now we come to the polytechnic engineer and his neat solution. He, we have noted, is rooted in another tradition, that of the polytechnic school founded by Napoleon, who asked his engineers: How do we get our troops across the Rhine? And the engineers answered: We build a bridge. The assignment is depoliticized in this way, and responsibility is clearly assigned. Napoleon gives the order and, if the bridge leads to war, then because that is what Napoleon wishes. The engineers come up with the solution, so if the bridge collapses under the weight of the cannons, they are to blame. If the cannons fire on people, the engineers remain innocent.

In the 1960s, the technical approach ceded to a methodical one. The engineer applies the following formula: define the objective, analyze the problem, reach a conclusion, draw up the plan, implement it, and monitor how it functions. This, so they say, renders the chosen solution compatible with other economic or ecological processes. The fact is, however, that it is difficult to define the objective the minute one begins work on a task. In consequence, far too much data is collated for analysis and ultimately cannot be put to use. That which goes by the name of conclusion is therefore an arbitrary dismissal of inconvenient information. To draw up a plan based on this conclusion is accordingly just as intuitive a matter as the traditional masterpiece. The plan is carried out to the letter and monitored only far too late, when everything has been done.

Neat solutions pollute our environment. I would mention the Aswan Dam, which has destroyed the ecosystem underpinning irrigation in Egypt; or the World Bank's construction of the Sardar Sarovar (Narmada) Dam in western India, which is currently displacing 260.000 small farmers; or the 2.400 pump stations likewise financed by the World Bank, which are meant to mitigate the impact of the irrigation system recently installed by engineers in the Indus estuary. The irrigation system has caused sea-salt that lay hitherto deep in the ground to permeate the topsoil and make it unfertile, so the salt water must now be pumped off. The available pumps were designed for freshwater, however, and will rust within a few years. But no matter: nobody yet has any idea where the power to run 2.400 pumps is supposed to come from.

Evidently the technicians behind neat solutions are always looking ahead to their next task. They follow the law Meadow described, which states that to redress a problem always leads to a bigger problem. It is clear, moreover, that a neat solution doesn't deliver a real solution, for this is not at all possible—it merely redistributes problems. The engineer thus never manages to turn misfortune into good fortune but only to allocate benefits and drawbacks to different people than before.

If we ask for a heart of flesh, here, then also for the sake of rules or planning methods which put the neat solution in context. In my opinion one shouldn't go about pretending to adore decision-making. It isn't necessary to decide everything today. Our successors are not any dumber than we are. Rather, they can see further into the future. We may therefore postpone a few decisions. We may also reach soft decisions that can be revised, if ever planning proves to have been mistaken. Even completed buildings need not imply a precise solution, but should remain convertible, able to serve freshly defined purposes. We should always work on an appropriate scale, such as 1:1, at best, or 1:1.000 or 1:10.000, at worst. We should experiment, but in a way such that we can break off the experiment. We should always remain aware that it is not happiness we bring, but rather a change for the better, for some, and a change for the worse, for others. This is why we should learn to resolve conflicts with empathy.

Let us consider teaching too. Students should be allowed to make mistakes. Making mistakes is the only way to learn. That is why they should be allowed to take on tasks they can fail at: not only textbook exercises that end well, or planning proposals that the professor's assistant has already trialed, or drawings that lack content but are accomplished to perfection. This is the reason why we haven't instigated the Bauhaus preliminary course in our new design faculty. We don't want an "apprenticeship" that proceeds step by step, whereby students are told at every step, "You may take the next step only when you have accomplished this or that to perfection," and "Only when you know this will you be allowed to know that." At our school one is allowed also not to know—and to act nevertheless.

And only now begins the actual sermon, with this point precisely: the stony heart presumes to know what it knows, whereas we are dealing with not knowing.

Now, this "not knowing" is an ancient term, and classical philosophers said long ago that, "I know that I know nothing" or "It is not given to man to attain complete knowledge." In the Judeo-Christian tradition, this approach to not knowing implied acknowledgement of Our Lord, who is omniscient on our behalf.

The new factor in our day is: the term is devoid of meaning. Our "not knowing" is not a temporary state; it neither refers to a potentially broader science nor is it a sign of modesty in the face of a comprehensive system of knowledge or of religion. Nietzsche's new message "God is dead" is a metaphor for the loss of any possibility of seeing our ignorance, our "not knowing" in relation to greater, intact knowledge. Our knowledge is not like the shards of a broken vase that might still be mended or, at the least, imagined still to be whole. There is no vase, and our shards cannot be made whole because they do not fit together.

And there we have the stony heart's solutions we know only too well: either to act as if nothing is going on, and to herald security even if it actually no longer exists; or to take doubt and skepticism so far as to suggest there might be a basis worth purging, one on which we might erect a new edifice of knowledge.

The heart of flesh goes forth from the devastated remains of its own fragmented knowledge in the midst of greater rubble. Lyotard calls these "narratives." I would now like to mention three such fragments or "narratives."

All of us running around at technical schools take a scientific view of the world, one that suggests natural processes are embedded in systems, and that all these systems are networked in turn to create a great, cosmic system. And this last certainty is precisely what we have lost—yet we are nonetheless incapable of abandoning our idea of it. Perhaps we obscure the image of this crystalline system, as Deleuze and Guattari do, and make of it a disordered rhizome, or a system no longer transparent. But nothing takes us beyond the concept we have of a system. And here, the hard heart springs back into action. The catastrophes I described earlier occurred because either we or the engineers went so far as to apply our concept of the

"One can say this much: our buildings work wherever they are put!"
Drawing: Lucius Burckhardt

systematic course of things to the act of planning, and thus to become system builders ourselves. That the world constitutes a system is a metaphor; one moreover, for which there is no guarantee. We cannot mistake this image for reality and tinker away at it.

Another narrative that we cling to nonetheless is Marxism. This too is a narrative insofar as it partially and incompletely explains the way of the world. The progression from Marxism to dialectical materialism and other universal models of the sort is nothing but folklore. Yet this by no means invalidates the explanatory power of Marxism—a term I take to include the revisionists Luxemburg, Hilferding, and those on the barricades in 1968. We should not believe, however, that Marxism might change the world. To believe that, and to use Marxism to that end, is to show one's stony heart. Yet our heart of flesh cannot do without Marxism as an additional narrative.

And finally, one of the greatest narratives we have is our Christian religion. For our fathers, it too was a means of explaining the world and they, hard-hearted as they were, consequently became men of great faith and men of great doubt. They wrote books, inquiring as to whether one may keep the Christian faith without believing in the resurrection of Christ. Such intellectual acts of prowess are alien to us. Neither our faith nor our doubt is that strong. Gianni Vattimo recommends "feeble thinking" (*il pensiero debole*), and I second that in recommending feeble faith. Christ has risen for my sake—but I have a hard time believing it. And this ability of mine, to live in such discrepancy, is implicit in my plea to leave me my heart of flesh. I will never be either a true believer or a true skeptic.

And, in conclusion, I'd like to make one more personal comment: on behalf of the government of Thuringia and in cooperation with others, I, in my capacity as founding rector, have founded the design faculty at the school of architecture and engineering, here in Weimar. The act of founding the faculty amounts to an incomplete blueprint, a blueprint that I now abandon with a soft heart, a heart of flesh. I ask others to assume the creative task of filling it with life, and I undertake to understand whatever my successors do. One cannot hold onto a thing until it turns out how one would like it to be. This too is an aspect of the heart of flesh.

Bibliography

DESIGN

Design Is Invisible: Design ist unsichtbar. — In: Helmuth Gsöllpointner, Angela Hareiter, and Laurids Ortner (ed.), *Design ist unsichtbar*, Vienna 1981. — In: Bazon Brock (ed.), *Die Kinder fressen ihre Revolution*, Cologne 1985, p. 42–48. — In: Hans Höger (ed.), *Design = unsichtbar*, Ostfildern 1995, p. 15–24. — In: Jesko Fezer and Martin Schmitz (eds.), *Wer plant die Planung? Architektur, Politik und Mensch*, Berlin 2004, p. 187–199. — In: *Le design au-delà du visible*, Les essais du Centre Pompidou, Paris 1991, p. 17–30. — In: Silvan Blumenthal and Martin Schmitz (eds.), *Design ist unsichtbar. Entwurf, Gesellschaft und Pädagogik*, Berlin 2012, p. 13–25. — In: Jesko Fezer and Martin Schmitz (eds.), *Lucius Burckhardt Writings. Rethinking Man-made Environments. Politics, Landscape & Design*, Vienna/New York 2012, p. 153–165. — In: Gaetano Licata e Martin Schmitz (eds.), *Lucius Burckhardt: Il falso è l'autentico. Politica, città, paesaggio, design, pedagogia*, Macerata 2017.

Invisible Design: Das unsichtbare Design. — In: *Basler Magazin*, supplement to the *Basler Zeitung* No. 44, 5.11.1983, p. 15. — In: Bazon Brock (ed.), *Die Kinder fressen ihre Revolution*, Cologne 1985, p. 48–53. — In: Silvan Blumenthal and Martin Schmitz (eds.), *Design ist unsichtbar. Entwurf, Gesellschaft und Pädagogik*, Berlin 2012, p. 25–34.

Criteria For A New Design. Kriterien für ein neues Design. — In: *werk-archithese* 64/4, 1977. — In: Bazon Brock (ed.), *Die Kinder fressen ihre Revolution*, Cologne 1985, p. 53–55. — In: Hans Höger (ed.), *Design = unsichtbar*, Ostfildern 1995, p. 60–61. — In: Silvan Blumenthal and Martin Schmitz (eds.), *Design ist unsichtbar. Entwurf, Gesellschaft und Pädagogik*, Berlin 2012, p. 34–38.

On the Design of Everyday Life. Design für den Alltag. — In: *Ästhetik im Alltag*, vol. 2, Offenbach 1977. — In: Bazon Brock (ed.), *Die Kinder fressen ihre Revolution*, Cologne 1985, p. 55–62. — In: Jesko Fezer and Martin Schmitz (eds.), *Lucius Burckhardt Writings. Rethinking Man-made Environments. Politics, Landscape & Design*, Vienna/New York 2012, p. 142–152. — In: Silvan Blumenthal and Martin Schmitz (eds.), *Design ist unsichtbar. Entwurf, Gesellschaft und Pädagogik*, Berlin 2012, p. 38–51. — In: Jesko Fezer and Martin Schmitz (eds.), *Lucius Burckhardt Writings. Rethinking Man-made Environments. Politics, Landscape & Design*, Vienna/New York 2012, p. 142–152. — In: Gaetano Licata e Martin Schmitz (eds.), *Lucius Burckhardt: Il falso è l'autentico. Politica, città, paesaggio, design, pedagogia*, Macerata 2017.

Design—Rite and Expression of a Hopeful Society. Design—Ritual und Ausdruck einer hoffnungsfrohen Gesellschaft. *Umriss* 1/2, 1984, p. 5. — In: Bazon Brock (ed.), *Die Kinder fressen ihre Revolution,* Cologne 1985, p. 62–64. — In: Silvan Blumenthal and Martin Schmitz (eds.), *Design ist unsichtbar. Entwurf, Gesellschaft und Pädagogik*, Berlin 2012, p. 51–54.

Design Implies Processes, Not Just Forms! Design heisst Entwurf, nicht Gestalt! — In: Internationales Design Zentrum (ed.), *Design?* vol. 1, Berlin 1970. — In: Bazon Brock (ed.), *Die Kinder fressen ihre Revolution*, Cologne 1985, p. 65–66. — In: Hans Höger (ed.), *Design und Politik—querfeldein* 1, FH Würzburg-Schweinfurt 2005, p. 98–100. — In: Silvan Blumenthal and Martin Schmitz (eds.), *Design ist unsichtbar. Entwurf, Gesellschaft und Pädagogik*, Berlin 2012, p. 55–58.

The Grammar of Reality. Die Grammatik der Wirklichkeit. — In: *Aargauer Blätter* Nr. 74, 1967. — In: Bazon Brock (ed.), *Die Kinder fressen ihre Revolution*, Cologne 1985, p. 67–68. — In: Silvan Blumenthal and Martin Schmitz (eds.), *Design ist unsichtbar. Entwurf, Gesellschaft und Pädagogik*, Berlin 2012, p. 58–61.

Urban Design and Its Significance for Residents. Die Stadtgestalt und ihre Bedeutung für die Bewohner. — Shortened in: Michael Andritzky, Peter Becker and Gerd Selle (eds.), *Labyrinth Stadt—Planung und Chaos im Städtebau*, Köln 1975., p. 126–128. — In: Bazon Brock (ed.), *Die Kinder fressen ihre Revolution*, Cologne 1985, p. 96–100. — In: Silvan Blumenthal and Martin Schmitz (eds.), *Design ist unsichtbar. Entwurf, Gesellschaft und Pädagogik*, Berlin 2012, p. 61–68. — In: Jesko Fezer and Martin Schmitz (eds.), *Lucius Burckhardt Writings. Rethinking Man-made Environments. Politics, Landscape & Design*, Vienna/New York 2012, p. 115–122. — In: Gaetano Licata e Martin Schmitz (eds.), *Lucius Burckhardt: Il falso è l'autentico. Politica, città, paesaggio, design, pedagogia*, Macerata 2017.

Heritage Preservation Is Social Policy. Denkmalpflege ist Sozialpolitik. Lecture given on the second day of the Hessian Heritage Preservation Conference, Kassel, 1976, published in the Conference Report. — In: *Denkmalpflege ist Sozialpolitik, Konferenzbericht der Projektgruppe GhK 1975*, Kassel 1977. — In: Bazon Brock (ed.), *Die Kinder fressen ihre Revolution*, Cologne 1985, p. 168–175. — In: Silvan Blumenthal and Martin Schmitz (eds.), *Design ist unsichtbar. Entwurf, Gesellschaft und Pädagogik*, Berlin 2012, p. 69–84.

The Shortsighted and Farsighted. Die Kurzsichtigen und die Weitsichtigen. — In: *Die Weltwoche* Nr. 12, 22.3.1978, p. 45–46. — In: Bazon Brock (ed.), *Die Kinder fressen ihre Revolution*, Cologne 1985, p. 83–87. — In: Silvan Blumenthal and Martin Schmitz (eds.), *Design ist unsichtbar. Entwurf, Gesellschaft und Pädagogik*, Berlin 2012, p. 85–91.

Quality… Qualität … — In: *Neue Zürcher Zeitung*, April 1967 — In: Bazon Brock (ed.), *Die Kinder fressen ihre Revolution*, Cologne 1985, p. 68–69. — In: Silvan Blumenthal and Martin Schmitz (eds.), *Design ist unsichtbar. Entwurf, Gesellschaft und Pädagogik*, Berlin 2012, p. 91–93.

On the Production of Counter-productivity. Produzierte Kontraproduktivität. — In: Quim Pintó (ed.), *Error Design—Irrtum im Objekt* (catalog of the eponymous exhibition held at the Kunsthalle Krems, 12.9–18.10.1998, and at the Museum für Gestaltung, Zurich, 12.12.1998–7.3.1999; Krems 1998, p. 16–17. — In: Silvan Blumenthal and Martin Schmitz (eds.), *Design ist unsichtbar. Entwurf, Gesellschaft und Pädagogik*, Berlin 2012, p. 93–98.

Nothing Simple about Simplicity. Einfachheit ist nicht einfach. — In: ifa-Institut für Auslandbeziehungen and Volker Albus (eds.), *bewusst, einfach—Das Entstehen einer alternativen Produktkultur*, exhib. cat., Stuttgart 1998, p. 68–89. — In: Silvan Blumenthal and Martin Schmitz (eds.), *Design ist unsichtbar. Entwurf, Gesellschaft und Pädagogik*, Berlin 2012, p. 99–106.

All Over the Place. Querbeet. — In: Andreas Brandolini *Kamingespräche—Designerinterviews und -monologe*, Kassel/Berlin 1994, p. 165–180. — In: Hans Höger (ed.), *Design = unsichtbar*, Ostfildern 1995, p. 105–115. — In: Silvan Blumenthal and Martin Schmitz (eds.), *Design ist unsichtbar. Entwurf, Gesellschaft und Pädagogik*, Berlin 2012, p. 107–122.

An Ecological Innovation. Eine ökologische Neuerung. — In: Hans Höger (ed.), *Design = unsichtbar*, Ostfildern 1995, p. 141. — In: Silvan Blumenthal and Martin Schmitz (eds.), *Design ist unsichtbar. Entwurf, Gesellschaft und Pädagogik*, Berlin 2012, p. 122–123.

SOCIETY

Good Taste. Der gute Geschmack. — In: Bazon Brock, H.U. Reck (eds.), *Stilwandel als Kulturtechnik, Kampfprinzip, Lebensform oder Systemstrategie in Werbung, Design, Architektur, Mode*, Cologne 1986, p. 37–52. — In: Hans Höger (ed.), *Design = unsichtbar*, Ostfildern 1995, p. 68–79. — In: Silvan Blumenthal and Martin Schmitz (eds.), *Design ist unsichtbar. Entwurf, Gesellschaft und Pädagogik*, Berlin 2012, p. 129–145.

Can A Shift In Tastes Be Planned? Die Stilgeschichte ist kein blosser Gänsemarsch. — In: *Die Weltwoche* No. 30, July 1984. — In: Bazon Brock (ed.), *Die Kinder fressen ihre Revolution*, Cologne 1985, p. 366–369, under the title: Ist Geschmackswandel planbar? — In: Silvan Blumenthal and Martin Schmitz (eds.), *Design ist unsichtbar. Entwurf, Gesellschaft und Pädagogik*, Berlin 2012, p. 145–149.

Beyond Utility Value. Jenseits des Gebrauchswertes. Excerpt from discussions of the "post-history" group (Linde Burkhardt, Annemarie Burckhardt, Lucius Burckhardt, Diedrich Diederichsen, Andreas Gram, Gianni Vattimo) at the "Wertewandel" (Shifting Values) conference held during the "Erkundungen" (Reconnaissances) design event, Stuttgart, 1986. — In: Hans Höger (ed.), *Design = unsichtbar*, Ostfildern 1995, p. 100–105. — In: *Kunst und Kirche*, No. 4, 2003, p. 188–190. — In: Silvan Blumenthal and Martin Schmitz (eds.), *Design ist unsichtbar. Entwurf, Gesellschaft und Pädagogik*, Berlin 2012, p. 149–156.

… In Our Minds. … in unseren Köpfen. — In: Lucius Burckhardt and Internationales Design Zentrum Berlin (eds), *Design der Zukunft: Architektur, Design, Technik, Ökologie,* Cologne 1987, p. 11–17. — In: Hans Höger (ed.), *Design = unsichtbar*, Ostfildern 1995, p. 94–99. — In: Silvan Blumenthal and Martin Schmitz (eds.), *Design ist unsichtbar. Entwurf, Gesellschaft und Pädagogik*, Berlin 2012, p. 157–164.

Dirt. Der Schmutz. — In: Werk und Zeit Nr. 3, 1980. — In (entitled Der Müll): Bazon Brock (ed.), *Die Kinder fressen ihre Revolution*, Cologne 1985, p. 324–326 (under the title "Der Müll"). — In: Silvan Blumenthal and Martin Schmitz (eds.), *Design ist unsichtbar. Entwurf, Gesellschaft und Pädagogik*, Berlin 2012, p. 165–169. — In: Jesko Fezer and Martin Schmitz (eds.), *Lucius Burckhardt Writings. Rethinking Man-made Environments. Politics, Landscape & Design*, Vienna/New York 2012, p. 166–169. — In: Gaetano Licata e Martin Schmitz (eds.), *Lucius Burckhardt: Il falso è l'autentico. Politica, città, paesaggio, design, pedagogia*, Macerata 2017.

The Night Is Man-made. Die Nacht ist menschgemacht. — In: Klaus Stanjek (ed.), *Zwielicht—die Ökologie der künstlichen Helligkeit*, München 1989, p. 143–150. — In: *Le design au-delà du visible*, Les essais du Centre Pompidou, Paris 1991, p. 31–42 (under the title "Et l'homme fit la nuit"). — In: Hans Höger (ed.), *Design = unsichtbar*, Ostfildern 1995, p. 30–31. — In: Silvan Blumenthal and Martin Schmitz (eds.), *Design ist unsichtbar. Entwurf, Gesellschaft und Pädagogik*, Berlin 2012, p. 169–180. — In: Jesko Fezer and Martin Schmitz (eds.), *Lucius Burckhardt Writings. Rethinking Man-made Environments. Politics, Landscape & Design*, Vienna/New York 2012, p. 179–188. — In: Gaetano Licata e Martin Schmitz (eds.), *Lucius Burckhardt: Il falso è l'autentico. Politica, città, paesaggio, design, pedagogia*, Macerata 2017.

Fake: The Real Thing. Das Falche ist das Echte. — In: University Linz Institute for Design (ed.), exhibition catalog "Jewelry–Signs on the Body", Vienna 1987, p. 55–60 (under the title "Plus toc que nature"). — In: Hans Höger (ed.), *Design = unsichtbar*, Ostfildern 1995, p. 62–67. — In: *Le design au-delà du visible*, Les essais du Centre Pompidou, Paris 1991, p. 53–60. entitled: *Plus toc que nature.* — In: Silvan Blumenthal and Martin Schmitz (eds.), *Design ist unsichtbar. Entwurf, Gesellschaft und Pädagogik*, Berlin 2012, p. 181–188. — In: Jesko Fezer and Martin Schmitz (eds.), *Lucius Burckhardt Writings. Rethinking Man-made Environments. Politics, Landscape & Design*, Vienna/New York

2012, p. 204–211. — In: Gaetano Licata e Martin Schmitz (eds.), *Lucius Burckhardt: Il falso è l'autentico. Politica, città, paesaggio, design, pedagogia*, Macerata 2017.

Recycled Regionalism. Regionalismus wiederverwendet. — In: Gottlieb-Duttweiler-Institut (eds.), Liegt die Zukunft der Stadt in der Agglomeration? Lectures at the Gottlieb Duftweiler Institute (GDI) Conference, 17–18 May 1984, organized in cooperation with the Schweizer Werkbund and Deutscher Werkbund. *GDI–Schriften zur Gesellschaftspolitik* 30, Rüschlikon 1984, p. 159–165. — In: Bazon Brock (ed.), *Die Kinder fressen ihre Revolution*, Cologne 1985, p. 327–331. — In: Silvan Blumenthal and Martin Schmitz (eds.), *Design ist unsichtbar. Entwurf, Gesellschaft und Pädagogik*, Berlin 2012, p. 189–197.

How Does Trash End Up In Museums? Wie kommt der Müll ins Museum? — In: Peter Noever (ed.), *Tradition und Experiment — Das Österreichische Museum für angewandte Kunst Vienna zum 125-jährigen Jubiläum*, Salzburg 1989. — "Mais comment les rebuts entrent-ils au musée?" In: *Le design au-delà du visible*, Les essais du Centre Pompidou, Paris 1991, p. 61–70, — In: Hans Höger (ed.), *Design = unsichtbar*, Ostfildern 1995, p. 24–30. — In: Silvan Blumenthal and Martin Schmitz (eds.), *Design ist unsichtbar. Entwurf, Gesellschaft und Pädagogik*, Berlin 2012, p. 197–205.

Color Is A Sign. Farbe ist Zeichen. — In: Arnica-Verena Langenmaier (ed.), *Die Farbe der Dinge: Farbgebung—eine Aufgabe des Design*, Munich 1994. — In: Hans Höger (ed.), *Design = unsichtbar*, Ostfildern 1995, p. 87–94. — In: Silvan Blumenthal and Martin Schmitz (eds.), *Design ist unsichtbar. Entwurf, Gesellschaft und Pädagogik*, Berlin 2012, p. 205–215.

Good Form and Good Color. Formvollendet (Gartenerdbeere). — In: *Form* Nr. 146, 1994, p. 19. — Under the present title in: Hans Höger (ed.), *Design = unsichtbar*, Ostfildern 1995, p. 139–140. — In: Silvan Blumenthal and Martin Schmitz (eds.), *Design ist unsichtbar. Entwurf, Gesellschaft und Pädagogik*, Berlin 2012, p. 216–217.

Bad Form. Die schlechte Form (Dinosaurier).— In: *Form* Nr. 145, 1994, p. 16. — In: Hans Höger (ed.), *Design = unsichtbar*, Ostfildern 1995, p. 137–139. — In: Silvan Blumenthal and Martin Schmitz (eds.), *Design ist unsichtbar. Entwurf, Gesellschaft und Pädagogik*, Berlin 2012, p. 217–221.

A Walk in Second Nature. Spaziergang durch die zweite Natur. — In: Bernard Lassus (ed.), *Hypotheses for a Third Nature*, Coracle Press, London 1992. — In: Silvan Blumenthal and Martin Schmitz (eds.), *Design ist unsichtbar. Entwurf, Gesellschaft und Pädagogik*, Berlin 2012, p. 221–224. — In: Jesko Fezer and Martin Schmitz (eds.), *Lucius Burckhardt Writings. Rethinking Man-made Environments. Politics, Landscape & Design*, Vienna/New York 2012, p. 226–231. — In: Gaetano Licata e Martin Schmitz (eds.), *Lucius Burckhardt: Il falso è l'autentico. Politica, città, paesaggio, design, pedagogia*, Macerata 2017.

University Planning and Urban Planning. Hochschulplanung und Stadtplanung. — In: *Der Bund* Nr. 99, 29. 4. 1968 (Special supplement). — In: Silvan Blumenthal and Martin Schmitz (eds.), *Design ist unsichtbar. Entwurf, Gesellschaft und Pädagogik*, Berlin 2012, p. 233–255.

Ulm Anno 5. On the Curriculum of the Ulm School of Design. Ulm anno 5 – Zum Lehrprogramm der Hochschule für Gestaltung in Ulm. — In: *Das Werk* 47/11, 1960, p. 384–386. — In: Hans Höger (ed.), *Design = unsichtbar*, Ostfildern 1995, p. 53–59. — In: Hans Höger (ed.), *Design und Politik—querfeldein* 1, FH Würzburg-Schweinfurt 2005, p. 93–97. — In: Silvan Blumenthal and Martin Schmitz (eds.), *Design ist unsichtbar. Entwurf, Gesellschaft und Pädagogik*, Berlin 2012, p. 255–264. — In: Jesko Fezer and Martin Schmitz (eds.), *Lucius Burckhardt Writings. Rethinking Man-made Environments. Politics, Landscape & Design*, Vienna/New York 2012, p. 35–43. — In: Gaetano Licata e Martin Schmitz (eds.), *Lucius Burckhardt: Il falso è l'autentico. Politica, città, paesaggio, design, pedagogia*, Macerata 2017.

The Exhibition Medium. Die Ausstellung als Medium. — In: *Der Monat* Nr. 196, 1965, 32–25. — In: Bazon Brock (ed.), *Die Kinder fressen ihre Revolution*, Cologne 1985, p. 118–124. — In: Silvan Blumenthal and Martin Schmitz (eds.), *Design ist unsichtbar. Entwurf, Gesellschaft und Pädagogik*, Berlin 2012, p. 264–274.

documenta urbana—what could that mean? documenta urbana – was könnte das heissen? — In: *documenta urbana—sichtbar machen*, exhib. cat., vol. 1/2, Kassel 1982. — In: Bazon Brock (ed.), *Die Kinder fressen ihre Revolution*, Cologne 1985, p. 113–116. — In: Silvan Blumenthal and Martin Schmitz (eds.), *Design ist unsichtbar. Entwurf, Gesellschaft und Pädagogik*, Berlin 2012, p. 275–280.

To Expect Quick Results from the Planned Reform Is to Underestimate the Braking Forces. Von geplanten Reformen eine rasche Wirkung zu erwarten, bedeutet eine Unterschätzung der Bremskräfte. — In: *Wirtschaftswoche* Nr. 12, 24. 3. 1972, p. 26. — In: Silvan Blumenthal and Martin Schmitz (eds.), *Design ist unsichtbar. Entwurf, Gesellschaft und Pädagogik*, Berlin 2012, p. 280–282.

From Design Academicism to the Treatment of Wicked Problems. Vom Entwurfsakademismus zur Behandlung bösartiger Probleme. — In: *Canapé News* Nr. 29, Experiment Canapé (closing report), ETH Zürich 1973. — In: Bazon Brock (ed.), *Die Kinder fressen ihre Revolution*, Cologne 1985, p. 226–230. — In: Silvan Blumenthal and Martin Schmitz (eds.), *Design ist unsichtbar. Entwurf, Gesellschaft und Pädagogik*, Berlin 2012, p. 282–290. — In: Jesko Fezer and Martin Schmitz (eds.), *Lucius Burckhardt Writings. Rethinking Man-made Environments. Politics, Landscape & Design*, Vienna/New York 2012, p. 77–84. — In: Gaetano Licata e Martin Schmitz (eds.), *Lucius Burckhardt: Il falso è l'autentico. Politica, città, paesaggio, design, pedagogia*, Macerata 2017.

On the Difficulty of Teaching Modesty. Über die Schwierigkeit, Bescheidenheit zu dozieren. — In: *urbanisme* Nr. 168/169, 1979, p. 86–88. — In: Silvan Blumenthal and Martin Schmitz (eds.), *Design ist unsichtbar. Entwurf, Gesellschaft und Pädagogik*, Berlin 2012, p. 290–297.

The Minimal Intervention. Der kleinste Eingriff — L'intervention minimale. A seminar in post-earthquake Belice (Sicily), 10–12. Sept. 1981. — In: *Bauwelt* 73/4, 1982, p. 127–130. — In: Fachbereich Architektur der Gesamthochschule Kassel (eds.), *Architektur für den Nutzer – Gebrauchsarchitektur* (The teaching of architecture with people in mind). Report Nr. 6 of the EAAE workshop of November 1982, Kassel 1984, p. 60–64. — In: Bazon Brock (ed.), *Die Kinder fressen ihre Revolution*, Cologne 1985, p. 241–247, under the title: Der kleinstmögliche Eingriff. — In: Silvan Blumenthal and Martin Schmitz (eds.), *Design ist unsichtbar. Entwurf, Gesellschaft und Pädagogik*, Berlin 2012, p. 297–304. — In: Markus Ritter and Martin Schmitz (eds.), *Der kleinstmögliche Eingriff oder die Rückführung der Planung auf das Planbare*, Berlin 2013, p. 167–174.

75 Years of Bauhaus—On the Tame Approach to Wicked Problems. 75 Jahre Bauhaus—Der gutartige Umgang mit bösartigen Problemen. — In: *Die Weltwoche* Nr. 65, 14. 8. 1994. — In: Silvan Blumenthal and Martin Schmitz (eds.), *Design ist unsichtbar. Entwurf, Gesellschaft und Pädagogik*, Berlin 2012, p. 305–312.

Not A New Bauhaus! Kein neues Bauhaus! — In: *Form* Nr. 144, 1993, p. 14. — In: Silvan Blumenthal and Martin Schmitz (eds.), *Design ist unsichtbar. Entwurf, Gesellschaft und Pädagogik*, Berlin 2012, p. 313–317.

A University Must Foster a Sense of Belonging and Hone Resistance at One and the Same Time. Die Schule muß zugleich Heimat sein und zu Widerstand reizen. — In: Silvan Blumenthal and Martin Schmitz (eds.), *Design ist unsichtbar. Entwurf, Gesellschaft und Pädagogik*, Berlin 2012, p. 317–330.

Do Examinations Make for a Better Education? Führen Prüfungen zu besseren Ausbildungen? Controversial discussion with Nikolaus Wyss. In: *STZ (Schweizerischen Technischen Zeitschrift*, Swiss Engineering) Nr. 9, 1996, p. 55. — In: Silvan Blumenthal and Martin Schmitz (eds.), *Design ist unsichtbar. Entwurf, Gesellschaft und Pädagogik*, Berlin 2012, p. 330–331.

Problem-oriented Project-based Teaching. Problemorientierter Projektunterricht. — In: Silvan Blumenthal and Martin Schmitz (eds.), *Design ist unsichtbar. Entwurf, Gesellschaft und Pädagogik*, Berlin 2012, p. 332–341.

The Sermon. Predigt in der Jakobskirche in Weimar, 30. 6. 1994. — In: Hans Höger (ed.), *Design = unsichtbar*, Ostfildern 1995, p. 216–221. — In: *Azimuts* 10/5, 1996, p. 34–38 (French). — In: Hans Höger (ed.), *Design education*, Milano 2006, p. 73–76 (Italian). — In: Silvan Blumenthal and Martin Schmitz (eds.), *Design ist unsichtbar. Entwurf, Gesellschaft und Pädagogik*, Berlin 2012, p. 342–349. — In: Jesko Fezer and Martin Schmitz (eds.), *Lucius Burckhardt Writings. Rethinking Man-made Environments. Politics, Landscape & Design*, Vienna/New York 2012, p. 232–238. — In: Gaetano Licata e Martin Schmitz (eds.), *Lucius Burckhardt: Il falso è l'autentico. Politica, città, paesaggio, design, pedagogia*, Macerata 2017.

Also available at Birkhäuser:

Jesko Fezer and Martin Schmitz (eds.), *Lucius Burckhardt Writings. Rethinking Man-made Environments. Politics, Landscape & Design*, Vienna/New York 2012.

Markus Ritter and Martin Schmitz (eds.), Burckhardt, Lucius. *Why Is Landscape Beautiful? The Science of Strollology*, Basel 2015.

Biographies

Lucius Burckhardt (* Davos, 1925) gained a PhD in Basel then became a research assistant at the Social Research Center at Münster University in 1955. A guest lectureship at Ulm University of Applied Arts in 1959 was followed from 1961 to 1973 by several teaching assignments, including a guest lectureship in sociology at the Architecture Faculty of the Swiss Federal Institute of Technology (ETH Zurich). He worked simultaneously as editor-in-chief of the journal *Werk* from 1962 to 1973, was First President of the German *Werkbund* from 1976 to 1983, and professor of the socio-economics of urban systems at the University of Kassel as of 1973. He was also a correspondent member of the German Academy of Urban and Regional Spatial Planning, a Chevalier dans l'Ordre des Arts et des Lettres, from 1987 to 1989 a member of the Founding Committee of Saar University of Visual Arts, and from 1992 to 1994 the founding dean of the Design Faculty at the Bauhaus University Weimar. In recognition of his life's work, he was awarded the Hessian Culture Prize for Outstanding Achievements in the Realms of Science, Ecology and Aesthetics in 1994, the Federal Prize for Design Promoters in 1995, and the Swiss Design Prize in 2001. Lucius Burckhardt died in Basel in 2003.

Book publications: *Wir selber bauen unsre Stadt* (with Markus Kutter), Basel 1953; *Achtung: die Schweiz* (with Max Frisch and Markus Kutter), Basel 1955; *Die neue Stadt* (with Max Frisch and Markus Kutter), Basel 1956; *Reise ins Risorgimento*, Cologne/Berlin 1959; *Bauen ein Prozess* (with Walter Förderer), Teufen 1968; *Moderne Architektur in der Schweiz seit 1900* (with Annemarie Burckhardt and Diego Peverelli), Winterthur 1969; *Der Werkbund in Deutschland, Österreich und der Schweiz*, Stuttgart 1978 (translated into Italian, French, and English); *Für eine andere Architektur* (edited with Michael Andritzky and Ot Hoffmann), Frankfurt/Main 1981; *Die Kinder fressen ihre Revolution (*edited by Bazon Brock), Cologne 1985; *Le design au-delà du visible*, Paris 1991; *Design = unsichtbar*, Ostfildern 1995; *Wer plant die Planung?- Architektur, Politik und Mensch*, Berlin 2004; *Warum ist Landschaft schön? Die Spaziergangswissenschaft*, Berlin 2006; *Design ist unsichtbar. Entwurf, Gesellschaft und Pädagogik*, Berlin 2012; *Lucius Burckhardt Writings. Rethinking Man-made Environments*, Vienna/NY 2012; *Der kleinstmögliche Eingriff*, Berlin 2013; *Wir selber bauen unsre Stadt* (with Markus Kutter), reprint Berlin 2015; *Why is Landscape Beautiful? The Science of Strollology*, Basel 2015; *Il falso è l'autentico. Politica, città, paesaggio, design, pedagogia*, Rome 2017 and *Landschaftstheoretische Aquarelle und Spaziergangswissenschaft*, Berlin 2017.

Silvan Blumenthal (* Ilanz/Grisons, 1980) completed his Master of Architecture at ETH Zurich in 2008. He worked as a practicing architect and continued his studies in the field of History and Philosophy of Knowledge at ETH Zurich. Author of *Das Lehrcanapé – Lucius Burckhardt und das Architektenbild an der ETH Zürich 1970–1973* (Basel 2010) and co-editor of *Lucius Burckhardt – Design ist unsichtbar: Entwurf, Gesellschaft und Pädagogik* (Berlin 2012). From 2009–2016 Silvan was a research assistant at Studio Prof. Gion A. Caminada at ETH Zurich. Currently he is a doctoral fellow at the Institute for History and Theory of Architecture at ETH Zurich.

Martin Schmitz (* Hamm/Westphalia, 1956) studied under Lucius Burckhardt in Kassel and had lectureships to date in Saarbrücken, Weimar, and Kassel. He is an independent publisher since 1989 and is the author of *Currywurst mit Fritten – Über die Kultur der Imbißbude* (1983). He was the curator of the movie program at documenta 8 in 1987, the "Dilettantism" conference in Görlitz in 1995, the *documenta urbana* symposium "Kunst plant die Planung" in Kassel in 2007, the international convention "Spaziergangswissenschaft: Sehen, erkennen und planen" in Frankfurt Main in 2008, and the 1st Lucius Burckhardt Convention in Kassel in 2014. He is co-editor of several books by Lucius Burckhardt: *Wer plant die Planung?*, *Warum ist Landschaft schön?*, *Design ist unsichtbar*, *Der kleinstmögliche Eingriff*, *Wir bauen selber unsre Stadt*, *Landschaftstheoretische Aquarelle und Spaziergangswissenschaft*, Berlin 2017 and *Lucius Burckhardt Writings*, *Why Is Landscape Beautiful?* and *Il falso è l'autentico. Politica, città, paesaggio, design, pedagogia*. Since 2013 professorship at Kassel University of the Arts. www.martin-schmitz.de

Index